ORIGIN OF JAGANNĀTH DEITY

Origin of Jagannāth Deity

Jitamitra Prasad Singh Deo

GYAN PUBLISHING HOUSE
NEW DELHI - 110002

ORIGIN OF JAGANNĀTH DEITY

(Religion)

Rs. 450

ISBN : 81-212-0351-X

I[st] Edition-1991
IInd Enlarged & Revised Edition-2003
Published by
Gyan Publishing House
5 Ansari Road, Daryaganj
New Delhi-110 002
Email : gyanbook@vsnl.com
Visit our Website at : http//www.gyanbooks.com

Lasertypesetting by: Tact Computer Graphics, Delhi
Printed at: Mehra Offset Press, Delhi

Dedicated at the sacred feet of Lord Jagannāth, who has revealed Himself through the Author

Contents

List of Illustrations and Maps

ILLUS TRATIONS

MAPS

Preface

The Study on 'Origin of Jagannāth Deity', is an individual work and the author has not received any project for it. Therefore, the author is unable to produce photographic illustrations and only three illustrations could be given.

When a study on the 'Origin of Jagannāth Deity', (the Lord of the Universe), is done, it is appropriate to know about Knowledge and Reality.

The Knowledge which is acquired from teachers and from books are imitative, repetitive, derivative and educative. Another Knowledge which is above these types of Knowledge is intuitive. Only intuitive knowledge reaches to the Reality.

Intuition means the power of the mind by which it immediately perceives the Truth of things without reasoning or analysis, a truth so perceived, is immediate knowledge in contrast with mediate.

The realised Souls, otherwise known as *Rishis* and *Yogis* in India are individuals of Intuitive knowledge in Human creation. The knowledge of intuition cannot be expressed in words fully, because it is the practical experience in Meditation. All the Holy books or scriptures of the world therefore indicate, but have failed to express the full Truth, the full consciousness or the full realisation.

With this information, let us know the view of Swami Śivananda on the four sources of knowledge. Swami Śivananda[1] has written that inspiration, revelation, insight, intuition, ecstasy. Divine sight and Paramananda state are the seven planes of knowledge. There are four sources of knowledge, viz. instinct, reason, intuition and Super-intuition or Brahma Jnana.

Instinct

When an ant crawls in your right arm, the left arm automatically moves towards the right arm to drive away the ant. The mind does not reason there. When you see a scorpion in front of your leg, you withdraw your leg automatically. This is termed instinctive or automatic movement. As you cross a street, how instinctively you move your body to save yourself from the cars. There is no vritti in such mechanical movement.

Instinct is found in animals and birds. In birds, the ego doesn't interfere with the free Divine flow and Divine play. Hence the work done by them through their instincts is more perfect than that done by human beings. Have you not noticed the excellent work done by birds in their building the wonderful nests ?

Reason

Reason is higher than instinct and is found only in human beings. It collects facts, generalises, reasons out from cause to effect, from effect to cause *(a priori* and *a posterior* methods of reasoning), from premises to conclusions, from propositions to proofs. If concludes, decides and comes to judgement. It takes you safely to the door of intuition and leaves you there.

Belief, reasoning, knowledge and faith are the four important psychic processes. First you have belief in a doctor. You go to him for diagnosis and treatment. He makes a thorough examination and then prescribes certain medicine. You take them. You reason out : "Such and such is the disease. The doctor has given me iron and iodide. Iron will improve my blood. The iodide will stimulate the lymphatics and absorb the exudation and growth in the liver. So, I should take it." Then the disease is cured of these drugs, in a month. Then you get knowledge of and perfect faith in the efficacy of the medicine and the proficiency of the doctor. Then you recommend to your friends this doctor and his drugs.

Intuition

Intuition is Spiritual Anubhava. Knowledge through functioning of Karana-Sarira is Intuition. Sri Aurobinda calls it Super-mind or Supramental Consciousness. There is direct perception of truth (Pratyaksha) or immediate knowledge through Samadhi. You know things by a flash. Professor Bergson preached about intuition in France to make the people understand that there is another higher source of knowledge than intellect. In intuition, there is no reasoning process at all. It is Pratyaksha. Intuition takes a man to the door of intuition and returns back. Intuition is Divya drishti. It is Jnana-Chakshu. Spiritual flashes and glimpses of truth come through intuition. Inspiration, revelation, spiritual insight come through Intuition.

Atma-Jnana

Atma-Jnana is above intuition. It transcends the Karana Sarira. It is the highest form of knowledge. It is the only Reality

In Intuitive knowledge, one individual attains Samadhi or Self-absorption. Samadhi starts with the absorption of Self in the duality of structure in consciousness and ends in the absorption of Self in identification with secondless unique Self. Self-absorption with duality of structure in consciousness is called Sabikalpa Samadhi. Self-absorption without any sense of duality is called Nirvikalpa Samadhi. Sabikalpa Samadhi is of four types and Nirvikalpa Samadhi is of two types, one having three sub-divisions.[2]

In Sabikalpa Samadhi the devotee has attained realization of his oneness with Spirit but cannot maintain his Cosmic consciousness except in the immobile trance state. By continuous meditation he reaches the superior state of Nirbikalpa Samadhi in which one moves freely in the world without any loss of God-perception.

In Nirbikalpa Samadhi the Yogi dissolves the last vestiges of his material or earthly Karma. Nevertheless, he still has certain astral and causal Karma to work out and there one takes astral and then causal re-embodiments on high-vibrational spheres.[3]

With this much information, let us peep into the types of Samadhi's definition of Sudhir Ranjan Sengupta[4] on Sabikalpa Samadhi and Nirvikalpa Samadhi.

These are briefly described below :

Sabikalpa Samadhi

(i) *Sabitarka Samadhi:* Self-absorption in the duality of Structure in consciousness with latent sense of controversy in the consciousness is called Sabitarka Samadhi.

(ii) *Sabichar Samadhi* : Self-absorption in the duality of structure in consciousness with a latent sense of discretion in the consciousness is called Sabichar Samadhi.

(iii) *Sananda Samadhi* : Self-absorption in the duality of structure in consciousness with an all-absorbing Bliss is called Sananda Samadhi.

(iv) *Sasmita Samadhi* : Self-absorption in the duality of structure in consciousness with a latest sense of Self-existence is called Sasmita Samadhi.

Nirvikalpa Samadhi

(i) *Bhaba Pratyaya Videha Samadhi:* Consists in Self-absorption without the least trace of duality in consciousness with complete Self-identification with Nature of God, without the light of consciousness. Bhaba-pratyaya Videha Samadhi has three sub-divisions viz. Prakriti Pratyaya, Aham Pratyaya and Mahat Pratyaya, i.e., Self-consciousness lost in nature and Self-consciousness lost in egotism and lost in Buddhisattva.

(ii) *Purna Pratyaya Samadhi* : Self-absorption in the secondless unique conscious Absolute Self of the Supreme Self without the least trace of duality is called Purna Pratyaya Nirvikalpa Samadhi. The Purna Pratyaya Nirvikalpa Samadhi is possible when the five waves of mind cease to function and the Sadhaka transcends the basic evolution. Purna Samadhi attained as a result of the realisation of the identity of Self with the Absolute Self of God without the least trace of duality in the Self-revealed consciousness liberates an individual soul from the ills of the World and World knows no other existence except the Supreme Being. The sages say that of these eight varieties of Samadhi, Purna Pratyaya Videha Samadhi alone can liberate an individual Soul.

With this background of Knowledge and Reality, a humble attempt has been done to unravel the Reality of Origin of Jagannāth Deity in this work. It was found that Scholarlistic approach of educative knowledge becomes entangled with the mysteries surrounding Lord Jagannāth and His Cult. Therefore, intuitive approach was done to reveal and it was found that the individuals of Nirvikalpa Samadhi create. Ādi Śaṅkarāchārya was one of such individual who in the commentary of Prasthānatrayi[5] established that Iśvara or the Puruṣottama stands for akṣara. Akṣara is the para Brahman, the Supreme Being. 'He does not perish when all beings perish.'[6]

The effort of this work has established that one icon of Buddha was installed as Jagannāth (Viṣṇu-Krshna) Deity by Ādi Śaṅkarāchārya and he was the founder father of Jagannāth Deity. As Jagannāth Deity unfold itself as Puruṣottama-Jagannāth, it is Akṣara (i.e. imperishable).

The author expresses gratitude to authors and scholars from whose works, extensive materials have been drawn for this study and is thankful to M/s Gyan Publishing House, for taking up the publication of this book. The author's wife Smt. Rajshree Devi needs reverence for she has taught the author to be revalorise.

Khariar **Jitamitra Prasad Singh Deo**

REFERENCES

1. Swami Śivananda, *Mind Its Mysteries and Control,* The Divine Life: Society, Shivanandanagar, 1974, pp. 27-29.
2. Sengupta, S.R., *Mother Cult,* Firma KLM. Private Limited, Calcutta, 1977, p. 106.
3. Paramahansa Yogananda, *Autobiography of a Yogi,* Jaico Publication, Bombay, 1971, p. 427.
4. Sengupta, S.R., *op. cit.* 1977: pp. 106-107.
5. Phani Mohanty, *The Concept of Purusa and Puruṣottama in the Commentary of Sankara on the Prasthanatrayi,* Garg Publications,. New Delhi, 1986, p. 49.
6. *Ibid.,* p. 55.

Abbreviations

AHOO	Sahu, N.K. (ed.), A History of Orissa, Vol. II, Susil Gupta (India) Ltd. Calcutta, 1956.
BIO	Sahu, N.K., Buddhism in Orissa, Utkal University, Cuttack, 1958.
CHOO	Rath, B.K. Cultural History of Orissa, Sundeep Prakashan, New Delhi, 1983.
CII	Corpus Inscriptionum Indicarum.
CPOSK	Singh Deo, J.P. Cultural Profile of South Kōśala, Gian Publishing House, New Delhi, 1987.
GOIMPR	Verma, R. (State editor), Gazetteer of India, Madhya Pradesh, Raipur, (Bhopal), 1973.
GOIOP	Kuanr, D.C. (State editor), Gazetteer of India, Orissa, Puri, (Cuttack), 1977.
HOO	Panigrahi, K.C., History of Orissa (Hindu period). Kitab Mahal, Cuttack, 1981.
IOO	Rajaguru, S.N. Inscriptions of Orissa, Bhubaneswar, 1966.
JBORS	Journal of the Bihar and Orissa Research Society.
JOMHS	Journal of Mahākōśala Historical Society.
MAR	Kosambi, D.D. Myth and Reality, Popular Prakashan, Bombay, 1983.

OHRJ	The Orissa Historical Research Journal.
OHC	Orissa History Congress.
PATSAIOC	Proceedings and Transactions of the Seventh All India Oriental Conference, 1933.
PHOTSKOSKAO	Nema, S.R. Political History of the Śōmavaṁśi Kings of South Kōśala and Orissa, Oriental Publishers, New Delhi, 1978.
TAGOI	Cunningham, A., The Ancient Geography of India, Varanasi, 1963.
TCHOI	The Cultural Heritage of India.
TCOIH	Kṛishṇamacharlu, Rao Bahadur C.R. (epigraphist), The Cradle of Indian History, The Adyar Library, Madras, 1947.
TCOJ	Mishra, K.C., The Cult of Jagannātha, Firma K.L. Mukhopadhyay, Calcutta, 1971.
TCOJATRTOO	Eschman, A.; Kulke, H. and Tripathy, G.C. (ed.), The Cult of Jagannāth and the Regional Tradition of Orissa, Manohar Publication, New Delhi, 1978.
THACOTIP	Majumdar, R.C. (ed.), The History and Culture of the Indian People, Bharatiya Vidya Bhavan, Bombay.
THOO	Mahatab, H.K., The History of Orissa, Cuttack.
THOMVIO	Mukherjee, P., The History of Medieval Vaishṇavism in Orissa, Asian Educational Services, New Delhi, 1981.
TRIHP	Sankalia, H.D., The Rāmayana in Historical Perspective, Macmillan India Limited, New Delhi, 1982.
TSBLON	Mitra, R. (ed.), The Sanskrit Buddhist Literature of Nepal, Sanskrit Pustak Bhandar, Calcutta, 1971.

One

Introduction

Culture of a locality, is the state of being cultivated or the refinement reached. So, the result of refine cultivation, at last becomes a type of civilisation. Culture is every aspect of civilisation and includes religion, which means faith in something higher and nobler, according to the conception of the people of the Society. Culture cannot be imposed on a society, it grows. Faith begins where reason ends. Knowledge which is acquired from teachers and books are imitative, derivative, repetitive and educative. The highest form of knowledge of Reality is intuitive. Intuition is the power of mind, by which it immediately perceives the truth of things without reasoning or analysis. Such intuitive knowledge is got through meditation. The knowledge of our Indian Rishis or Sages was intuitive. The full experience of intuition, cannot be expressed abundantly. Therefore, reality gets lost in the mundane creation.

The culture of Upper Mahānadi river, which comprised the South Kōśala state of early and medieval periods had spread far and wide. L.P. Pandey[1] had traced the similarity of the Cave Men's art of Upper Mahānadi valley and America. The resemblance was the marks of hands with fingers. Pandey surmised this hand-mark may be a symbol, meaning the protecting and ever-helping hand of the Great Mother. Even Ujjain once formed a part of South Kōśala.[2]

Since 1968, the author had been doing archaeological field surveys, discoveries, study of antiquities of Upper Mahānadi valley and writing for different research journals, bulletins, papers, weeklies and magazines. Finally, a critical study was done and published in a book form named, *Cultural Profile of South Kōśala.*[3] An attempt was done to show the flow of culture from Upper Mahānadi valley to the Lower Mahānadi valley and how the eastern part of South Kōśala, now comprising the Western part of modern Orissa Province, played the pivotal role. The work was a successful attempt of critical historical narration. In the 'Religion' chapter of this work, new hypothesis was given.

More advance and intensive research was taken up in 'Religion', of Upper Mahānadi valley. It was found that the religious revolution of India and religious revolutionary essence of Mahānadi valley culture, was the evolution or origin of Jagannāth Deity and Jagannāth Cult.

The findings and advancement of knowledge through archaeological research, induced the author to compile them in book form. This book is named *Origin of Jagannāth Deity,* because it is found that much of Human refinements, which developed in Upper Mahānadi valley, have influenced or found their safe base in coastal area of Lower Mahānadi valley.

It is not easy to get at the real facts regarding the Origin of Jagannāth Deity, as the whole question has been purposely obscured, so as to give it the appearance of antiquity. Further the growth of myth and ceremony has invested the dominant form of Jagannāth Cult with organised full rituals. The Myths have been written and rewritten by Brahmins to suit themselves. According to F.E. Pargiter,[4] the sources for the older period survive as Purāṇas (='the ancient stories'), which in their present form, are only religious fables and cannot, with whatever historical content the works once possessed heavily encrusted by myth, diluted with semi-religious legends, effaced during successive redactions copied by innumerable, careless scribes; so that one finds great difficulty in restoring as much as the King-lists.

The autor claims that the religious revolution of India in general and Mahānadi river vally in particular, resulted in the development of Jagannāth Deity and Cult.

Prevalent views on the Origin of Jagannāth Deity has been given in the Puri District Gazetteer.[5] For ready assess, it has been quoted below thus :-

"Attempts have been made by scholars to trace the Origin of Jagannāth to the Buddhist, Jaina, Savara, Vedic or Brahmanical sources. The western scholars like Mr. Slevens, Prof. Wilson, James Fergusson and General Cunningham were among the early advocates of the Buddhist origin of Jagannāth. It is known from history that Buddhism had a strong foothold in Orissa from the Pre-Christian era." According to Rajendra Lala Mitra[6], "during the four centuries preceding the Christian era, Orissa generally and the district of Puri in particular were under the domination of the Buddhists". After the conquest of Kalinga by Asoka in circa 261 B.C. Buddhism must have got an extra impetus under royal patronage. It is also evident from the accounts of the famous Chinese traveller Hiuen Tsang that Mahayana form of Buddhism flourished in Orissa in the 7th century A.D. The advocates of the Buddhist origin of Jagannāth believe that Puri was an ancient seat of Buddhism and the worship of Jagannāth is a relic of some Buddhist Cult. The story of Buddha's tooth-relic, as it is found in the 12th century Sinhalese work 'Dathavamsa', written by one Dhammakitti Thera, was once in wide circulation. It is mentioned in this story that the sacred tooth of Buddha remained for centuries at Dantapura in Kalinga. This Dantapura was identified by some with Puri. King Guhasiva of Kalinga worshipped the sacred tooth in a temple, but a King who ruled at Pataliputra forcibly took it away from him. Subsequently the sacred relic was restored to Guhasiva, but while fighting with a powerful neighbouring King he fell in the battle. In order to fulfil the wishes of her deceased father, princess Hemamala surreptitiously conveyed the sacred relic in her hair to Ceylon in about 300 A.D. where it is worshipped to this day. Basing on this legend Fergusson writes there can be little doubt but that the temple (of Jagannāth at Puri) now occupies the site where formerly stood the Dagoba containing the celebrated tooth-relic.[7] Sir Alexander Cunningham in his works *The Stupa of Barhut* and *The Bhilsa Topes,* advocated the view that the figures of Jagannāth, Subhadra and

Balabhadra had been derived from the Buddhist Tri-Ratna or Triple-Gem symbol signifying Buddha, Dharma and Sangha, set up together in one of the Sanchi sculptures. In the *Ancient Geography of India,* Sir Alexander Cunningham[8] has stated, "The three shapeless figures of Jagannāth, and his brother and sister, are simple copies of the symbolical figures of Buddhist Triad Buddha, Dharma and Sangha, of which the second is always represented as a female. The Buddhist origin of the Jagannāth figures is proved beyond all doubt by their adoption as the representative of the Brahmanical avatāra of Buddha in the annual almanacs of Mathura and Benares". The Indian scholars like N.N. Bose, Rajendra Lala Mitra, Dr. Harekrushna Mahtab and others have also supported the Buddhist view of Jagannāth. By referring to a stone of Asokan polish with the symbols of Buddha, Dharma and Sangha at the top, recently discovered at Bhubaneswar and now preserved in Ashutosh Museum of Calcutta Dr. Mahatab[9] observes, "The Symbols are a little different from those found out at Sanchi and other places but the Bhubaneswar symbols are almost exactly like the images of Jagannāth, Balabhadra and Subhadra. The Bhubaneswar discovery proves that in Orissa, the worship of the symbols was prevalent since the Asokan period." According to Dr. Mahatab the Savaras of Orissa were converted to Buddhism during the reign of Asoka and worshipped the Tri-Ratna symbol placed in a Buddhist Stupa at Puri. Later in the 7th or 8th century when Buddha was considered as an Avatara of Viṣṇu, Jagannāth was also considered to be an Avatara of Viṣṇu. Gradually Buddhism lost itself in Vaiṣhṇavism.[10]

"Late Pandit Nilakantha Das is the Chief exponent of the Jaina origin of Jagannāth. According to him Jagannāth is primarily a Jaina institution. He has tried to identify the Nilamadhava of the legends with the famous Kalinga Jina of history. "This Jagannāth, it appears, was there in the coast of Kalinga (present Orissa) as a piece of black stone which was called Kalinga Jina or symbol of Jina in Kalinga. Later on it was somehow analysed and the analytic name Nilamadhava was given to it".[11] Pandit Das believes that under the stress of the Sunya or nihilistic theory which developed out of the Mahayanic system of Buddhism, 'the Jain symbol', i.e., the stone called Kalinga Jina, came to be explained as Nila (black, nothingness) Ma (mother, creative energy) and Dhava (white, i.e., the phenomenal Universe)".[12] Thus the images of Jagannāth (of black colour representing Sunya), Suvadra (the creative energy), and Balabhadra (of white colour representing the phenomenal Universe) have evolved from Nilamadhava or the old Kalinga Jina. Pandit Das further adds, "Nilamadhava, therefore, represents a philosophy which means from a noumenal nothingness was produced a full phenomenal appearance, and this was on account of Ma (mother element or producing principle)."[13] Sudarsana, according to him is the Hindu name given to the old Jaina symbol; 'Dharma-Chakra, and Kaivalya (liberation), a term so exclusively common in Jagannāth, has been derived Jaina sources. Kedarnath Mohapatra, the distinguished historian, and Pandit Binayak Misra are among the other advocates of the Jaina view of Jagannāth. These two scholars have even tried to identify Indradyumna, the legendary founder of the Jagannāth worship at Puri, with Kharavela, the great Jaina emperor of Kalinga.[14]

"Jagannāth is regarded as Daru Brahma i.e. Godhead manifested in a wooden image. The worship of Daru as Brahman is traced to the Vedic sources, and to the Bhagavat Gita.[15] Pandit Nilakantha Das in an article, 'The Cult of Jagannāth', writes, "It may be mentioned here that in the Vedic literature of Rigveda (X-81-4) the word Wood (Daru) is used to indicate the material of which the Universe (Jagat) is made. Jagannāth is specifically known as 'Daru Brahman' (World substance symbolised in Wood) both in the Puranās and by the people."[16] Jagannāth has also been identified with the mystic bijamantra OM. Mono Mohan Ganguly is of the opinion that Buddhism is an off-shoot of the Hindu religion and the idea of the Tri-Ratna has been taken from the parent stock. "I believe the figure of Tri-Ratna has been copied from the triliteral syllable *aum* (OM), and hence is due to the resemblance of the figures of the Brahmanical triad of Jagannāth, Subhadra and Balaram to the holy Pranava.[17] Mr. Peterson also trace the origin of Jagannāth to the adoration of the mystic syllable A.U.M. coalescing into Om.[18]

Prof. Prabhat Mukherjee in his book *The History of Medieval Vaisnavism in Orissa*, apparently admits the deformed uncouth figures of Jagannāth to be due to its Savara origin, but traces the influence of Kṛishṇa-Vasudeva worship of the Bhagavata Cult on Jagannāth during the Gupta rule which was marked by the spread of Vaiṣhṇavism all over India. According to Prof. Mukherjee, in about 5th century A.D. Sankarshna and Vasudeva came to be known as Jagannāth and Balaram in Orissa.[19] "The Brihat Samhita or Varahamihira (6th century A.D.) enjoins to place Ekanamsa between Baladeva and Kṛishṇa (Ekanamsa Karya devi Baladeva Krishnyomadhye). In the Harivamsa, Ekanamsa is spoken of as the daughter of Nanda, and also as the sister of Balarama and Kṛishṇa."[20] So, under the inflence of Bhagavata Cult Ekanamsa came to be worshipped as Subhadra and was placed between Balabhadra and Jagannāth.

"Many arguments and counter arguments have been put forth by the scholars in supports of their respective views regarding the Origin of Jagannāth as referred to above, but no one has been able to deny the intimate association of the Savaras with Jagannāth worship even from its very inception. The story of finding Viṣṇu with the Savaras appear in different forms in Oriya folk-lore, medieval Oriya literature and the Puranās. One of the versions of the story is briefly as follow :

"After Viṣṇu saved the world from deluge in his Baraha incarnation, Brahma asked him of the means of Salvation of all creatures. Viṣṇu said, "I am being worshipped as Nilamadhava on the Blue Hill in Purushottama Kshetra. The highest form of Salvation could be attained by beholding me there." This was a cause of apprehension of Yama, the God of death, as he could not discharge his duties properly. On Yama's request Viṣṇu assured him to disappear from the Blue Hill after some days.

"The sacred Rohini Kunda was situated to the west of the all bestowing Kalpa-Vriksa whose branches had spread for one Krosa. The shrine of Nilamadhava was situated to the west of the Kunda, known to all excepting the Savara who worshipped him and the Gods who came to pay their daily oblations at his altar. In Satyayuga the pious and learned King Indradyumna of the Solar dynasty ruled in Avanti. He was anxious to see Viṣṇu. A wandering Sanyasin informed him that God himself was being worshipped as Purushottama on the Blue Hill in Odra Desa. Indradyumna sent Vidyapati, the brother of his family priest, to Utkala as his emissary. Vidyapati came to Utkala and settled in a Savara village situated to the west of the Blue Hill. After being acquainted with Visvavasu, the fowler, Vidyapati revealed to him the secrets of his mission and entreated him for a sight of Nilamadhava. He also told the fowler that his royal master would not touch food until his return. Out of compassion for the King Visvavasu took Vidyapati through a narrow track and showed him the Shrine of Nilamadhava. After seeing Nilamadhava Vidyapati returned to Avanti.

"In the meanwhile in order to fulfill His pledge given to Yama. Lord Viṣṇu made the Shrine of Nilamadhava invisible under the sand. When Indradyumna accompanied by Narada set out with a vast army and reached the borders of the kingdom of Utkala, its King informed him about the disappearance of Nilamadhava. Indradyumna was completely disheartened with the news, but sage Narada assured him that God would reappear in the form of Daru (a log of wood). Thus being consoled Indrayumna visited the Blue Hill and offered a thousand aswamedha sacrifices there.

"On the closing day of the aswamedha sacrifice Nilamadhava appeared to Indradyumna in a vision, and at his bathing time the attendants came and informed him that a Daru with four branches was floating on the Sea. The King with due ceremony brought the Daru and placed it on the Mahavedi. While discussing with Narada about fashioning the log into an image, the King heard a voice from heaven saying, "God Himself will make His own image. The aged carpenter standing with his tools should be shut up a room for fifteen days and utmost secrecy should be maintained about the construction of Image." Things were arranged accordingly and at the end of the allotted time Jagannāth, Balabhadra, Suvadra and Sudarsana appeared on the Mahavedi. Being directed by a voice from heaven the King adorned the images with silken cloth and painted them with their respective colours. He also built a temple one thousand cubits high to install the images.

"Indradyumna went to heaven to invite Brahma to consecrate the temple. Brahma was listening to music, and the time that intervened amounted to many ages of mortal life. In the meanwhile a King named Gala had taken possession of the temple and was worshipping an image of Madhab in it. At last Brahma came, Indradyumna and Gala were reconciled to each other and the image of Madhab was shifted to a smaller temple. Brahma consecrated the temple and the images. After leaving the temple in charge of Gala, Indradyumna proceeded to Brahmaloka.

"A slightly different version of the story is found in the Musali Parva of the Mahabharata written by the great 15th century Oriya poet Sarala Das. According to him, Narayana or Savarinarayana was being worshipped by the Savaras in the forest and being informed about it, King Galamadhava of Kanchi proceeded to the Savara village to take possession of the Deity. But the Deity had disappeared in the meanwhile. King Galamadhava was angry with the Savaras thinking that they had hidden the Deity, and waged a war against them. He had killed all the Savaras, excepting one, when the voice of Viṣṇu from heaven asked him to desist from the holocaust as the Savaras were His great devotees. God Viṣṇu also cursed Galamadhava that his entire line would be extinct. The story of Indradyumna begins after this. Lord Kṛishṇa was killed by the arrow of Jara, a fowler, Arjun consigned the body of Kṛishṇa to flames, but the flames could not consume it. Being directed by a voice from heaven Arjun threw the body of Lord Kṛishṇa into the Sea, and at length it floated in the form of a Daru to Nilasundara on the shores of the Sea. Jara had followed the body of Kṛishṇa along the Sea coast. King Indradyumna, knowing that Viṣṇu will appear at Nilagiri (the Blue Hill), had constructed a temple there with the help of the Brahmin Viswavasu. Kṛishṇa informed Jara in a dream that He would appear in Rohini Kunda in the shape of Daru (log of Wood) Indradyumna got the information from Jara and sent his men to lift the Daru from Rohini Kunda, but all his efforts failed. Then being directed by the Lord in a vision,

Indradyumna employed the services of Jara, the fowler, and Vasu, the Brahmin ; who jointly lifted the Daru from Rohini Kunda, Jara and Viswakarma together fashioned the log into the three images of Balavadra, Suvadra and Jagannāth who, according to poet Sarala's version, stood for Siva, Bramha and Viṣṇu respectively.[21] The incompletion of the images is ascribed to the opening of the door before the allotted time.

"The worship of Jagannāth by the Savaras also finds mention in other Oriya texts like the 'Daru Brahmagita' of Jagannāth Das (16th century A.D.) and the Deulatola by Nilambara Das (17th century A.D.). The Daitas who are hereditary servitors in the temple of Jagannāth at Puri, claim their descent from the Savaras and the Deities are left to their sole care during the Snana yatra and the Car festival. They also observe the funeral rites of Jagannāth during Nabalakebar when the Deities, being made of Wood, change their body every 12-18 years.

"Hunter remarks,[22] 'The very origin of Jagannāth proclaims him not less the God of the Brahmanas than the low-caste aboriginal races.' After narrating the story of Indradyumna in his 'Orissa', Hunter further adds, 'In the foregoing legend we find the aboriginal people worshipping a blue stone in the depths of the forest. But the Deity has grown tired of the Jungle offerings of the primitive people, and longs for the Cooked food of the more civilised Aryan race. When the Aryan element at length comes on the scene, the rude blue stone disappears, and gives place to a carved image. At the present hour, in every hamlet of Orissa, this two-fold worship co-exists. The common people have their shapeless stone or block, which they adore with simple rites in the open air, while side by side with it is a temple to one of the Aryan Gods with its carved images and elaborate rites."[23]

"W.J. Wilkins[24] has also traced the origin of Jagannāth worship to tribal source, 'The probability being that He (Jagannāth) was the local divinity of some, now unknown tribe, whose worship was engrafted into Hinduism, and the God when admitted into the pantheon was regarded as another manifestation of Viṣṇu."

"Dr. Benimadhav Padhi in his book *Daru Devata* has

traced the origin of Jagannāth to the Daru worship by the Savaras in the pre-historic times. Tree worship is a very ancient Cult. The proto-australoids worshipped the ficus tree and their religion was known as the 'Cult of Ficus Tree'. Gradually tree worship has spread into other religions. Till today the Savaras or Sauras of Ganjam and Koraput districts worship tree as their 'Kitung', which in Saura language means God. They believe that their 'Kitung', dwells in a tree, outside their village. They never cut the tree which they call Jagant (a special name of Kitung), nor cut any other tree in the area where it stands. They also believe that their Kitung has ten incarnations which is exactly similar to the concept of ten incarnations of Viṣṇu. The word Jagannāth is never a Sanskrit word, nor a Pali word ; presumably it is the Sanskritised form of the austric word 'Jaganta'."[25]

The purpose of quoting from Puri district Gazetteer was to acquaint with the prevalent opinions, on the origin of Jagannāth Deity. Myths, legends, traditions and literatures have encompassed Jagannāth Deity so much that a scholar[26] thinks of Jagannāth Deity as 'The Mysterious Jagannāth.'

No doubt tradition preserves the culture of a Nation. The view of C.R. Krishnamacharlu[27] is appropriate, when he states that scientific study of evidences available and construction of history do not logically speaking, consist, as is generally imagined now a days merely in the exposition of the archaeological, epigraphical and numismatic evidence only, since these do not reach effectively and satisfactorily the distant limits in the past to which, literature and traditions, better custodians, in some respects, of the Nation's historic memories, extend. Who can reach or count the sub-strata of monumentary relics that have undergone submergence, layer over layer, with the passage of time ? The top most layer of the monuments is at best only a partial evidence for the last chapter of the history of the nation.

Literature and traditions are better custodians no doubt. About Indian mythology and the mythology of popular Hinduism, R.N. Dandekar[28] illustrates, "Mythology is very aptly described as the language of the primitive. What the early man failed to express satisfactorily through the medium of words, he tried to express through the medium of mythological concepts. In their primary form, therefore, myths cannot be said to be the result of poetic invention in the sense which these words now bear. If philosophy attempts to discover the ultimate Truth, mythology must be said to represent the human effort to attain at least to the penultimate truth, of which all experience is the temporal reflection. As a matter of fact, it is possible to psycho-analyse, so to say, a people by means of a critical study of its mythology.[29] Through their numerous legends of cosmogony, of Gods, and of heroes, the Indians have given expression fuller and finer than any other people in the World—to their beliefs, ideals and traditions.

"Early Vedic Mythology : In the absence of any literature belonging to the pre-Vedic period we cannot make any statement regarding the mythological concepts which were then prevalent. Considering that the Vedic religion is a growth of many centuries and has been elaborated by the fertile and subtle brains of a number of generations of active people, it becomes quite understandable that it should defy any attempt at a sweeping definition in one word. What is true of Vedic religion is equally true of Vedic mythology, for in the concept of Indian religion, particularly Vedic religion, the elements of religion, mythology and magic, are inextricably interlaced. It has been suggested that the early Vedic religion is 'Naturalism' pure and simple ; and Vedic mythology can be studied in its proper perspective only on the background of the history of the development of human thought as a whole. It must be emphasized that Vedic mythology is essentially an evolutionary mythology. It has reacted to the many vicissitudes in the life of the Vedic Indians, and, with each vicissitude, new elements have been introduced into the personality of a Vedic God. It is this dynamic process that has been responsible for the complex character of Vedic Gods. It is, however, not altogether impossible, through a critical study of Vedic literature with the aid of comparative philology comparative mythology and anthropology, to determine, on the one hand, the order in which particular Gods have, at different stages, dominated

Vedic mythology, and, on the other, to fix the priority of the various elements in the personality of an individual God and thus to present, as it were, a picture of his 'becoming' "—" The mythology of popular Hinduism has always tended to become richer and richer, as time passed, on account of the addition of legends pertaining, on the one hand, to the victories of the numerous Gods, Goddesses and Godlings over the various rākṣasas or Titans of Hindu mythology, and, on the other, to their acts of grace in respect of their devotees and worshippers. There was further added to Hinduism an ever increasing mass of mythological details, whose origin can be traced to various minor Cults, such as the Serpent-worship and the worship of graha-devatās (planetary deities) and grāma-devatās (village deities). Again, we must not forget the large number of legends occasioned by the remarkably ingenious manner in which the characters of certain ancient sages, like Narada, have been developed by the fertile mythological imagination of Hindu poets, bards and minstrels. Philosophy is often described as the foundation of religion, ritual as its super-structure and mythology as its detailed decoration. In the case of Hinduism, however, mythology is not merely its decoration; it is its essential constituent factor. Mythology is at once the strength and weakness of Hinduism-Strength, because mythology represents some of the distinctive features of Hinduism, such as toleration, broad sympathy, liberal outlook, and dynamically assimilative and, at the same time, elevating power; and weakness, because there is the danger of the true spirit of Hinduism being undermined by the weight of its mythological richness."

H.D. Sankalia[30] had very successfully approached to reach the historical reality of *Rāmayana* description, through archaeological method. D.D. Kosambi[31] had shown, how *Bhagavad-Gita* is a remarkable interpolation. The approach of these two scholars invoked the author to study the culture of Mahānadi valley, through archaeological findings. The cream of Mahānadi valley culture, is the evolution or origin of Lord Jagannāth Deity. There are many archaeological findings of early medieval period in India. Through the comparative and critical study of early medieval archaeological findings, the author has approached to study the Origin of Jagannāth Deity and it has been studied that the decadence of Buddhism in India Religious revolution of India, specially of Mahānadi valley, resulted in the foundation of Jagannāth Deity and its Cult.

The research oriented work has been divided into eight chapters. Chapter I, deals with the introduction. Chapter II, deals with the Religious Revolution of Mahānadi valley. Buddha has been acknowledged as an Avatara of Viṣṇu and this has been discussed in Chapter III. Chapter IV, deals with Buddha alias Jagannāth, as an Avatara of Viṣṇu, in Mahānadi valley and its evolution as Puruṣottama-Jagannāth. Reverence and dishonour of Śaṅkarāchārya at Jagannāth temple of Puri is dealt in Chapter V. Jagannāth as a single Deity was established first, it developed to Jagannāth Trinity and it has been dealt in Chapter VI. Jagannāth Deity evolved to be worshipped as Dadhibaban, Patitāpabana and Trutiya Deities. This evolution is discussed in Chapter VII. In Chapter VIII, a critical review of Dr. K.C. Mishra's view is done. At last the Conclusion is given.

REFERENCES

1. Pandey, L.P. "Similarity of the Cave-Men's Art in India and America, *PATSAIOC,* 1933, pp. 239-242.
2. Pandey, L.P. "Was Ujjain Even in Mahakōśala,"*JOMHS*, Vol. II, pp. 10-12.
3. CPOSK, passim.
4. Pargiter, F.E. *The Purāṇa text of the Dynasties of the Kali Age,* Oxford, 1913, passim, as referred by Kosambi, D.D. *An Introduction to the Study of Indian History,* Popular Prakashan, Bombay, 1975, p. 2.
5. *GOIOP,* pp. 797-804.
6. Mitra, R.L. *The Antiquities of Orissa,* Vol. II, Calcutta, 1882, passim.
7. *Ibid.,* p. 176.
8. *TAGOI,* pp. 430-431.
9. *THOO,* Vol. II, 1960, pp. 520-521.
10. *Ibid.,* pp. 521-523.
11. *OHRJ,* Vol. VII, No. 1, p. 7.

12. *Ibid.*
13. *Ibid.* p. 8.
14. Padhi, Benimadhab-*Daru Devata,* (Oriya), Cuttack Student's Store, Cuttack, 1964, p. 36.
15. Das, Pandit Suryanaryana-*Oriya Sahitya-ra-Itihas,* (Oriya), Part I Cuttack, (?), pp. 454-458.
16. *Orissa Review,* Vol. XXVI, No. 12, Cuttack, p. 25.
17. Ganguly, M.M. *Orissa and Her Remains—Ancient and Mediaeval (District Puri),* Thacker Spink & Co. Calcutta., 1912, pp. 406-407.
18. *AHOO,* p. 277.
19. *THOMVIO,* p. 17.
20. Behera, K.S. *Orissa Review,* No. 11, Cuttack, p. 3.
21. Mohanty, A. (ed.), *Sarala Mahabharata, Musali Parva,* Cultural Affairs Dept. Bhubaneswar, 1965, p. 116.
22. Hunter, W.W. *Orissa,* Vol. I, London, 1872, pp. 88-89.
23. *Ibid.*, pp. 94-95.
24. Wilkins, W.J. *Hindu Mythology,* p. 208.
25. Daru Devata, pp. 52-54.
26. Mahtab, H.K. "The Mysterious Jagannāth and Problems of History of Orissa," *OHC.* Proceedings of the Annual Session, B.J.B. College, Bhubaneswar, 1979, pp. 1-7.
27. *TCOIH,* pp. 2-3.
28. Dandekar, R.N., "Indian Mythology," *TCHOI,* Vol. II, The Rāmakrishna Mission Institute of Culture, Calcutta, 1969, pp. 223-224, 238-239.
29. For instance, see H. Zimmer, *Māyā : Derindische Mythos* (1936).
30. *TRIHP,* passim.
31. *MAR,* pp. 15-18.

Two

Religious Revolution of Mahanadi Valley

I

Like the Indus valley civilization in the west, the Gangetic valley civilization in the north, the Brahmaputra valley civilization in the east, the Mahanadi valley civilization flourished in the south-east of ancient Jambudwipa. Two rivers have been flowing through Orissa and the Oriya Nation : the first is Mahanadi and the second is Lord Jagannāth. Like Jerusalem for the Christians, Mecca for the Muslims, Puri-Jagannāth is the ultimate goal for the Hindus. Puri-Jagannāth is deemed to be the confluence of the people of all religions-Hinduism (Sakta, Śiva, Vaiṣhṇava, Ganapatya, etc.), Buddhism and Jainism irrespective of their caste, colour, creed and language.[1]

The glories of the source of Mahanadi river are much. Sihawa, situated to the south of modern Raipur district of Madhya Pradesh, is the source of the river Mahanadi. Greater part of the country lying between Dhamtari and Sihawa tract is a rocky ground covered with thick forest, scenery of which is very pleasant and attractive. A temple, situated to the north of the door of Karneshwara temple has an inscribed slab bearing the Saka year 1114, corresponding to A.D. 1192. The inscription refers this Sihawa area, to have been the place of Devarhada tirth or the sacred Lake of the Gods. Rishi

Shringin is still worshipped here, the belief being that it was the place of his hermitage. In fact, the large part of Sihawa tract was once regarded as sacred. The tract also yielded some remains and inscriptions relating to Jainism. Inscriptions are of Vishva-Somasena. The village Ratawa, eight kilometres away from Sihawa, is said to be the place of Angirasa Rishi and the village Mechuka, some 32 kilometres away, contained the hermitage of Muchkunda. Jagapal's inscription in Rajim temple refers to this tract by the name Mechka-Sihawa. Deokhut is about 13 kilometres from here. The name appears to be the corrupt form of Deo-kut which means the hillock of Gods.[2]

While doing study on the subject 'The Cult of Jagannāth,' for his D.Phil thesis, K.C. Mishra[3] had given impartial views, when he stated that Sarala Das, a famous poet of Orissa of the early 14th century, suggests that Jagannāth was brought to Puri from Śavarinārāyāna. He had well balanced the opinion, when he wrote,[4] "There is however, a clue to determine the existence of a Rastradevata in Dakṣiṇa Kōśala at Śavarinārāyāna and another in Kalinga at the Mahendra, they were taken to be the family Gods of the royal families of these Kingdoms." While giving the background of the Cult of Jagannātha, K.C. Mishra[5] very boldly and frankly mentioned that the Mahanādi or Chitrotpala flowed through the regions of the early Pāṇḍu-vaṁśi Kings of Sirpur in Dakṣiṇa Kōśala with its group of temples at Rājim and Śavarinārāyāna, and through the newly developed Suvarṇapura of the Sōmavaṁśī Kings, while it also drained in the districts of Puri and Cuttack. It may be suggested that civilisation progressed through the course of this river to the coastal regions of Orissa from the far-away hinterland of Madhya Bhārata.

In the meantime Satyanarayan Rajaguru[6] had made and is making untiring efforts by referring to the Telugu translation of Madalapanji, preserved at Madras Government Oriental Manuscript Library, and is claiming that on the top of Mahendra mountain Jarasabara Chief was residing, who was worshipper of 'Paraoamani.'

Tradition has associated the worship of the Deity Puruṣottama with the name of Indradyumna. In the

Mahābhārata[7] we find mention of a legendary King named Indradyumna. The King has been described there as one who performed a thousand sacrifices. It is said there that the cows brought for the sacrifices made a pond with their hooves, which was named after the King. The epic story of Indradyumna and the tank-named after him, appears to have helped develop the traditional association of King Indradyumna and Indradyumna Sarovara with Puruṣottama-Jagannāth.[8]

S.N. Rajaguru[9] identifies Indravarman, the King of the Gaṅga house of Śvetaka as Indradyumna, and holds him to be responsible in installing Lord Jagannāth at Puri.

The Gaṅga house of Śvetaka was established in 6th century A.D. and the Śvetaka house appears to have been completely extirpated by Anantavarman Choḍagaṅga about the close of the eleventh century. The above identification of traditional Indradyumna, with Gaṅga King Indravarman, as done by S.N. Rajaguru cannot be accepted, because; as it is going to be dealt, the early medieval period witnessed the synchronisation of different religions or faiths.

The study on the Cult of Lord Jagannāth is so heterogeneous that while writing the paper, 'The Cult of Jagannāth,' for the second time. K.C. Mishra[10] changed his view and stated :

> "In our opinion, there is every probability that God Narayana was installed on the Mahendra mountain and was worshipped by Matharas for a long time. It is presumed that prior to this period, the Sabaras worshipped some Gods on the mountain whose names are not yet ascertained. When the Matharas came they overpowered the Sabaras and took possession of their Deity. The next dramatic change came when the Gaṅgas arrived on the scene and began worshipping the Deity as Gokarneswara. The Gaṅgas were worshippers of Śiva and the Deity was worshipped as Svayambhu by Sailodbhavas prior to them. It is interesting to observe that an identified Deity beginning with the Sabara worship became Narayana with the Matharas, Svayambhu with the Sailodbhavas and Gokarneswara with the Gaṅgas. The Sailodbhavas were the worshippers of both Viṣṇu and Śiva and this is proved from a number of copper plate grants they have donated. In course of time, their attachment to Viṣṇu,

became more and they worshipped the Deity perhaps on the Mahendra mountain as Chakradhara Madhava or Bhagavan Madhava. This is an interesting development which traced the metamorphosis of the Deity at Mahendra Giri from an unknown Deity aboriginal in origin to Narayana or Viṣṇu. In course of time, this is supposed to have been transferred to Puri in a complex and mysterious manner."

In spite of all these facts, it is known that the culture of Orissa is much indebted to Upper Mahanadi valley. R.V. Russell and Hiralal[11] have well recorded the Tribal legends of the Savaras and state that local tradition traces their origin to the celebrated Seori of the *Rāmayana,* who is supposed to have lived somewhere near the present Seorinarayana in the Bilaspur district and to have given her name to this place. Ramchandra in his wanderings met her there, ate the plums (berries), which she gathered for him after tasting each one herself and out of regard for her devotion permitted her name to precede his own of Narayan, in that given to the locality.

During the *vanavasa*, Rāma arrived on the shore of the Pampa lake and saw the Savari-asrama, situated in Savarivana, also called Matunga-vana. It was there, Savari worshipped Rāma by offering ripe berries after tasting them. The site came to be known as Savari-narayana, and it is the earliest Vaiṣhṇav worship in eastern India.

Another legend of Upper Mahanadi river valley recorded by R.V. Russel and Hiralal states that the Savaras were created for carrying stones for the construction of the great temple at Puri and for dragging the Car of Jagannāth, which they still do at the present time. Yet another connecting them with the temple of Jagannāth states that their ancestor was an old Bhil hermit called Sawar, who lived in Kharod, two miles from Seorinarayan. The God Jagannāth had at this time appeared in Seorinarayan and the old Sawar used to worship him. The King of Orissa had built the great temple at Puri and wished to install Jagannāth in it, and he sent a Brahman to fetch him from Seorinarayan, but nobody knew where he was except the old hermit Sawar. The Brahman besought him in vain to be allowed to see the God and even went so far as to marry his daughter, and finally the old man consented to take him blindfold to the place. The Brahman, however, tied some mustard seeds in the corner of his cloth and made a hole in it, so that they dropped out one by one on the way. After some time they grew up and served to guide him to the spot. This story of the mustard seeds of course finds a place in the folk-lore of many nations. The Brahman then went to Seorinarayan alone and begged the God to go to Puri. Jagannāth consented, and assuming the form of a log of wood, floated down the Mahanadi to Puri, where he was taken out and placed in the temple. A carpenter agreed to carve the God's image out of the log of wood on condition that the temple should be shut up for six months while the work was going on. But, some curious people opened the door before the time and the work could not proceed and thus the image of the God is only half carved out of the wood upto the present day. As a consolation to the old man the God ordered that the place should bear the hermit's name before his own as Seorinarayan.

The Bilaspur district Gazetteer,[12] also records the legend of Seorinarayan thus. "There is a story that once the place was a forest inhabited by an old Sawara or Saoner, who worshipped Jagannāth, the Deity was afterwards removed to the temple of Jagannāth at Puri, by a Brahman. But as a reward for the faithfulness of the old Sawara, Jagannāth wished that, the name of the place of his concealment should contain the names of both the worshipper and the worshipped. Hence the place came to be called Sawar-Narayan of Seorinarayan. Close to Mahanadi, there is a small tank, known as Rohini-Kund in which the bones of the dead are immersed."

Puruṣottama was worshipped on the Sea shore at Puri and there are lot of traditions about it.[13] Sarladīs, the famous poet of Orissa, in the Vanaparva and Musaliparva gives the traditional narration how Śõmavaṁśi King Galamadhava brought the Lord Sabarinarayan to Puri. This is the earliest recorded oral transmission from generation to generation and therefore remains uninterpolated. This handed down belief or practice is recorded in the Puri District Gazetteer[14] thus : "A slightly different version of the story is found in the Musaliparva of the *Mahabharata,* written by the great 15th century Oriya poet Saraladas. According to him Narayana or Savarinarayana was being worshipped by the Savaras in the forest and being informed about it, King Galamadhava of Kanchi proceeded to the Savara village to take possession of the Deity. But the Deity had disappeared in the meanwhile. King Galamadhava was angry with the Savaras thinking that they had hidden the Deity, and waged a war against them. He had killed all the Savaras, expecting one, when the voice of Viṣṇu from heaven asked him to desist from the holocaust as the Savaras were His great devotees. God Viṣṇu also cursed Galamadhava that his entire line would be extinct."

The worship of Jagannāth by the Savaras also finds mention in other Oriya texts like the "Daru Brahmagita" of Jagannāth Das (16th century A.D.) and the "Deul tola" by Nilambara Das (17th century A.D.). Gopinath Mohapatra[15] gives a perplexed opinion, when he states that Śavarinārāyāna was being worshipped by the Savaras on a hill called 'Dhauli', near Bhuvaneswar, Orissa. It has been mentioned in Musaliparva of Sarala Mahabharata[16] that in Satyayuga the God hold or bear the name of Śavarinārāyāṇa. It doesn't mean that Śavarinārāyāṇa was worshipped on a hill called 'Dhauli,' near Bhuvaneswar. The view of learned Scholar Gopinath Mohapatra is incorrect and cann't be accepted.

It seems, Basudev Sahu[17] has followed Gopinath Mohapatra and emphasised that Śavarinārāyāna is worshipped near the Rohinikunda at Puruṣhottama Kshetra and Sarala Das suggests that Śavarinārāyāna was worshipped near Dhauli mountain of Bhubaneswar. The view of Basudev Sahu is erroneous and cannot be accepted. Śavarinārāyāṇa is a Universally known site, on the Upper Mahanadi valley. This is within the distance of about three miles, from the confluence of the river Jonk and the Mahanadi.[18]

V.V. Mirashi[19] says that an old temple of Viṣṇu exists at Śheorinārāyan, perhaps erected by a collateral branch of the Royal family (i.e. Kalachuris of Ratnapur). This temple of Śheorinārāyan alias Śavarinārāyāna can be dated to 12th century A.D. because in this period, the Kalachuris of Ratnpur became most powerful and occupied the whole of South

Kōśala region.Śavarinārāyāna Deity might have been worshipped throughout the country, but the original site of Śavarinārāyāna is located on the confluence of Mahānadi and Sibnath alias Seonath rivers. It is but natural that Śavarinārāyāna site should be located at a little distance in the outskirt of Dandakaranya.

H.D. Sankalia[20] states that the mention of Savari-asrama is also important for tracing Rāma's route to Lanka. At present, the place known as Śavarinārāyāna or Śheorinārāyan in the tourist map of Madhya Pradesh is situated about 40 kms. (or 30 miles) south-east of Bilaspur. This is the heart of the Ādivasi area, where, besides Savaras, there are Gonds and several other aboriginal tribes. The present site is situated on the northern asrama, or the asrama was situated somewhere in this region.

Śheorinārāyan plates of Ratnadeva II,[21] Śheorinārāyan stone inscription of Jajalladeva II[22] and Śheorinārāyan statue inscription[23] are the epigraphical proofs which speak of the Upper Mahanadi valley, well known place of pilgrimage on the left bank of Mahanadi. Sabari temple of Kharod, situated in the vicinity of Śheorinārāyan site and Sabari river alias Kolab river, which flows in Koraput district, commemorate Ram-bhakta Savari.

Śivalinga worship existed in India since remote past and the whole Mahānadi valley was not deprived of it. Śivalinga came into existence long before the advent of image worship.[2r] It has been earlier stated that Śavarinarayan, is the earliest site of Vaiṣhṇav worship in eastern India. Turturia is situated on the right bank of Balamdi Nala, 11 kilometres above its junction with the river Mahanadi. According to local tradition, Turturia is said to be the seat of the hermitage of Sage Valmiki and the birth place of Lava and Kusha, the twin sons of Sita. On one of the pillars of the grey sandstone is found a single line of inscription in Gupta characters which were damaged, when washed and cleaned. The only letters "ro Bhagavato" could be read. These pillars resembling those found at Besnagar and Deogarh, are of late Gupta age.[25]

J.N. Banerjea[26] refers to the inscribed Viṣṇu image, now

worshipped at Burhikhas in Bilaspur district and states that one or two stone images of Vaiṣhṇavite deities are, however, known, which can be dated probably in the second century before the Christian era, if not earlier. Another inscribed Viṣṇu image dated to 2nd century B.C. is at Malhar.[27] These two inscribed Viṣṇu images are the earliest inscribed Viṣṇu images of India. This shows that Upper Mahānadi valley had the Vaiṣhṇav impact for the first time. Further J.E. Brockington[28] informs that in India the earliest temple of Rāma is the Rajivalocana temple at Rajim.

The ring-stones are found throughout the Mahānadi valley. The stone rings of ancient finds can profitably be compared with the Cakras and Yantras of modern times, which were utilised by the Saktas in the ritualistic worship of the Great Mother.[29] The YONI discovered at Maraguda valley[30] and preserved as the private possession of the author, may be regarded as the earliest Sakti worship of Chalcolithic age in Mahānadi valley. These show that Śaiva, Vaiṣhṇav and Sakta worship had early beginning in Upper Mahānadi valley.

R.C. Das[31] very interestingly mentions, "In the context of the history of Orissa and the evolution of its society and culture since ancient times, it is an interesting point as to whether Sri Jagannāth represents the stage of the development of Orissan society from the "bicameral stage'' to the "conscious stage" and from the hunting and food-gathering stage to the agricultural stage—In that case, His age might in all probability, extend up to *Rig-Veda / Atharva Veda* where mention has been made of Apurusa Daru/Daru-worship."

From the archaeological remains of Upper Mahandi valley, it is known that Religious synthesis took place.[31] The worship of Puruṣottama-Nrsimha, can be traced from the inscription of Lakshmana temple at Sirpur,[33] for the first time. Viṣṇu and Śiva were given equal status side by side, on the same platform or Vedi, and therefore Hari-Hara Cult developed.[34] The author's field survey in 1984 camė across Hari-Hara images at Junagarh and Sankusgarh in Kalahandi district. The Hari-Hara images have Urdhva-linga (penis erectus) and shows erotic element.

Jaina Harivamsa Purāṇa records that Mahavira preached

his sermons in Kalinga. Further Avasyakasutra tells that Mahaviraswami during his religious tours visited Toshali, the capital of Kalinga. The early spread of Jainism in Orissa is evident from these traditions and it will be reasonable to conclude that Jainism made its first appearance in this country in 6th century B.C. Avadānaśataka[35] states that Buddha had visited South Kōśala and had stayed in the then capital of South Kōśala for three months. The long stay of Buddha at South Kōśala seems to have influenced the people so much that they named a river as *Rahul,* after the name of the son of Buddha, *Rahul* is a tributary of Tel river and flows in Kalahandi district. The visits of Mahavira and Buddha seems to have great impact of their teachings, in the whole Mahānadi valley.

Traces of Vajrayana Buddhism is found at Malhar,[36] whose excavation report places those findings within circa, B.C. 350 to 300. A.D. About 1st or 2nd century A.D. Maḥāyāma Buddhism blossomed into its full glory under the care of Nagarjuna, who lived at Po-lo-mo-lo-ki-li, as described by Hieun Tsang.[37] In the words of Nilakantha Das,[38] the South Kōśala region, i.e. the region of Raipur, Sambalpur, Patna upto Baudh, was in those times, i.e., about the 5th century A.D. and onwards, called the Uddiyāna regions.[39] Uddiyāna seems to be a Buddhistic term meaning Yāna or the way of religious thinking and practice by the Uddās or the land inhabited or influenced by them. These Uddās appear to be a race of the Savaras or the Austrics greatly influenced by some Dravidians or atleast the rudiments of the Dravidian language in later times. They perhaps came to these regions mostly by sea routes by the Bay of Bengal and inhabited the uplands of Utkala from where they gradually shifted to this region on their way to the Kangoda region in later times. The word Uddayāna somehow became Uddiyāna under the influence of the contiguous or intermingling Dravidians. For even now the Dravidians, specially the neighbouring Telugus say Uddivādu (Uddiwādā) where they mean the land of the Uddas or the Oriyas. Thus Uddiyana indicates a religious designation like Mahayāna, etc., signifying some particular ways of thinking and practice which were in vogue in the regions referred to. This word Uddiyāna, in course of time, was used to indicate the name of a place where this Yana was in vogue. This was perhaps so on account of the most palatable and therefore the most outstanding religion called Buddhism of *Mahasukha* (great pleasure) of sexual enjoyment, later on Hinduised into the Sahajiya or the Gaudiya Vaiṣṇava Cult of Bengal.

Further N. Das[40] mentions that the people of the Uddiyāna or ancient South Kōśala or Kōshala, a tract mainly inhabited by the Savaras with some intermingling of the Oddas, as has been indicated, seems to have social and other similar connections with the eastern people, i.e., the people of Utkala, Radha, East Bengal and Assam.

Vatsyayana,[41] in his Kumasutra deals about the women of different countries and informs that the women of the Stri Rajya and of Kōshala, are full of impetuous desire, their semen falls in large quantities, and they are fond of taking medicine to make it do so. Richard Burten and F.F. Arbuthrot, the translators of Vatsyayana's Kamasutra have mentioned (Oudh) by the side, where Kōśala is mentioned and thereby have meant North Kōśala. It should be noted that when Vatsyayana wrote Kamasutra in fourth or fifth century A.D.[42] there was no existence of North Kōśala and South Kōśala is mentioned here, because Stri Rajya is associated with it.

So, as the women of the South Kōśala are full of impetuous desire, they are fond of rushing on with impetus or violence, vehement and acting with headlong energy in sex act. In the words of A.R. Sharif,[43] the women of Kōśala enjoyed thrashing of their private parts. They also resorted to the artificial lingam (phallus) for sexual satisfaction.

In these circumstances of all-round synchronisation, it was befitting that a unique culture developed and that was the Jagannāth Culture. Nilakantha Das[44] says, "Yet this Tantra of the mother cult in later times somehow mixed up with Śūnyavāda (nihilism) of Buddhism which came out of Mahāyāna school of it, in the Terais of the Himalayas upto Nepal, East Magadha and Bengal, where, in later times, it developed Mahāsukha (great pleasure derived from ecstasy of the sex act) of Bajrāyana and Sahajayāna as a substitute for

Nirvana. About the 7th or the 8th century A.D. this aspect had developed in the Tantric region of Uddiyana whose King Indrabhuti who was the disciple of Ananga Bajra, a Bengali prince and Laxminkarā, the sister of Indrabhuti and the Queen of Jalendra, the King of Lankapuri, or the present Patna district, are found to have preached things perhaps imitated in long practice from the so-called Siddhas like Ananga Bajra, whose book "Prājnopāya Binischayasiddhi," speaks of sexual excesses in very horrible and nauseating terms.[45] Indrabhuti's famous book, *Jnanasiddhi* begins, "I bow to Jagannāth who is worshipped by all Jains and who also represents all Buddhas and in perfection is like the all pervading sky."[46]

N.K. Sahu[47] emphasises Indrabhuti, the Raja of Sambhal (Sambalpur), who has been assigned to have ruled during the dark period of the history of South Kōśala, according to the author,[48] to have been the propounder of Vajrayana Buddhism. He was the first Siddha to identify Buddha with Jagannāth and he was the worshipper of Jagannāth whom he prays at several places of his famous work *Jnanasiddhi.* Before Indrabhuti there was no conception of Jagannāth as a God to be worshipped. In Sanskrit literature Jagannāth as a Deity is unknown before *Jnanasiddhi.* Jagannāth mentioned in the Shantiparva of the *Mahabharata* of Bangabasi edition and even in early publication of Bangabasi edition is an interpolation as this is not found in Poona edition or Kumbakoram edition and even in early publication of Bangabasi edition. Puri (Puruṣottama Puri) is the Seat of Puruṣottama and not of Jagannāth. In the 10th century A.D. a religious revolution synthesised Jagannāth of Sambalpur with Puruṣottama of Puri.

The earliest mention of Puruṣottama is found in Rigveda couplet *(Rig veda,* X -155-3). During Rigveda period there was physical geography of Saptasaindhava alias Saptasindhu[49] and there was no peninsular India then. Even Lord Buddha is addressed as 'Puruṣottama,' in Samudrabanika Jataka of Pali literature, (vide : Satapathi, S.N. "Greater Indian conception in Orissan Culture," *Amrutayana,* (Oriya monthly magazine), ed. Gita Hota, Bhuvaneswar, October, 1988, p. 31.) The *Anarghara-ghava Natakam* of Murari Misra,[50] assigned to 9th century A.D., refers to God Purusottama who was worshipped on the sea shore. The Sarada Devitemple inscription (circa. 10th century A.D.) of Maihar (Satna district, Madhya Pradesh) mention Purusottama Kshetra in Odra country.[51] Reference to Purusottama Kshetra has been made in the Baramdeo temple inscription dated in the Kalachuri era 840 or 1088 A.D., and in the Nagpur stone inscription of the Rulers of Malva, dated 1104 A.D.[52] The latter inscription clearly mentions that Purusottama is situated on the eastern ocean. These views seem to support N.K. Sahu that Puri (Purusottama Puri) is the seat of Purusottam and not of Jagannāth. Even H.K. Mahatab[53] after much study has declared that Jagannāth has been referred to for the first time in *Jnanasiddhi,* of Indrabhuti written in circa. 717 A.D.

It becomes necessary to know the use of the title Jagannāth and how it came into use in Sanskrit literature. H.V. Stietencron[54] states that it appears that the decisive factor in bringing about the correlation of 'Jagannātha' with Viṣṇu was Sāktism and more particularly the enormous popularity of one of its most important texts, the *Devi Mahatmya.* The text which was composed by a gifted poet in the late Gupta or early medievel period and therefore became an integral part of the *Markaṇḍeya Purāṇ,* refers in its first chapter to Viṣṇu as Jagannāth. Its influence was considerable, as can be proved by the countless images of the Goddess in her various aspects which are inspired by the descriptions of the *Devi-Māhātmya.* And it was mainly due to this text that the combination of the title 'Jagannāth' with Viṣṇu became known throughout India. But in the *Devi-Mahatmya,* the reference is to Viṣṇu as primordial Deity, sleeping on the cosmic waters. It is not to the particular God enshrined in a temple at Puri or elsewhere, nor to Puri's wooden images, of unique and unmistakable shape which later became constitutive for all Jagannātha temples in India.

So, it can be said that the title Jagannāth has been used in Sanskrit literature, in *Markandeya Purāṇa* for the first time, whose present composition form is late Gupta period. R.C. Hazra[55] while dating *Devi-Māhātmya* is of opinion that chapters LXXXI-XCIII of the Markandeya Purāṇa constitute an independent and complete work called 'Devi-Māhātmya, alias Candi or Saptasati,' which must have been inserted into it, at a comparatively late date, but certainly not later than 600 A.D.

Further Stietencron[56] is of opinion that the title, *'Jagannātha'* (Lord of the World) itself is unspecific. It has been applied to Buddha, to Śiva and to Viṣṇu. Its uncompounded variant Jagatoùnātha was similarly used for each of these three Deities. The same is true for its synonyms 'Lokanātha, and 'Lokesvara' which could be used for Śiva, Viṣṇu and a form of the Bodhisattva Avalokiteśvara. Other titles Iśvara (ruler) or Paramesvara (supreme ruler) were equally unspecified upto the post Gupta period and could be applied both to Viṣṇu and Śiva. All these terms simply denote the all-embracing power of protection and Lordship vesting in the Supreme God.

In Padma Purāṇa (chapter 70, sloka 1.), Maheśa has been addressed as Jagannātha. In the same Purāṇa (chapter 17, sloka 51.), Puruṣottama has been called as Jagannātha. R.C. Hazra[57] thinks that Vamana, Liṅga, Varaha, Padma, Agni, Skanda, Brahma-Vaivarta and Bhavisya, are the results of destructive recasts and Padma Purāṇa has late appendages composed after 800 A.D, and 900 A.D. *Padma Purāṇa* cannot be dated earlier. Jagannāth, a form of Viṣṇu is also mentioned in the *Trikandāsesha Abhidhama,* of Puruṣottma Dev, a supplement of the famous Amarakosha, compiled in the 9th century A.D.

Gopinath Mohapatra[58] has created a confusion by stating that in 8th century A.D. a descendant of Gopal, the Pala King of Bengal was Anangavajra, whose Guru Padmavajra, as Buddhist Tantric, composed Hevajratantra and is mentioned there that Jagannāth and Katyayani were worshipped in Odra-desa. D.C. Sircar[59] dates this *Hevajratantra* to 8th century A.D. If it is accepted, Gopinath Mohapatra has argued that the worship of Jagannāth might have been started by 7th century A.D. N.N. Bhattacharyya[60] also mentions that *Hevajra-tantra* may be a work of circa 8th century A.D.

About the middle of 8th century A.D. Gopāl, founded of ruling dynasty in Bengal, which came to be known as Pala.[61] The Pala rulers were all Buddhists, and during their long rule, extending over nearly four centuries, Buddhism found a safe refuge in Bihar and Bengal after it had ceased to have any footing in the rest of India, with the exception of Kashmir, Nepal and a few isolated regions.[62]

About Padmavajra and Anangavajra, N.K. Sahu states[63] :

Padmavajra

According to Tārānāth, Kaṁbala and Padmavajra jointly introduced the Hevajratantra into Buddhism, and Padmavajra also called Saroūuhavajra was the famous disciple of Kukuripada, who is said to have introduced the Heruka Sadhana and other Tantras from the land of Dākini.[64] Padamvajra is widely known by his great work *Guhya Siddhi,* which is regarded as an authoritative text on Tantrayān.

Anangāvajra

Padmavajru's worthy discriple Anañgavajra was a contemporary of Kambalapada, and he is described in the History of the 84 Mahasiddhas as the son of King Gopala, whose time has been fixed about the middle of the 8th century A. D. He wrote several works on the Hevajratantra, enunciated by his teacher Padmavajra, but he is particularly famous for his work Prajñopaya-Viniśchaya-Siddhi where he has boldly and lucidly explained the teachings of Vajrayana.

N.K. Sahu[65] further mentions that the *Kālikā Purāṇa* declares God Jagannātha and Goddess Kātyāyani as the presiding deities of Odra Pitha, mentioned as one of the four Piṭhas along with Kāmarupa, Purṅagiri and Jālandhara.[66] Mahākātyāyni is described in the Prachi Mahatmya as the consort of Sobhanesvara Śiva, and as a fearful Goddess in the Prachi valley of Orissa, to whom meat and wine were freely offered for propitiation.[67] The popularity of this Goddess in Orissa is amply evidenced by the fact that Tribhuvana Mahadevi, the Bhauma-Kara Monarch (896 A.D.) of Orissa compares herself with Kātyāyini at the time of her accession to the throne at Guheśvarāpaṭaka (Virajā)[68] and it may be said that this deity is no other than the Goddess Virajā of that Capital City. Attention may also be drawn to the fact that the Kubjikā Tantra, which is considered to be fairly early work mentions Viraja as the Goddess of Uḍḍiyāna,[69] while the Brhan-nila-Tantra also declares that Bhairavi (the consort of Jagannātha Bhairava) is the Goddess of Uḍḍiyāna.[70] It has already been mentioned that the term 'Jagannāth,' was used for Viṣṅu, Śiva and Buddha. Hence, the term 'Jagannāth.' used in Hvajratantra is addressed to Buddha image and Buddhist worship in Odradesa. The term 'Jagannāth,' used in Buddhist Tantra scriptures and Hindu Tantra, before 9th century A.D. volumes are used for Buddha and Śiva.

In this way the title 'Jagannāth,' evolved in late Gupta period. By ignoring the development or historicity of this Title, R.P. Misra[71] forms an opinion, when he states, 'The Cult of Jagannāth is undoubtedly a growing religion of assimilative toleration. Although scholars have tried to trace its origin from the age of *Rig veda* by the arbitrary interpretation of a doubtful *Rig vedic* verse 10/155/3, it is reasonable to accept that it originated in the lap of Non-Aryan culture as similar suggestions are revealed from the Purāṇas, from traditions, from the dominant aniconic features in holy triad of this Cult and from the funeral rites of the Non-Aryan Diata-patis who perform them for the forsaken old images in the Navakalevara rituals. Notwithstanding the multilateral philosophi sation of scholars, it is probable that it was a development of the deification of megalith which prevailed among the Savaras, Bondās, Gudba, Paraja and the Kandhas of Orissa as early as first century A.D. in fulfilment of the veneration of the deceased ancestors and dedication to the deities. This deity was originally the Jagannātha or Jagnaila as the Savaras called it, it was Janga as the Gandās call it and it was Jagaboi as the Bonds and Gadba called it. It assumed the name Nilamadhava in the Sailodbhava age in Orissa because of growing influence of Bhagavatism and esoteric semblance between the religious practices of its own and those of the Vaiṣhṇavite Cult of Madhava, both of which embodied the then vow of Mauna Dhyana and Yoga. The Non-Aryan Bhauma-Karas believing their origin from Viṣṇu and being the rulers of an age of religious amalgam most probably elevated this deity which was no other than a log from Non-Aryan oblivion. As nostone images of Jagannāth is yet traceable from the wombs of antiquities, its exaggerated Indranila shape from Purāṇas cannot be believed. The Bhaumas the Non-Aryan Kings of the Aryan and Non-Aryan populace of Orissa got it carved into three images in recognition of Trinity of Hinduism, Trisarana of Hinayana and Mahayana, Triratna of Jainism, Divya, Vira and Pashu; three aspects of Hindu Tantricism, Kaya Vajra; Vak Vajra and Chitta Vajra of Tantric Buddhism, Mahakali; Mahalakshmi and Mahasarasvati of Hindu Saktism and the mystical triad of other religions. It is during the Bhauma period that Anangavjra and his disciple Indrabhuti called these deities as Jagannāth and retained the ideals of the religious synthesis of this Cult adorning Jagannāth with the epithet. Sarvajinavararchitam, Sarva Buddhamayam, Sarva-lokahitanu-Kampi etc. The Sōmavaṁśi also patroned this Cult with the construction of temple for this Cult. Shankara recognised the greatness of the original Site of this Cult and established Bhogavardhana Matha here to signify it as the Vaikuntha of Vaiṣhṇavism, Bhogavati heaven of Buddhism and Bhoga Sarthavati of Jainism."

The view of H.C. Das[72] is worth quoting, "The Rudrayamala and Tantra-Yamala of the 10th century A.D. refer to Jagannātha as the famous Shrine of Utkala. Similarly Kalika Purāṇa (11th century A.D.) clearly speaks of Jagannātha as Bhairava and Katyayani as Bhairavi in Orissa (Uḍḍiyāna). Śri Śaṅkarāchārya's visit to Puri and establishment of Govardhana Matha is an epoch making event particularly in reference to Śri Jagannātha. The Anargharaghava Nataka of Murari Mishra (850 A.D.) referring to God Puruṣottama on the Sea-shore, Trikand Desa of Puruṣottama Deva identifying Jagannātha as Viṣṇu, reference to Jagannātha, Śiva, Brahma, Hari, Viṣṇu, Hrisikesa by Siddhasena Divakara, a Jaina writer of eminence (9th century A.D.), the Tantric Yamala describing Darurupi Jagannātha as the main Deity of the Puruṣottama Kshetra in Utkala prove the existence of the Cult of Jagannātha since 8th century A.D. if not earlier.

"We are, therefore, prone to believe the authenticity of the temple chronicle with regard to the construction of earlier Jagannātha temple by Yayati Kesari. On the basis of these records I am of the view that there was certainly an edifice in existence prior to structure erected by the Kesari King. Possibly the Bhaumas who were great builders might have constructed a temple for the shrine of Jagannātha in 8th/9th century A.D. I have assigned the important Sakta shrines of Puri like Bankimuhana Rāmachandi, Vimala, Bali Harachandi to the Bhauma period and the Seven Mother Goddesses on the edge of Markandeswar tank to the Śōmavaṁśi epoch. It will, therefore, be reasonable to believe the existence of the shrine of Jagannātha in some form or other at this time under the patronage of the Bhauma and Sōmavaṁśi rulers. My contention that an edifice existed before it was reconstructed by the Kesari King, is avered by the corroborative evidences and literary references."

No doubt, the tribal elements have entered Jagannāth Cult but the views of R.P Misra and H.C. Das are objectionable, because the Bhauma Kara Kings were votaries of different religious Cults viz. Buddhism, Śaivism and Vaiṣṇavism. They fostered a spirit of tolerance and harmony among the followers of different religious sects and thus brought a significant change in the religious field.[73]

Late K.C. Panigrahi[74] was also not free from this trend of thought, when he mentioned that the probable course of the history of Jagannātha seem to be that in the earliest times of his existence he was a Brahminical deity, worshipped as an altar as described in the Vana Parva of the Māhabhāratā. The altar was probably a wooden one and like the image of Jagannātha, liable to be renovated every twelve years. It next came to the custody of the Savaras who seem to have been the rulers of the region. Then the Bhaumas came from Assam in the first part of the eighth century A.D., ruled over Orissa, obtained the Shrine from the Savaras, got the Wooden altar carved into three images, enshrined them in a temple built on the spot and gave it the name Nilachala which was the name of the famous shrine of Kamaksya in their home land of Assam. Since the early Bhauma rulers of Orissa were Mahayana Buddhists, it is most likely that the three images carved represented Tri-ratna as suggested by General Cunningham and explained by Mahatab. In the next two political periods Yayati I of the Sōmavaṁśi dynasty and Chodaganga of the Gaṅga dynasty built spectacular temples in the Shrine, which gradually became famous as a great religious centre of the Hindus. The survivals of the first two temples built in the Bhauma and Sōmavaṁśi periods, might still be lying in different parts of Puri, used as later fixations. Puri has not yet been archaeologically surveyed.

"References to Lord Jagannātha or his Shrine at Puri in the medieval Sanskrit works, are many. The Sanskrit work Jnansiddhi assigned to the eighth century A.D. and attributed to Indrabhuti, opens with a salute to Jagannātha worshipped by "all Sages who have conquered all their desires." The word Jagannāth in this sense also occurs in several other verses of the same work. In these references the word has been used in its etymological sense meaning 'the Lord of the Universe' but some scholars through a forced interpretation maintain that the Jagannātha of the verses refer to Lord Jagannāth of Puri. This interpretation cannot be accepted. A definite reference of Lord Jagannātha of Puri occurs in the Sanskrit drama Anargha Raghava Natakam of Murari, assigned to the medieval period. The Sutradhara of the drama clearly states that it was meant to be staged in festival of Lord Puruṣottama of the sea shore studded with the Tamala trees. The famous astronomer Satananda clearly states that he was a resident of Puruṣottama and that his famous work *Bhasvati* was completed in the Kaliyuga year 4200 or 1099 A.D., which falls in the closing part of the Sōmavaṁśi rule."

K.C. Panigrahi has done the gross mistake of not differentiating the names or titles, 'Puruṣottama' and 'Jagannātha', hence this confusion.

Biswarup Das[75] deals with the religious aspect of Bhauma-Karas in a balanced manner and states that a cardinal feature of the religious history of India during the eighth and ninth centuries of the Christian era was that members of the same royal family were followers of different religious Cults. The founder of the Gujarat Pratihara dynasty was a worshipper of Viṣṇu while his three descendants were devotees of Śiva, Bhagavati and Sūrya. But the most typical example is furnished by the Bhauma-Karas. Some members of this Royal family were devout Buddhists, whereas others were great patrons of Vaiṣṇavism or Śaivism. There is even an instance of the husband and wife of this family belonging to different religious persuasion...........Indeed in the medieval period such a state of things came to pass in the field of religion not only in Orissa but also in other parts of India. The Pala King Narayanapala was an ardent Buddhist (Paramasaugata), but built and endowed a temple of Śiva and attended the ceremonies of Brahmanas with punctilious sincerity.[76] Similarly, the Pala ruler Dharmapala granted land to the Brahman as for the worship of Brahmanical Gods.[77] D.C. Sircar[78] rightly observes that this "seems to point to a rapprochement between Śaivism and Buddhism". The Raṣṭrakuta (Gujarat branch) King Dantivarman was a staunch follower of Brahmanism and a great patron of Buddhism.[79] Thus we come across royal families, though staunch supporters of a particular faith, held other faiths in high reverence. As a result, wide and sympathetic toleration became the characteristic of the religious history of India during the medieval period. This led to a Catholicism which supplanted narrow sectarianism.

"The Bhauma-Karas, in harmony with the sentiment of the age, became eclectic in their belief." So, it was the period of Religious Eclecticism.

Further, towards the fall of this dynasty in 9th century A.D. when Murari Misra survived, an entirely different description of Puruṣottama, is found in Murari's 'Anarghar-ghava-nātakam,'and in several texts belonging to the Gaṅga period, notably the *Gitagovinda* (12th century A.D.), the Utkala khanda of the *Skanda Purāṇa* (early 14th century A.D,), the *Kramadipika* (middle, 14th century A.D.) and some Jagannātha passages of the *Rudrayamalatantra* (probably 14th century A.D,). They describe Puruṣottama clearly in the form : Puruṣottama, seated on a lion throne, is joined with his consort Kamala (Lakshi). The God is four-armed, wearing crown and all ornaments. He carries a lotus (padma) in his upper right hand and the disk (Cakra) in his upper left hand. With his lower left arm he embraces his consort Kamala who is sitting on his left thigh, pressing her slightly against himself and touching her left breast with his hand, while his right lower hand is raised towards her breast in amorous play. The Goddess who is also fully adorned with ornaments, has put her right arm around his neck, her hand resting gracefully on his right shoulder. With her left hand she, too, holds a lotus flower. And She is looking at his face which is lovingly turned towards her.[80]

So, it seems that all-round religious synchronisation was continuing in the whole Mahānadi valley during early medieval period. The advent of Ādi Śaṅkarāchārya during this period, was a boon to the spiritual revolution, as a great impetus, it received from the spiritual genius, who was born in the Chera country about the year 788 A.D.[81] In the course of his Digvijaya, Sankara visited Puri and established Govardhana Matha. It seems, during the period of Śaṅkarāchārya, Puri had become great and famous as Puruṣottama Kshetra. It seems Śaṅkara had visited Puri before Murari Misra survived, because during Murari Misra's time, the description of Laxmi-Narayan is known, as stated above.

Sachidananda Misra[82] mentions that before Śaṅkara, there was no worship of Puruṣottama-Jagannāth at Puri. Puri was a Śaiva Kshetra and it seems Śaṅkara installed Jagannāth, while establishing Govardhana Matha there. Misra comes to this opinion because, as he mentions that Śaṅkara established Govardhana Matha in the east, whose Kshetra's name is Puruṣottama,' the Matha's Devi is 'Vimala' and Deva 'Jagannāth.'

Jagannātha seems to have been the Deva of Govardhana Matha. but Jagannātha worship had not become popular as the presiding Deity of Puri, then. Puri was then a Śaiva Kshetra. Late Kedarnath Mohapatra[83] was also of the same view, when he stated that after Śaṅkarāchārya installed the Vaiṣhṇav deity Jagannātha, as the male Deity of Govardhana Matha at Puri, established by him, later it became popular.

The view of H.V. Stietencron[84], is interesting, when he states that since the Jagannātha iconography has preserved visible features of Ekapada Bhairava, the Hinduization must have occurred under Śaiva auspices (even if possibly including Narasimha elements), and not under Vaṣṇava ones which would have excluded the Bhairava form, when at a later stage the Vaiṣṇavas accepted the Wooden God, they emphasized only the Narasimha element while the Bhairava element was largely excluded from theology and ritual. They may partly explain why only the iconography of Jagannātha has retained traces of Bhairava while the ritual has not.

About the 9th century or the 10th century A.D. Bhairava was made a Vaishanava Deity and came to be known as Puruṣottama of the Gita.

A. Eschmann, H. Kulke and G.C. Tripathi[85] are of the opinion that association between the original God Jagannātha-Narasimha and the Deity Puruṣottama might have begun at the time of Yayati. The opinion, "Buddhism of Orissa became Hinduised round about the tenth century when Śaivism made a dent in the region," of H.K. Mahatab,[86] is also interesting, because it shows the evolution of Lord Jagannātha.

II

There are scholars of traditional trend also and they are Harekrushna Mahatab, Surendra Mohanty and Kṛishṇa Chandra Panigrahi. H.K. Mahatab[87] had begun his first study by mentioning that the origin of Jagannātha worship is shrouded in mystery. In 1979, Mahatab[88] read a paper named, "The Mysterious Jagannāth and Problems of History of Orissa," in the Annual Session of Orissa History Congress. Mahatab writes, "The history of Orissa or for the matter of that of the Oriya society centres round the institution of Jagannāth who remains as mysterious as ever. The latest addition to numerous theses on Jagannāth of Orissa is a masterly work published in 1978, entitled *The Cult of Jagannāth and the Regional Tradition of Orissa.* The book is an anthology of twenty-five articles contributed by competent research scholars of established merit who worked on a project sponsored by the South Asia Institute of the University of Heidelberg and financed by the German Research Council during 1970-75.

"The articles have been edited by Anncharlott Eschmann, Hermann Kulke and Gaya Charan Tripathy. The authors of the articles have bestowed remarkable care and energy on the subjects they have dealt with. As far as I know the details of the Cult of Jagannāth from various angles have not been so elaborately dealt with by any scholar or a group of scholars as have been done by the writers in this book of 1978.

"In view of the ability and scholarly reputation of the authors, particularly of the time and energy they have put in this work, one would think not only twice but many a time before making any observation with regard to any point of research which has been as thorough as it could be. Even then I venture to make a few observations with full knowledge of my limitations as a casual student of research. The learned authors have started from the period when Brahminism was revived with full vigour, suppressing Buddhism of about a thousand years. Therefore, research of the full history of the evolution of Jagannāth from a tribal deity to the position of an "ageless one" was not seriously undertaken by the authors."

The authors criticised by H.K. Mahatab have well dealt with the Tribal studies in the above mentioned book. For an individual, who is traditional minded and thinks of Jagannāth as "The Mysterious Jagannāth," there is no patent medicine, because one is drowned in tales, beliefs or practices and handed over oral or literatures, transmitted from generation to generation. In research methods, opinion should be based on findings and their proper identificational study. Truth should be exposed and not imposed.

The only mistake, the German scholars did was that, they didn't extend their study to the Upper Mahānadi valley. They had to limit their study to Orissa Province, because the German University had financed for research study, on the Cult of Jagannātha, in Orissa Province only and were bent to prove the tradition of the Tribal origin of Jagannāth, with preconceived idea of recorded tradition.

A book named, *Lord Jagannātha : The Microcosm of Indian Spiritual Culture.* written by Surendra Mohanty[89] and published by Orissa Sahitya Akademi, during the celebration of Silver Jubilee of the Akademi, contends the traditional views of Jagannātha only. The view of K.C. Panigrahi as stated earlier is also traditional.

The views of scholars of traditional opinions are of gross

mistake, because they do not differentiate the terms, 'Puruṣottama' and 'Jagannātha', hence this confusion. Puri was and is Puruṣottama Kshetra from time immemorial and after Jagannātha was installed as Presiding Deity, it came to be known as 'Puruṣottama-Jagannātha.'

As already observed the period of Bhauma-Karas was the period of Religious Eclecticism. The view of Mayadhar Mansinha, on visible struggle for synthesis, seems to support the view of the author. Mansinha[90] states, "There is evidence of religious struggle in ancient Orissa, between the follower of Śiva and the Buddha in the Bhaskareswar temple at Bhuvaneswar, where nothing but an Asokan pillar has been converted into a Lingam, its very unusual height betraying the vandalism too obtrusively. On the other hand, we have proof of a most happy reconciliation between mutually-warring sects on the enchantingly sculptured walls of the Mukteswara temple (8th-9th centuries A.D.).[91] Here is a Śiva temple where images of the Buddha and the Jaina Tirthankaras have been carved along with those of Durga, Lakulisa, Surya, Ganesha, Saraswati and many other Sectarian Hindu Gods and Goddesses. Jagannātha, as he is at present was probably not known or had not caught the imagination of the Hindu masses by the time of construction of this temple, as its liberal minded artists did not place him in the assembly of Orissa's Gods and Goddesses. But in the Konarka temple (13th century A.D.) there is a remarkable place of sculpture, proclaiming religious Universalism. Here Jagannātha as he is now, appears as the Central Deity, surrounded by Durga, Śiva and other Hindu Gods and Goddesses. So, we may be justified in supposing that it was the Mahayanic Buddha, Dhamma and Sangha that gradually became Jagannātha, Balabhadra and Subhadra, the present trinity in the Shrine of Jagannātha, between the 8th and the 12th centuries A.D."

Lichchhavi rulers of Nepal have made great contribution to Lord Jagannātha of Puri. It is known that the Raja of Nepal has special privilege or an advantage granted or enjoyed, when he enters the Jagannātha temple of Puri. The welcome address to him, goes thus : "Oh ! the "descendant of the Surya-vansi Lichchhavi King, while your ancestor Maharaja

Sankaradeva was ruling, a Salegram having both Sankarsana and Vasudev signs were found from the pious Ganduki river. Because of that, he was able to sing with spiritual energy. Being descendant of that great Royal family, you are requested to pay your homage to Śri Jagannātha etc."[92]

It is worth giving the genealogy of the Lichchhavis of Nepal.[93]

Vṛishadeva
|
Śaṅkaradeva
|
Dharmadeva
|
Mānadeva
|
Mahideva
|
Vasantasena (Vasantadeva)
|
Śivadeva I
|
Aṃsuvarman
|
Jishṇugupta
|
Narendradeva
|
Śivadeva II
|
Jayadeva

Anirudha Das[94] is of opinion that it is known from inscription that Harshagupta the King of South Kōśala had married the daughter of Sūryavarman, the King of Magadha. His daughter Rājyamati, was married to Nepal Raja Jayadeva. R.C. Majumdar[95] emphasises that Jayadeva ruled in Nepal during the first half of the eighth century A.D. and Jayadeva married Rājyamati, daughter of Śri Harshadeva, King of Gauda, Odra, Kalinga, Kōśala and other countries, who was descended from the race of Bhagadatta. The identity of this King Harsha is not yet satisfactorily established.

Even though the identity of King Harsha is not yet satisfactorily established, it can be claimed that King Harsha here, can be identified with Sōmavaṁśi King Harshagupta of South

Kõśala. In 7th and 8th centuries A.D. there was no existence of North Kõśala State and the King, having influence in the territories of Gauda, Odra, Kalinga, Kõśala and other countries, can be assigned to King Harshagupta of South Kõśala only.

Further Anirudha Das[96] refers to "Mudala Siddhi," palm-leave manuscript and states that two living Salegrams were donated by Nepal King Śaṅkaradeva for Balabhadra and Subhadra. About Lord Jagannāth the mysterious.

According to Anirudha Das and Sadāsiva Ratha Sharma[97], Yayati Kesari was the second builder of Jagannāth temple. Surendra Mohanty[98] thinks that the third wave of Sanskritisation of Lord Jagannāth took place during the period of Yayāti. Now, it is proper to look into the deeds of the famous Sõmavaṁṣī King Yayati I.

Sõmavaṁśi King Mahā-śivagupta Yayāti I, whose reigning period is assigned circa 960-988 A.D.[99] or circa 925-955 A.D [100] immediately after ascending the throne, followed, the policy of expansion like his father. His first task was to expand the Sõmavaṁśi Kingdom in the east. According to the old tradition of the Madalapanji, K.C. Panigrahi[101] states that the re-establishment of the shrine of Jagannātha at Puri with a temple built there was another great work of Yayati. In the words of H.V. Stietencron,[102] "We have seen that two important elements of the later Jagannāth Cult, namely (i) the connection of Puruṣottama, with Narasimha and (ii) the juxtaposition of Viṣṇu and Śiva on a common platform (Vedi) were possibly introduced into Central Orissa from the West along the Mahānadi river. Both elements were present in the Western hill tracts of Orissa around A.D. 900 They could advance further down into the coastal area in the middle of the 10th century when Yayāti I established the Sõmavaṁśi rule in Utkala." Herman Kulke[103] follows the tradition of Madalapanji and mentions 'the Raktabahu tradition,' which seems to be a creation (or interpolation), to show the ancientness of Jagannātha. It has no historicity.

The above mentioned tradition of Madalapanji seems to be a creation to show the ancientness of Jagannātha. If Buddha, as Jagannāth, was worshipped by Indrabhuti in 8th century

A.D. then, it would not have been possible of any Jagannāth Deity to have been installed at Puri. So, it seems a religious revolution synthesised Jagannāth of Indrabhuti with Purushottama of Puri in 10th century A.D. and Yayati I was responsible for this Religious revolution synthesis of installing Jagannāth as Presiding Deity of Puri. Therefore, Yayāti's work at Puri was both political and religious and hence spectacular. Because of this, probably, Yayati Kesari is almost a household name in Orissa and all living monuments, irrespective of their age, are generally attributed to him.[104] Though Yayati belonged to a Śaiva dynasty, it was probably with him, that the second wave of Viṣṇuism reached coastal Orissa. Moreover, he must have been familiar with Hinduized cults of posts: the Khambheśvari worship is known in Western Orissa since 500 A.C..... The association between the original God Jagannātha-Narasiṁha and the Deity Puruṣottama might have begun at the time of Yayāti.[105]

III

For exposition of more Reality or Truth, the traditions should be given up. Two such examples of Madalapanji may be stated. Raja G.C.H. Jagadeb[100] has tried to expose that traditional narration of Madalapanji and informs that the last Gaṅga King Matta Bhanu Deb started drinking liquour from his 15th Anka. In the 17th Anka of the King, enemies invaded the country and killed the successors of the King. So Kapilendra though a Śuryavaṁshi was taken as an adopted son of Gaṅgavamsa King, who succeeded him in 1357 Sakabda or 1435 A.D. G.C.H. Jagadeb had done the gross mistake of being traditional. Because tradition always does not have truth, one should try to expose more truth, which is done in research methodology with the assisting evidences. The adoption of Kapilendra by the last Gaṅga Gajapati is never followed by any research scholar. Prabhat Mukherjee[107] claims that Kapilendra seized the throne of Orissa and K.C. Panigrahi[108] informs that Kapilendra usurped the Throne.

Another tradition of Madalapanji as stated by S.N. Rajaguru[109] is that the popular tradition is that Kala Hammira, the progenitor of the Parlakimedi line, was the first son among the 18 sons of Kapilenradeva who left their parental home and established petty Kingdoms in the border areas of Utkala. Kalā Hammira came to the South and lived in Kimidi country which was extended from Kalahandi to Kalinga (coastal land) and from the river Riṣhikulya upto the Lāngulya. In the above mentioned study, S.N. Rajaguru has tried to prove the Gaṅga origin of the Khimundi house with little success, but in a later study, S.N. Rajguru[110] claims the ruling house of Parlakhemundi to be of Gaṅga dynasty, with Gajapati epithet, Chandravaṁśī and Atreya gotra. Rajguru argues that Kapilendra's gotra was Gautama, while Parlakhemundi's Gaṅgas are of Atreya gotra, so the first Gaṅga who established himself at Khemundi was not a son of Kapilendra. To show the Gaṅga origin of Khemundi house, S.N. Rajaguru mentions that when Anantavarma Chodagaṅga Deva won Utkala and shifted his headquarters to Cuttack, he left Paramardi Deb alias Permandi Deb to rule the South. Paramardi Deb's son was Chodagaṅga Deva, not to be mixed with the great King, with the same name. This Chodagaṅga Deva, the son of Paramardi Deb is referred in the inscription of Kedaresvara temple[111], Bhubaneswar, whose descendants ruled Khemundi.

For knowing more reality or truth, through research, sometimes old traditions has to be given up, because no progress in any walk of life is possible without leaving the present state and moving forward to win a new state of greater glory.[112]

Savaras no doubt exist in Mahendragiri area of Ganjam district, who have the tradition of making Neem-wood images, Savaras live elsewhere also. Without being more dynamic in research, S.N. Rajaguru[10] is trying to prove that the culture of the Savaras of Mahendragiri has influenced the growth of Jagannāth cult mostly. It should be observed, as shown in this study that the influence of Savarinarayan of Upper Mahandi has much impact on Jagannāth Cult, than any other place. Of course, there were alround influence of the Lower Mahanadi valley later.

Another tradition of Satyabadi is recorded by J.D. Begler[114] which states : 'There is a famous temple at Satyabandi which is, I believe, noticed in Dr. Rajendra's work. Two Brahmans of Seorinarayan, it is related, agreed that if they had a son and a daughter respectively, they were to be given in marriage to each other. When the time came and the father of the daughter went to demand the fulfilment of the promise, the other met him on the way and refused. Thereupon, he appealed to the Raja of Kalinga, who was the paramount sovereign, for redress ; the Raja naturally demanded witnesses, the man said he could produce none, as no one was present when the compact was made near a stone. The Raja refused to entertain his plaint without evidence, the man came to the stone where the promise had been made, and earnestly prayed to the Deity of the Stone to help him, the Deity told him to go back to the Raja and that he would follow, "but" said the Stone (or the Deity within the Stone), "if you look back I will not go." The man rose and departed and he could hear the footsteps of the God following him, till, at the spot where the temple stands, the ground being covered with soft grass, the foot-steps of the God were no longer audible, the Brahman turned back to ascertain if he was being followed and that very instant the Stone stood still and has remained immovable ever since; the man related the whole story to the Raja, who came to see the prodigy and ordered the other Brahman to fulfil his promise on the evidence of the Stone, he also built the temple enshrining the Stone, and the name Satyabadi owes its origin to this circumstance. I did not see the temple but I mention the story as it is a wide and well known one and I heard it near Seorinarayana, not from a Brahman, but from a Saora, who has no faith in the Brahmanical Deities. The story would lead to the influence that at some remote period the Kings of Kalinga regained over Seorinarayan, and if over Seorinarayan, than over the whole of Chhattisgarh. I would in connection with this recall the title *Trikalingadhipati* applied in some inscriptions to the Sovereigns who ruled over Jabalpur as well as Katak."

From the archaeological discoveries it is known that the Sōmavaṁśīs who established themselves in Upper Mahānadi valley, gradually extended their empire to the coastal belt of

Orissa. So, it is but natural that there was cultural flow or link of Upper and Lower Mahānadi Valleys.

The Upper Mahānadi valley comprised the South Kõśala State of ancient and medieval periods. Because of local influence Śiva Lingas came to be named Kõśaleśvara Liṅgas and the Kõśaleśvara temple at Baidyanath is an example. Few Kõśaleśvara Śiva temple[115] (circa, llth century A.D.) at Bada Kanjia in Puri district is an example. Few years back, Sasanka Shekhar Panda[116] has traced a temple on the mountain top in Surada village area, five km. to the east of Balangir. This temple is called Kõśaleśwar temple locally and is surrounded by five small temples. The temple has been assigned to Sõmavaṁśi period and is a plain stone temple, without any sculptural art. One small temple is completely in ruin, while the other four small temples are of Rāmachandi, Bhairabi, Brushabha (Nandi) and Khasua. Radhagobinda Das[117] describes it as Kusaleswar temple and in support of the temple's name, as mentioned by him, set forths the example of Kusalesvar temple of Deogaon in Keonjhar district. R.P. Mohapatra[118] deals with the temple of Deogaon in Keonjhar district and calls it Kusaleswar temple. His argument is that it is understood from the local people that in the past, the area was in dense forest. The Śivalinga was traced amidst thick growth of Kusa grasses on the bank of the river Kusei (Kusabhadra), a tributary of the Vaitarani by following the missing black cow, which was daily offering milk at this place. As the Śivalinga was traced amidst Kusa grasses, the Liṅga derived its name from the said grass and came to be known in the neighbourhood as Kusaleśwar. On the other hand, the God being located near the river Kusei for which it might have been known in the name of Kusaleśwar. Some other believe that, the Liṅga after recovered, said to have fulfilled the desires of all the devotees through blessings for which the local people regard it as Kusaleśwar or the God of all blessing. The Kusaleśwar temple of Baidyanatha in Balangir district may have name bearing in the name of this temple.

This statement of R.P. Mohapatra is an interpolation. The temple of Baidyanath is named *Kosaleśvara,* and not Kusaleśvar. It is a misunderstanding of him. The Śiva temple at Deogaon should be named Kosaleśvara also, because it is the flow of culture of Upper Mahānadi valley or of South Kōśala, which has flowed down the Mahānadi. This is an example how reality gets lost through spurious insertions of slang in names, because of affluence. For the emphasis of the term, *Kosaleśvara,* Pandit Nilakantha Das[119] may be quoted, when he states that from about the 10th century A.D., i.e. from the time of the Kōśhala King of Orissa, the word Iswara, such as, Kōśhaleswara, Kapoteśwara, Beleśwara, Balukeśwara, was also used in place of Nātha. This is a peculiar feature specially of Kalinga part of Orissa, and to some extent in Kōśala as well as properly Uddiyana part.

The study of South Kōśala shows that the Pīnduvṁśīs alias Sōmavaṁśī moved to the eastern part of Kōśala and coastal belt of modern Orissa, where they came to be known as Sōmavaṁśi of Orissa. Their contribution to the Orisan culture was much and it finds expression in the words of B.K. Rath[120] thus.

"The Śōmavaṁśī rule in Orissa ushered in a great change in the political and cultural life of the people and the Sōmavaṁśī Kings are best remembered for their contribution to the development of the Cultural heritage of the Oriya people. Geographically the present state of Orissa owes its origin to Sōmavaṁśi rule in Orissa when the distinct and different geographical units of ancient Orissa, viz. (Utakala, Kōśala, Kalinga, Kongoda and Odra were brought under the control of a single administration. With this integrated political system, based upon a strong Kingdom with secured boundary lies, the pace was set in motion for an all-round development in the field of learning, religion, art, architecture and other cultural aspects of life. There was a fusion of thoughts and practices under the Sōmavaṁśi imbibed from the different Cultures of the different regions, along with the process of geographical unification and political integration, which later changed into a grand culture synthesis. This phenomenon is evident from the large number of monuments and sculptures of the period, these we have inherited today. These archaeological evidences, belonging to different religious thoughts, provide us with an adequate ideas about the development in religion, art and architecture that took place under the history".

In the early medieval period religious synchronisation and evolution or growth of Jagannāth Culture was felt in Mahānadi valley. In the words of A.L. Basham,[121] while in northern India Hindu culture declined somewhat after the Gupta age, in the Deccan it flourished and advanced. By this time Āryan influence had penetrated the whole of the peninsula, and the contact of Āryan and Dravidian produced a vigorous cultural synthesis, which in turn had an immense influence on Indian civilization as a whole.

Another example of the influence of "Kōśala," name is Kausalya Gaṅga, which owes its name to "Kōśala," and its location is about 8 km. from Bhubaneswarm, on the State Highway No. 8 towards Puri. There is a tank named Kausalyaganga which is famous for pisciculture. In the middle of the tank there is an island, the remain of a palace. According to the Madalapanji, the tank was dug by Gangeswara Deva of Gaṅga family.[122]

REFERENCES

1. Deka, K.C. "Contribution of Orissa to Indian Culture and the Worship of Lord Jagannātha," *Unmana*—Souvenir of Akhil Bharat Jagannātha Consciousness Conference. Cuttack, December 28-31, 1984, ed. Subas Pani, Charana Gosthi, Cuttack, p. 63.
2. *GOIMPR,* pp. 565-566.
3. *TCOJ,* p. 17.
4. *Ibid.,* p. 13.
5. *Ibid.,* p. 23.
6. Rajaguru, S.N. "Kiṁḅadanti-a-Itihasikata", *Sahara Śrī Khetra,* (Oriya), ed. Sahu, K. Sabara Sanskrutic Gabesana Kendra, Koraput 1988, pp. 88-97.
7. *Māhabhāratā.* III, Chapter 198, Sloka I.
8. *TCOJ,* p. 73.
9. Rajaguru, S.N. *op. cit.* 1988, p. 91.
10. Mishra, K.C."The Cult of Jagannāth," *Sidelights on History and Culture of Orissa,* ed. Das, M.N. Vidyapuri, Cuttack, 1977, p. 382.

11. Russell, R.V. & Hiralal, *The Tribes and Castes of the Central Provinces of India,* Vol. IV, Cosmo Publication, Delhi, 1975, pp. 502-503.
12. *Madhya Pradesh District Gazetteers, Bilaspur,* Bhopal, 1978, pp. 524-525.
13. *TCOJ,* pp. 77-100.
14. *GOIOP,* pp. 802-803.
15. Mohapatra G. *The Land of Viṣṇu : A Study of Jagannātha Cult,* B.R. Publishing Corporation, Delhi, 1977, pp. 7 & 26.
16. Mohanty, A. (ed.), *Sarala Māhabhāratā—Aswamedha, Musali and Swarga rohana parva,* (Oriya), Cultural Affairs Dept. of Govt. of Orissa, Bhubaneswar, 1970, p. 83.
17. Sahu, B. "Sri Jagannāth's History," (Oriya) *Sahitya Uchhaba (Lekhaka Samukhya),* ed. Dhala, B.K. Bhubaneshwar, 1981, passim.
18. *TCOJ,* p. 17.
19. Mirashi, V.V. CII, Vol. IV, Part I, Ootacamund, 1955, p. clxiii.
20. *TRIHP,* pp. 63-64.
21. Mirashi, V. V. *op. cit.* Vol. IV, Part II p. 419.
22. *Ibid.,* p. 519.
23. *Ibid.,* p. 582.
24. Siddhantashastree, R.K. *Śaivism through the Ages,* Munshiram Manoharal, New Delhi, 1975, p. 50.
25. *GOIMPR,* pp. 572-574.
26. Banerjea, J.N. "The Worship of Images", *THACOTIP,* Vol. II, The age of Imperial Unity, 1968, p. 452.
27. Parimoo, R. "Weapons of Gods as Embodiments of their Power", *OHRJ,* Vol. XXXI, No. 1, p. 85.
28. Brockington, J.L. "The Rāmayana in the Context of Indian Culture," *OHRJ,* Vol. XXIX, No. 1, p. 5.
29. Banerjea, J.N. *The Development of Hindu Iconography,* University of Culcutta, 1956, p. 489.
30. (i) Singh Deo, J.P. "Yoni Discovered at Maraguda Valley, Orissa", *Essays on History, Education and Culture, Comparatives,* Nos. 3 & 4, Institute of Comparative Studies, Bhubaneswar, pp. 149-152.
    (ii) Singh Deo, J.P. "Systematic Archaeological Exploration and Excavations required in Western Orissa", *OHRJ,* Vol. XXXII, Nos. 3 & 4, pp. 7-9.
31. Das, R.C. "Sri Jagannāth Some New Dimension", *OHRJ,* Vol. XXIX, No. 1, pp. 47-48.
32. Singh Deo., J.P. "Religious Cults of South Kōśala," *SOUVENIR,* 422nd Geeta Gyana Yagna of H.H. Swami Chinmayananda,13th to 20th January 1987 at Raipur, Madhya Pradesh, pp. 23-26.

33. *IOO,* Vol. IV, 1966, p. 69.
34. Stietencron, H.V. "The Advent of Vaisnavism in Orissa", and "The Śaiva Component in the Early Evolution of Jagannāth", *TCOJAT-RTOO,* 1978, p. 15, 122.
35. *TSBLON,* Sanskrit Pustak Bhandar, Calcutta, 1971, p. 20.
36. Bajpai, K.D. & Pandey, S.K. *MALHAR,* 1975-77, Dept. of Ancient History, Culture and Archaeology, University of Saugar, 1977, p. 35.
37. Watter's, *Yuan Chwang's Travels in India,* Part II, (?), p. 201.
38 Das, N. "Oriya Language and Culture", *OHRJ,* Vol. VIII, part I, pp. 5-6.
39. *OHRJ,* Vol. VII, No. 1, p. 14.
40. Das, N. *op. cit.,* p. 7.
41. *Vatshyayana's Kamasutra,* translated by Burton, R. & Arputhrcot, F.F. Orient Paperbacks, Delhi, 1977, p. 75.
42. Devasthali, G.V. "Literature", *THACOTIP,* Vol. III, 1970, p 324.
43. Sharif, A.R. "Kamasutra, time tested Classic on Man-Woman Relationship" *MIRROR,* ed. Prabhu Govind, Vol. XXI, No. I, Bombay, November, 1985, p. 44.
44. Das, N. *op. cit.*, p. 24.
45. "Two Vajrayana Works", Gaekwad's Oriental Series, No. XLIV, pp. 24-25.
46. "Jnanasidhi of Indrabhuti", Gaekwad's Oriental Series, No. XLIV Chapter I, passim.
47. Sahu, N.K. "Padmasambhava (Appendix III)", *Gazetteer of India Orissa, Sambalpur,* ed. Senapati N. Cuttack, 1971, pp. 96-97.
48. *CPOSK,* p. 160.
49. (I) Ragozin, Z.A. *Vedic India : As embodied principally in the Rig veda,* Munshiram Manoharlal, New Delhi, 1962, passim.
    (II) Singhal, J.P., *The Sphinx Speaks—The Story of Pre-historic Nations,* Sadgyan Sadan, New Delhi, 1963, pp. 1-11.
    (III) Bhargava, ML, *The Geography of Rgvedic India : A Physical Geography of Sapta Saindhava,* The Upper India Publishing House Ltd., Lucknow, 1964, passim.
50. *OHRJ,* Vol. III, No. 1, pp. 9-10.
51. *Epigraphia Indica,* Vol. XXXV, pp. 171-178.
52. *THOO,* Vol. II, Cuttack, 1960, p. 515.
53. *OHRJ,* Vol. XXX, Nos. 2, 3, & 4, p. 15.
54. Stietencron, H.V. "Early Temples of Jagannātha in Orissa : The Formative Phase", *TCOJATRTOO,* p. 62.
55. Hazra, R.C. "The Pūrṅas", *The Cultural Heritage of India,* Vol. II, The Rāmakrishna Mission Institute of Culture, Calcutta, 1969. p. 236.

56. Stietencron, H.V. *op. cit.* p. 61.
57. Hazra, R.C. *op. cit.* pp. 260-61.
58. Mohapatra, G. *Sri Jagannāth Tatwa,* (Oriya), Nalanda, Cuttack, 1989, p. 217.
59. Sircar, D.C. *The Sakta Pithas,* Motilal Banarsidās, Delhi, 1973, p. 12.
60. Bhattacharyya, N.N. *History of the Tantric Religion,* Manohar Publications, New Delhi, reprint 1987, p. 65.
61. Majumdar, R.C. "The Palas", *THACOTIP,* Vol. IV, 1964, p. 44.
62. *Ibid.,* p. 270.
63. *BIO,* pp. 165-166.
64. See R. Bhattacharya in, *J.B.O.R.S.,* 1928, p, 341ff; Sādhana Māla II p. XIII ff.
65. Suhu, N.K., *op. cit.* pp. 145-146.
66. उड्पीठं पश्चिमेतु तर्थवोडेश्वरों शिवां।

    कात्यायनीं जगन्नाथं उडेशंव प्रपूज्यत्।।

    Kālika Purāṇa, Vangavāsi edition.
67. Mahākātyayini is also known as Chaṇḍaghaṇṭa. For her description vide : Prāchi Māhātmya, chapter VI. See also K. Misra, KOṆĀRKA. p. 39.
68. Vide. J.B.O.R.S. II, pp. 419-427.
69. Kubjika Tantra (Patala VII), the same quoted in the Prāṇatoṣani Tantra (Vasumati edition), p. 234.
70. The Tantra Chudāmoni and the Bṛhan-Nila-Tantra (D.C. Sircar, *The Sākta Pithas,* pp, 21-22) both contain a list of 50 Pithas. The difference between these two lists, is that in the former 'Uḍḍisa' is mentioned in between Hastināpura Pitha and Prayāyaka, whereas in the latter 'Uḍḍinapura' occupies a place between Gajahvayapura and Prayāga.
71. Mishra, R.P. "National Integration of India and the Cult of Jagannāth", *SOUVENIR,* UGC. National Seminar on National Integration in India and the Cult of Lord Jagannāth, 25th, 26th & 27th December 1987, D.A.V. College, Titilagarh, pp. 33-34.
72. Das. H.C. *Cultural Development in Orissa,* Punthi Pustak, Calcutta, 1985, p. 11.
73. Subuddhi, U. *The Bhauma-Karas of Orissa,* Punthi Pustak, Calcutta, 1978, p. 11.
74. *HOO,* pp. 338-339.
75. Das, B. *The Bhauma-Karas-Buddhist Kings of Orissa and their Times,* Oriental Publishers, New Delhi, 1978, pp. 141, 158-159.

76. *Indian Antiquary,* Vol. XV, p. 304. Bhagalpur charter of Narayanapala.
77. *Epigraphia Indica,* Vol. IV, p. 243.
78. Sircar, D.C. *Studies in the Religious Life of Ancient and Medieval India,* Motilal Banarsidas, Delhi, 1971, p. 187.
79. *Epigrapia Indica,* Vol. VI, p. 293.
80. Stietencron, H.V. "Early temples of Jagannātha in Orissa : The Formative Phase", *op. cit.* 1978, p. 69.
81. *THACOTIP,* Vol. IV, The Age of Imperial Kanauj, 1964, p. 304.
82. Misra, S. "Sri Purushottama Vigraha Pratistha", (Oriya), *SOUVENIR.* UGC. National Seminar, D.A.V. College, Titilagarh, 1987, pp. 27-35.
83. Mohapatra, K.N. "Cultural Evolution of Jagannātha", *Sri Jagannātha Sanskruti,* (Oriya), ed. Orissa Cultural Forum, Bhubaneswar 1978, p. 122.
84. Stietencron, H.V. "The Śaiva Component in the Early Evolution of Jagannātha," *TCOJATRTOO,* p. 122.
85. *Ibid.,* p. 177.
86. Mahatab, H.K. "The Mysterious Jagannāth and Problems of History of Orissa," *OHC,* Proceedings of the Annual Session B.J.B. College, Bhubaneswar, 1979, p. 5.
87. Mahatab, H.K. *THOO,* Vol. II, Cuttack, 1960, p. 504.
88. Mahatab, H.K. "The Mysterious Jagannāth and Problems of History of Orissa," *op. cit.* 1979, pp. 1-7.
89. Mohanty, S. *Lord Jagannātha—The Microcosm of Indian Spiritual Culture,* Orissa Sahitya Akademi, Bhubaneswar, 1982, passim.
90. Mansinha, M. *The Saga of the Land of Jagannātha,* J. Mohapatra & Co. Cuttack, (?), p. 163.
91. Panigrahi, K.C. *Archaeological Remains at Bhubaneswar,* Orient Longmans, New Delhi, 1961, p. 92.
92. Das, A. & Sharma, S.R. *Sri Jagannāth and Nepal,* (Oriya) Vidyaputi, Cuttack, 1986, pp. 3-4.
93. *THACOTIP,* Vol., III, The Classical Age, 1970, pp. 720-21.
94. Das, A. *SABARA,* (Oriya), Sathi Mahal, Cuttack, 1969, pp. 38-39.
95 *THACOTIP,* Vol. III, The Classical Age, 1970, pp. 137-38.
96. *SABARA,* (Oriya), *op. cit.* p. 49.
97. *Sri Jagannāth and Nepal.* (Oriya), *op. cit.* p. 32.
98. Mohanty, S. *Lord Jagannātha,* Orissa Sahitya Akademi, Bhubaneswar, 1982, p. 12.

99. Nema, S.R. *Political History of the Śōmavaṁśi Kings of South Kōśala and Orissa,* Oriental Publishers & Distributors, New Delhi, 1978, p. 204.

100. *CHOO,* p. 51 and p. 62.

101. *HOO,* p. 105.

102. Stietencron, H.V. "The Advent of Viṣṇuism in Orissa," *TCOJA-TRTOO,* p. 16.

103. Kulke, H. "Early Royal Patronage of the Jagannāth Cult," *TCOJA-TRTOO,* p. 140.

104. *HOO,* p. 106.

105. Eschmann, A., Kulke, H. and Tripathi, G.C. "The Formation of the Jagannātha Triad," *TCOJATRTOO,* pp. 176-177.

106. Jagadeb, Raja G.C.H. *Uthai Empire under Gaṅga Kings,* Berhampur, 1977, p. 62.

107. Mukherjee, P., *The History of the Gajapati Kings of Orissa and their Successors,* The General Trading Company, Calcutta, 1953, p. 24.

108. *HOO,* p. 190.

109. Rajaguru, S.N., *History of the Gaṅgas,* Part II, Orissa State Museum Bhubaneswar, 1972, p. 72.

110. Rajaguru, S.N. "Short History of Parlakhimundi Rajabansa", (Oriya), *History of the Formation of the Orissa State,* ed. Patnaik, N.C. available at "Baruda", Karyalaya, Berhampur, 1986, pp. 41-42.

111. Rajaguru, S.N. *Inscription of Orissa (c. 1045-1190 A.D)* Vol. III, part I, Bhubaneswar, 1960, Kedaresvara temple inscription Nos. 173 & 194.

112. Swami Chinmayananda, *A Manual of Self Unfoldment,* Central Chinmaya Mission Trust, Bombay, 1985, p. 111.

113. Rajaguru, S.N. "Nilagiri and Mahendragiri," *Utkal Prasanga,* (Oriya), Rathayatra Special issue, ed. Champati Rai, Cuttack, July, 1984, pp. 5-8.

114. Beglar, J.D. *Archaeological Survey of India,* Vol. XIII, Varanasi, 1970, pp. 98-99.

115. Ray, P.K. "Archaeological Treasures of Orissa," *Our Cultural Heritage, (SOUVENIR),* Golden Jubilee Celebration of the Orissa State Museum, 1984, ed. Subas Pani, Bhubaneswar, p. 11.

116. Sasanka Sekhar Panda, "Kosaleśwar Śiva temple at Daspur Surda" ; *ORISSA REVIEW,* Vol. XLIII, No. 3, October 1986, ed. Patnaik, J.N. Bhubaneswar, pp. 47-52.

117. Das, R.G. "Surda village of Balangir and Kusaleśwar temple", (Oriya), *SAPTARSI,* Oriya monthly magazine, Sambalpur University, January, 1987, pp. 17-19.
118. Mohapatra, R.P. "Archaeological Remains of Kusaleśawar Temple of Deogaon," *OHRJ,* Vol. XXXI, No. 1, pp. 36-42.
119. Das, Pandit Nilakantha, "Oriya Language and Culture", *OHRJ,* Vol. VIII, No. 1, p. 25.
120. *CHOO,* p. 153.
121. Basham, A.L. *The Wonder that was India,* Delhi, 1982, p. 75
122. *GOIOP,* p. 737.

Three

Buddha Acknowledged as an Avatāra of Viṣṇu

The period of Gautama Buddha was within sixth and fifth century B.C. Buddha taught for 45 years through conversation, lectures and parables. His methods of teachings were unique. He walked from town to town, accompanied by his favourite disciples and followed by many devotees. He took no thought for tomorrow and contented to be led by local admirers. Ordinarily he stopped near some village and pitched his camp in some garden or wood or on some river bank. The afternoons were given to meditation and evening to instruction.

The philosophy of Buddhism is intensely rational. The first Sermon of the Buddha which is embodied in the 'Dhamma Chakka Pabattana Sutta', clearly states the essential doctrines of Buddhism. The four great truths are (i) Sorrow, (ii) the cause of Sorrow, (iii) the Remedy for Sorrow and (iv) the Path. Life is full of Sorrow. All is transient, sorrowful and full of pain. The cause of this Sorrow is birth, which is again caused by desire for earthly things and material enjoyments which are incapable of satisfaction and therefore lead the individual from birth to rebirth. The cessation of this desire will remove the cause of this Sorrow, namely birth. This cessation can be achieved by right faith, right thought, right action, right speech, right means of livelihood, right endeavour, right remembrance and right meditation, the eight fold path. This path is the middle path avoiding the two extremes, sensuality on the one side and extreme asceticism on the other.

According to Buddha, 'Let a man overcome anger by kindness, evil by good-victory breeds hatred, for the conquered is unhappy. Never in the World hatred ceases by hatred, hatred ceases by love.'

Buddha's conception of religion was purely ethical. He did not care for worship or rituals. He put all his emphasis on conduct. Buddha's view was that saintliness and contentment were to be found not in the knowledge of the Universe and God, but in selfless virtuous labour.

Thus the philosophy of Buddhism is intensely rationalistic. It believes in the law of Karma and rebirth. That is, a man reaps the consequences of his own actions in the previous existence. The cause of human suffering is birth and it is within the power of man to get rid of rebirth and the consequent suffering.

In Buddha's philosophy there was no place for heaven, purgatory or hell. He repudiated animism in every form. Matter has force and all substances motion. Life is change, a neutral steam of becoming an extinction. The soul is a Myth. The mind is a ghost. All that exists is the sensations and perceptions themselves following automatically into memories and ideas.

The Buddhist Nirvana is the release from rebirth. It does not formally deny the existence of God, but does not mention Him as a necessary factor for the attainment of Nirvana. Thus, it lays an emphasis on the individual exertion at Self improvement and homo actions as a means to attain it. Buddhist scriptures used the term 'Nirvana' as signifying a state of happiness attainable in one's life through the complete elimination of Selfish desires, the liberation of the individual from rebirth, the annihilation of the individual consciousness, the union of individual with God and a heaven of happiness after death. To achieve this *Ahṁisā* (non-violence) was one of the medium. The importance of *Ahiṁsā* is recognised in Hinduism, Jainism, Buddhism, Christianity and other religious systems. It is possible that the adoration of Buddha's foot prints was borrowed from the conception of Viṣṇu's pada. The influence of the Gitā on Buddhist works like the 'Saddharma-puṇḍarika, Mahāyāna Śraddhotpāda,' etc., is unmistakable. On the other hand, the full development of the avatāravāda seems to have influenced by the conception of the former Buddhas, some of whom were worshipped in their own Stūpas as early as the third century B.C. That a large number of Buddhists were admitted into the fold of the Vaiṣhṇavas towards the close of the Hindu period is suggested by the inclusion of Buddha in the list of Viṣṇu's avatāras[1]. In this manner the relation of Bhagavatism with other creeds continued.

About the Avataras of Viṣṇu, D.C. Sircar[2] informs the conception of the Vāmana (Dwarf) avatāra associated with Viṣṇu, and that of the Varaha (Boar), Matsya (Fish) and Kurma (Tortoise) avatāras not yet connected with that God, are to be found in the Śatapatha and other Brahmānas.ùù In the Taittirtya Āranyaka the earth is said to have been raised from the waters by a black boar with a hundred arms. This work also alludes to the Nrisiṁha or Man-Lion.——The Gitā and some other sections of the *Māhabhāratā* represent Viṣṇu as an ideal Divinity and an almighty Saviour, working for the salvation of mankind and delighting in both moral goodness and ritualistic purity, and as incarnating himself from time to time in human or animal form in order to maintain the standard of righteousness in the world. But the theory of avatāra presents only a stage of development in the *Māhabhāratā,* the earlier sections of the epic not containing any list of the incarnations. Traditions regarding the number of avatāras varied, and the later lists of the ten avatāras, sometimes adhered to, very often give different names. The avatāra theory, which apparently underwent several stages of evolution, seems to be based on old tales of strange animals with mysterious powers of assistance; but many of them had originally nothing to do with Viṣṇu. The Buddhist conception of the Pratyeka-Buddhas might have influenced the development of the theory.

"In a passage of the late Nārāyaṇiya section of the *Mahābhāratā* mention is made only of four avatāras, viz. Boar, Dwarf, Man-Lion and Man (Vāsudeva-Kṛishna). In another passage of the same section, the deified beings Rāma Bhārgava and Rāma Dāsarāthi are added to the list making a total of Six avatāras, while a third passage gives the list of ten incarnations, by adding Haṁsa, Kūrma, Matsya and Kalki, to the above Six." About the age of *Māhabhāratā* epic composition, M.A. Mehendale[3] is of opinion that scholars hold widely divergent views on the subject, but we may accept for all practical purposes the one expressed by Dr. Winternitz in the following words : "The *Mahābhāratā* cann't have received its present form earlier than the 4th century B.C. and later than the 4th century A.D."

Bhagavadgitā has been incorporated in the *Mahābhāratā.* Although its composition period cannot be definitely dated, it is generally referred to the first or second century before Christ.[4] D.D. Kosambi[5] is of the opinion that Gitå may be dated between 150-353 A.D., nearer the later than the earlier date. Swami Chinmayanada'' claims Badarayana, who has been identified as Vyasa the author of the *Gitā.*

The theory of avatāra or incarnation is mentioned in the Gitā which declares Kṛishṇa to be the Purushottama or Perfect Man. "Though unborn and eternal, I take charge of prakriti and am born through recourse of maya," says Kṛishṇa,[7] and this happens "when piety (Dharma) wanes and unrighteousness rears its ugly head." An avatāra is, generally speaking, a limited manifestation of the Supreme, but the Gitā seems to take it as the descent of the whole God into Man. In a sense every individual human being is an avatāra; only it is enveloped in ignorance and is a veiled manifestation, whereas the Divine avatāra with a conscious being is none else but God, who limits Himself for a definite purpose and fulfils Himself in the World. This possibility of an avatāra at the time of a World crisis is indeed, a most heartening Spiritual message of the *Gitā.*[8]

Matsya Purāṇa gives a list of ten incarnations, there were three Divine avatāras, viz. Nārāyana, Narasiṁha and Vāmana, as well as seven human avatāras, viz. Dattatreya, Māndhatṛi, Rāma son of Jamadagni, Rāma son of Dāśaratha, Vedavyasa, Buddha and Kalki. The same section occurs in the *Vāyu Purāṇa* with the substitution of Kṛishṇa for Buddha. The Harivaṁśa gives a list often incarnations which omits Matsva, Kurma, one of the Rāmas and Buddha, but adds Lotus, Datta (Dattātreya), Keśava, and Vyāsa. There are three lists of the avatāras in the *Bhāgavata Purāṇa*; but they do not agree with one another. One of these lists, according to which the incarnations are really innumerable, mentions no less than 24 avatāras. The Ahirbudhnya Samhitā, probably assignable to a date earlier than the eighth century, speaks of 39 vibhavas (manifestations) of the Supreme Being. Other Pāncharātra works like the Vishvaksena-Saṁhitā mention Buddha Arjuna and others in the list of secondary avatāras.[9]

Varāha Purāṇa mentions ten incarnations and Buddha has been accepted as an avatāra in it.[10]

According to R.G. Bhandarkar,[11] *Bhāgavata purāṇa* enumerates the incarnations in three different passages. Rṣabha, son of Nābhi and Merudevi is also mentioned.——Rṣabha, from the parentage given here and other indications, appears clearly to be the same as the first Tirthankara of the Jainas. He was probably raised to the dignity of an incarnation as the Buddha of the Buddhists was.

The earliest Dāśāvatāra temple[12] at Deogarh (Jhansi district, Uttar Pradesh), assigned to Gupta period, is a testimony of the popularity of Dāsāvatāra or Ten incarnations of Viṣṇu worship. At Tālā, in Bilaspur district, Madhya Pradesh, two dilapidated temples named Devrani and Jethani are found. The colossal nature of the stone sculptures lying around the ruined Jethani temple suggests that this temple was originally quite grand. Some of the Sculptures have a height of 4 metres to 5 metres. The images of Naṛasiṁha, Buddha and a few other deities have been identified. The temple may have been a Daśāvatāra shrine. In point of time this temple is earlier than the Devrani temple. It can be assigned to the 4th century A.D.[13]

Originally a Buddhist monastic excavation, the Daśavatāra

Cave-temple at Ellora was converted into a Hindu shrine under Rashtrakuta patronage in the eighth century A.D[14]

Buddha is recognised as an avatāra in the Daśāvatāra-charita of the Kāshmirian author Kshemendra (circa. 1050), A.D. and in the Gitagovinda of Jayadeva (circa. A. D. 1200) of eastern India.[15] Gradually the conception of Ten avatāras of Viṣṇu became prevailing.

Buddha-avatāra is one of the prominent Avatār. According to R.K. Pandey[16] Buddha avatār was to discriminate between right and wrong before the World, this avatār of Viṣṇu came as the Buddha, who later on addressed men all over the World to choose between two things, paths and principles not merely on the basis of senses but also on the basis of reason and rational capacity granted to men and men alone.

Swami Prahad Giri[17] has also written on 'अवतारबाद और जगन्नाथ' mentions of आदिबौद्धअवतारजगन्नाथ and mentions:

"कुतुब मीनार के पार्श्ववर्ती हिन्दु स्थापत्य में दशावतार की चित्रमूर्ति है, उसी में बुद्धवतार के स्थान पर भोगमण्डपस्थित मूर्ति के सदश आकृति वाले निराकार मध्य स्तूप का प्रदर्शन किया गया है। जितेन्द्रनाथ मुखर्जी ने स्वयं रचित ग्रंथ में जगन्नाथजी, बुद्ध के स्थान पर ग्रहण किया है। उत्काल में यमधर्म बिहार, घन्टशिला रत्नगिरि, अइरगढ़ बिहार प्रभृति बौद्ध बिहार थे। यमधर्म बिहार में भी त्रिनिराकार मूर्ति या जगन्नाथ रछश मूतियाँ प्रतीक उसासनों के बीच में आयी है। इन्द्रभूमि में जगन्नाथ, बुद्ध अवतार, प्रबुद्ध बुद्ध अवतार तथा सर्व जनार्चित जगन्नाथ बुद्ध कह कर उद्घोष किया है। सरलादास, अच्युतानन्द दास, यशोवन्त आदि प्रमुख प्राचीन उत्कलीय कवियों ने तथा परवर्ती मध्यकालीन कवियों ने जगन्नाथ को बुद्ध नाम से अभिहित किया हैं तथा प्राचीन चित्रकला में भी जगन्नाथ जी बुद्ध के स्थान पर आये है। बुद्ध पूर्णिमा के दिन बैशाखी व्रर्ती के लोग सौगत नारायण मन्दिर में जो पारम्परिक मण्व्र से पुष्पाज्जलि देते हैं वह इस प्रकार है

"जय विष्णु जगन्नाथ आदि बुद्ध सनातनम।
बैशाख–व्रतकृत्यस्य यत्फलं (तत् फलम) देहि में विभुम्।"[18]

REFERENCES

1. Journal of the Royal Asiatic Society of Bengal, Letters, Calcutta, Vol. XV, p. 101, as quoted in *THACOTIP*, Vol. II, 1968, p. 450.
2. Sircar, D.C. "The Avatāras of Viṣṇu," *THACOTIP*, Vol. III, The Classical Age, 1970, pp. 420-421.
3. Mehendale, M.A. "The Māhabhāratā," *THACOTIP*, Vol. II, The Age of Imperial Unity, 1968, p. 251.
4. Sircar, D.C. "Bhagavadgitā or Gitā," *THACOTIP*, Vol. II, The Age of Imperial Unity, 1968, p. 440.
5. *MAR*, p. 16.
6. Swami Chinmayananda, *Vedanta the Science of Life*, Part I, Central Chinmaya Mission Trust, Bombay, 1983, p. 9.
7. *Gitā*, IV. 6.
8. Sircar, D.C. "Bhagavadgitā or Gitā" *op. cit.* 1968, p. 445.
9. Sircar, D.C. "The Avatāras of Viṣṇu," *op. cit.* 1970, p. 421.
10. Bhandarkar, R.G. *Vaiṣṇavism, Saivism and Minor Religious Systems*, Indological Book House, Varanasi, 1965, p. 42.
11. *Ibid.*, 1965, p. 42.
12. Vats, 'The Gupta Temple at Deograh' *Memoirs of the Archaeological Survey of India*, No. 70.
13. Bajpai, K.D. & Pandey, S.K. *MALHAR* 1975-77, University of Sagar Sagar, 1977, p. 37.
14. George Michell, *The Hindu Temple*, B.I. Publications, New Delhi, 1977, p. 103.
15. Sircar, D.C. "The Avatāra of Viṣṇu" *op. cit.* 1970, p. 421.
16. Pandey, R.K. *The Concept of Avatārs*, B.R. Publishing Corporation, Delhi, 1978, pp. 29-30.
17. Giri, Swami Prahad-"अवतारवाद और जगन्नाथ", *UNMANA*, Souvenir of Akhil Bharat Jagannāth Consciousness Conference, Cuttack, December 1984, (Hindi section), pp. 10-18.
18. *Ibid.*, p. 17.

Four

Puruṣottama Buddha Jagannāth, as an Avatāra of Viṣṇu, in Mahānadi Valley and its Evolution as Puruṣottama-Jagannāth

Cosmos means the World or Universe as an orderly or systematic whole. Vedic culture deals with cosmogenic principles. Therefore, Vedic culture assimilates everything into its fold. One of such act was to incorporate one iconic feature of Buddha's image as Jagannāth Deity of Vedic alias Hindu religion.

In Samudrabanika Jataka (Pali literature), Buddha has been addressed as Puruṣottama.[1]

Bhāgavata religion popularised the worship of Avatāras, i.e. descents or incarnations of Viṣṇu, in Gupta period. D.C. Sircar[2] states that Buddha is recognised as an avatāra in the 'Daśāvatāra-Charita,' of the Kashmirian author Kshemendra (circa. A.D. 1050), and in the *Gitāgovinda,* of Jayadeva (circa. 1200), A.D. of eastern India. Jayadeva sings in praise of Kṛishṇa who is Viṣṇu himself, and of his ten avatāras, viz. Fish, Tortoise, Boar, Man-Lion, Dwarf, Rāma Bhargava, Rāma Dīsarathi, Rāma Haladhara, Buddha and Kalki. The same names are found in a well known Purāṇic verse enumerating the ten avatāras, which is quoted in a Mamallapuram (near Madras) inscription of about the eighth century A.D. In the foot-note D.C. Sircar mentions that the beginning of Buddha's inclusion in the list of the ten avatāras must be assigned to a date earlier than the eighth century. (Memoirs of the Archaeological Survey of India, No. 26, p. 5).

One of the earliest image of Viṣṇu showing the incarnation aspect is found preserved at the State Museum, Lucknow. This image of Viṣṇu, under reference, bears no crown. This Deity has been shown with small curls similar to those of the Tirthaṅkara and the Buddha figures.[3]

The post Gupta period witnessed the religious synchronisation in India level. The Yogasana Viṣṇu images, found in Sagar district of Madhya Pradesh are the strong examples, to show the synchronisation of Buddha and Viṣṇu. V.D. Jha[4] writes, "The Yogasana form of Viṣṇu has been described in 'Siddhartha Samhita,' 'Baikhana Sagamu' and 'Chaturvarga Chintamani (II, 114).' The Deity, seated in Padmasana pose on a lotus seat with the front hands placed in dhyana mudra, is known as Yogesvara Viṣṇu or Yoga-Narayana".

"This form of Viṣṇu is regarded as the composite form of Viṣṇu and Buddha. Even the accessary figures of the Naga and the lotus in Yoga murti are also typically Buddhist features. Dhyani Buddha is always shown two-armed and unornamented, whereas, the four-armed icons of Yoga-Viṣṇu are adorned with ornaments".

"The mediaeval icons of Yoga-Viṣṇu have been noticed at Deori, Marh Piparia, Bina and Baleha in Sagar district. Back hands of the four-armed icon at Bina are broken, front hands are placed on the lap in Yoga mudra. The Deity is adorned with a halo, kirita mukuta, ear-rings, necklace, ekavali, srivatso, arm-bands, beaded wrist-lets, sacred thread and a drapery; eyes slightly closed. Three beheaded male seated in Padmasana pose flanked by a standing female figure are shown at the top. The male figures are those of Brahma, Viṣṇu and Mahesa. The female figures should be identified with those of Bhu Devi and Laksmi respectively. The four armed female figures are shown holding Kamandalu in front left and abhaya in back right hand; front right dangling on the side, back left holds indistinct object. A male figure is shown standing on each side of the Deity."

"Śiva liṅga and Nagas flanked by disc and conch are shown on the lower relief. Two male devotees on each corner are seated with folded hands, 8th century A.D." V.D. Jha's view as stated above mentions three beheaded males seated in Padmasana pose flanked by a standing female figure are shown at the top. The male figures are those of Brahma, Viṣṇu and Mahesa.

These three figures cannot be accepted as Brahma, Viṣṇu and Mahesa, because the two figures on either sides are seated in bhumi-spara mudra and the centre figure is seated in Dhyani mudra. These three figures at the top of the Yogasana Viṣṇu image might represent Buddha himself. The Yogasana Viṣṇu images of Sagar district are additional prove, to ascertain the synchronisation of Buddha and Viṣṇu. Yogesvara Viṣṇu sculptures are very rarely represented, but a Yogasthanaka-Murti, dated to 12th century A.D., Stone image hailing' from Sarisadah, 24 Parganas, Bengal (exhibit No. 2592 in the Indian Museum) illustrates many traits of Yogesvara Viṣṇu Mention may be made of Yoga-asana Viṣṇu images found at Mathura museum (exhibit No. 379), at Khajuraho and Kallesvara temple at Bagali (Biliary district) of the later Chalukya period.

In Buddhist literature, "बोधिचर्यक्तार", Buddha is named as 'Jagannāth,' which goes thus :

अद्यैव शरणं यामि जगन्नाथ न् महावलान्।
जगद्रक्षार्थमुद्यु क्तन् सर्वत्रासहरान् जिनान।।

"बोधियर्यावतार 2/48"

Another simultaneity of Buddha and Viṣṇu can be found in Tantric literature, 'Brahmayamala.' Pranab Bandyopadhyay[5] gives the account of an episode in it thus : "Vashistha started off at Kamakshya, the famous pitha (Shrine) in Assam, and that he was told to proceed to Nilachala (the blue mountain) where he worshipped the Supreme Goddess of Kamrupa (Kamakshya). He was told that Viṣṇu in the form of Buddha knew the rituals of 'Cinacara.' So, Vashistha went to Malcachina which is situated on the slope of the Himalayas."

It seems, the Tantric literature 'Brahmayamala', was written after Jagannāth was installed as a Vaiṣhṇav Deity at Puri (Nilachala). Jagannāth has been described as the famous Deity of Odra or Utkal in the famous Tantric works like Kālikā purāna, Rudrayāmala, Brahmayāmala (as already stated) and Tantrayāmala, which were written in circa. 950 A.D. (Mahatab, H.K. *The History of Orissa,* Vol. II, Cuttack, 1960, p. 514).

In the Mahānadi valley, the earliest Dasavatār chisled images are found at the ruined Jethani temple of Tālā, situated on the bank of river Manihari, dated to 4th century A.D. as stated in last chapter and in the Ramchandra temple at Rajim. Rajim is situated at the confluence of Pairi and Mahānadi rivers, in Raipur district of Madhya Pradesh.

W.W. Hunter[6] informs that "Vaiṣhṇavism at Puri is but the successor of the older Buddhistic creed." A. Cunningham[7] states, "I have found these same three rude Jagannātha figures are used in all the Native Almanacs of Mathura and Benaras as the representative of Buddha in the Buddha Avatara of Viṣṇu" So, it seems that it was all India practice of depicting Buddha, with the shape of present Jagannāth Deity. With reference of including Buddha as an incarnation, example can be given, to a panel with last four incarnations of Viṣṇu viz. Ram Balarama, Buddha and Kalki, in Mathura museum.[8]

Rajim[9] has been listed under the chalcolithic site. At Rajim the chalcolithic Black-and-Red were having characteristics of chalcolithic affinity and microliths, from the mounds situated on the right bank of river Mahānadi have been collected. This proves Rajim to have been an ancient site.

From the inscription of the Nala dynasty[10] in Rajivalochana temple, it is known that the Nala dynasty built the temple of Viṣṇu originally in 7th century A.D.

Another inscription[11] known as "Rajim stone inscription of Prithvideva II: Kalachuri year 896," in the same temple, records the construction of a temple of Rāma and the grant of the village Salmaliya for the purpose of the naivedya or offerings of food to the Deity by Jagapala. In the foot-note V.V. Mirashi states that we learn that a King of the Nala dynasty originally built the temple of Viṣṇu. Jagapala seems, therefore, to have only repaired or rebuilt the temple. With this background of the inscriptions of Viṣṇu alias Rajivalochana temple, it can be confirmed that originally the temples of Rajivalochana and Rāma of Rajim were constructed in 7th century A.D. and the Kalachuri inscription of 12th century A.D. only shown that these temples were rebuilt.

On the door lintel of Rāma alias Rāmchandra temple of Rajim,[12] Daśāvatāra images are chiseled. The place of Buddha, represents the figure of Jagannāth. So it seems that by 7th century A.D. the making of Buddha image, like the present Jagannāth shape had already started in the iconographic aspect of Upper Mahānadi valley and the shape of Jagannāth icon, in the panel of Daśāvatāra, at Rajim site, is the earliest icon of present Jagannāth's shape in Mahānadi valley, chiseled on stone.[13]

The Lakshmana temple of Sirpur was dedicated to Viṣṇu, as his Avataras are carved on the stone door jamb and there is a figure of Varaha on one of the broken plasters[14] Raipur district Gazetteer[15] also confirms that down the two outer sides of the door-jambs are the incarnations and other scenes, while the inner sides are adorned with pairs of human figures. Pyarelal Gupta[16] confirms that ten avatāras of Viṣṇu are chiseled on the stone door jamb of this Lakshmana temple. The figure of Dhyani Buddha is found to represent the avatāra of Buddha. A.P. Sah[17] doubts whether during that period, the concept of all the ten avatāras was known to the people of Orissa cann't be said with certainty.

The title 'Jagannāth' (Lord of the Universe) is used for the first time in 'Devi Mahatmya', of *Mārkandeya Purāṇa,* whose composition form is late Gupta period,[18] but certainly not later than A.D. 600.

Further Stietencron[19] is of opinion that the title 'Jagannāth' itself is unspecific. It has been applied to Buddha, to Śiva and to Viṣṇu. Its uncompounded variant Jagato-natha was similarly used for each of these three Deities. The same is true for its synonyms 'Lokanātha,' and 'Lokeśvara,' which could be used for Śiva, Viṣṇu and a form of the Bodhisattva Avalokiteśvara. Other titles like Iśvara (ruler) or Paramesvara (Supreme ruler) were equally unspecified upto the post Gupta period and could be applied both to Viṣṇu and Śiva. All these terms simply denote the all embracing power of protection and Lordship vesting in the Supreme God.

In one of the early composed Hymn, 'Śiva Bhujangam' Śankarāchārya had addressed Śiva as, 'Jagannāth'. It goes thus :-

जगन्नाथ! मन्नाथ! गौरीसनाथ!
प्रपन्नानुकम्पिन्! विपन्नार्त्तिहारिन्।
महस्तोममूर्ते! समस्तैकबन्धे।
नमस्ते नमस्ते पुनस्ते नमोऽस्तु।।

(*Sankara the Missionary,* Central Chinmaya Mission Trust, Bombay, 1978, p. 129). So, it is definite that till the composition of 'Śiva Bhujangam,' Jagannāth was not yet installed as a Deity.

K.C. Mishra[20] observes, "In 1200 A.D. a Buddhist Pilgrim named Lāmā Tārānatha[21] gave an account of a mysterious tradition regarding the construction of a Buddha image, which has some resemblance with the constructions of the image of Lord Jagannātha. A certain Brāhmin named Kalyana wanted to make an image of the Buddha. Accordingly, he built a temple and brought many carpenters including Viśvakarmā to make the image. The temple was to be closed for 7 days so that the construction of the image could be completed. After 5 days, Kalyāṇa's mother apprehended the death of her son inside the temple. So, he opened it before the stipulated period was over, and found there an image half made. Such a tradition is also prevalent in Orissa regarding the construction of the image of Jagannāth.

"An archaeologist, L.A. Waddell, while giving an account of the Bauddha ruins of Munghyr has said that the people called the place, where the ruins of Bauddha temples are found. 'Indradyumna Gada."[22] In the history of the construction of the temple of Jagannāth there is also the mention of the name of a King named Indradyumna who is said to be the first builder of the temple. So, it is evident that the tradition associated with Jagannāth was not localised in Orissa, but popular throughout India witn certain alterations." The same is the Tale of the making of the Buddha image at Bodh Gaya in Bihar.

Swami Prahad Giri[23] mentions,

"साँची में मिले हुए धर्मयन्त्रों की जगन्नाथ मूर्ति के साथ पूर्ण रूप से समानता है।"

Buddhist stupas and ruins of Sānchi, Bharhut and Bodh-Gaya are dated to B.C. 1st century by Nihar Ranjan Ray.[24] In these Buddhist structures, the image of Buddha is depicted as modern Jagannāth Deity. So, it can be said that from B.C., 1st century the practice of making images of Buddha like the modern Jagannāth Deity had started.

H.K. Mahatab[25] remarks that recently a stone of Asokan polish with the symbols of Buddha, Dharma and Sangha at the top has been found out at Bhubaneswar and is now preserved in the Ashotosh Museum of Calcutta. The photograph of the stone with the symbols is appended herewith. The symbols are a little different from those found out at Sanchi and other places but the Bhubaneswar symbols are almost exactly like the images of Jagannātha, Balabhadra and Subhadra. The Bhubaneswar discovery proves that in Orissa the worship of the symbols was prevalent since the Ashokan period.

Even though the title 'Jagannāth' has been used for Viṣṇu and Śiva, as seen above, the shape of 'Jagannāth' emerged to represent Buddha, in the Daśāvatāra panel of Rāmchandra temple at Rajim, in 7th century A.D. in Mahānadi valley, as already observed at Mathura and Benaras.

The territory of Saṁbhala, in Uḍḍiyāna was ruled by Indrabhūti, in 8th century A.D. N.K. Sahu[26] identifies Sambhala with modern Sambalpur and states that the note-worthy fact is that Indrabhūti opens his famous work Jnānasiddhi[27] with an invocation to Lord Jagannātha, a Deity intimately associated with Orissa and with no other country of India far less with the Swat valley. A large number of poets and philosophers of Orissan literature are found invoking and saluting Jagannātha in their works, which seems to be one of the characteristics of the writers belonging to Orissa, and so, on this analogy it may not be unreasonable to accept Indrabhūti as belonging to Orissa (i.e., modern province of

Orissa). Indrabhuti has used the title or name 'Jagannāth', for addressing Buddha, in his excellent work 'Jnanasiddhi.' This is not to be confused with the Jagannāth Deity, which came into existence, as dealt in this work, after Indrabhūti.

Even though, no archaeological findings of Indrabhuti are found in Sambalpur area, so far, there is ground to locate Sambhala in Sambalpur region, because Indrabhūti has invoked Jagannātha in his composition, Jagannātha is associated with Mahānadi valley as discussed and the existence of the Muchalinda Buddha and Buddha in the pose of the first Sermon at Sarnath, at Ganiapali, proves that a Muchalinda Buddha monastery existed there, which can be dated to 5th century A.D. and Muchalinda Buddhas are not frequent in India.[28] One Muchalinda Buddha image is found in the Sculpture shed at Sripur (modern Sirpur, located in Raipur district of Madhya Pradesh), maintained by Archaeological Survey of India.

Further, the excavation at Nagraj site, has exposed a Buddhist monastery datable to 4th-5th century A.D. According to the excavator N.K. Sahu,[29] this monastery (newly excavated) is the earliest of this kind in Orissa. Even in India, a structural monastery of this magnitude is rare during the 4th-5th century A.D.

As already observed, Buddha alias Jagannāth as an avatāra is found at Rajim, datable to 7th century A.D. and as Indrabhūti worshipped Buddha as Jagannātha, it is reasonable to locate Saṁbhala, in Mahānadi valley. So, the idol of Buddha alias Jagannāth, which was worshipped by Indrabhūti, datable to 8th century A.D. should be taken as the next image of Buddha alias Jagannāth in Mahānadi valley.

Arjun Joshi[30] suggests that it may be said that an important Cave in the Court Samalai hill near Sonepur as attributed by the local people as the earliest Seat of the worship of Lord Jagannātha. It appears that Jagannātha of Raja Indrabhūthi was installed in that Cave giving rise to the tradition, which is current even in the present day. The Court Samalai hill requires proper archaeological survey for coming to a definite conclusion. It is to be observed that Indrabhūti was worshipping Buddha and had addressed Buddha as Jagannāth (i.e., the

Lord of the Universe). It never meant or means the Jagannāth Deity which was installed later.

The ten Avatāras are chiseled round about the Viṣṇu image, where Daśāvatāra, following the suçcession or manner of ten avatāras, as mentioned by Kashmirian author Kshemendru and Jayadeva, is found at Saintala, şituated in Balangir district of Orissa. N.K. Sahu[31] informs that Saintala is a village on the Balangir-Titilagarh road, 21miles south of Balangir. It is also a Railway station on the Sambalpur Titilagarh line. The village is notable for the old Chandi temple which is now in ruins.The Goddess who is a form of Mahishamardini Durga has now been installed on the mound formed by the ruins of her former temple. Some Sculptural pieces and the broken door jamb with the figures of Gaṅga and Jamuna have been preserved and they indicate a high standard of workmanship of the old temple. Two broken images of Viṣṇu surrounded by his ten incarnations have been discovered in the village and those have been attributed to the 9th century A.D. The fact that the ideology of ten incarnations of Viṣṇu was known in this part as early as the 9th century A.D. is very significant specially because such ideology had not been developed in the Coastal region of Orissa.

In this way, the shape of Jagannātha representing Buddha, became associated. Ten Avatāras or Daśāvatāra images are found in the Laxmana brick temple of Sirpur (Raipur district), Indralath brick temple of Ranipur-Jharial (Balangir district), around the Viṣṇu image collected from Ratanpur and preserved at Mahanta Ghasi Das Museum (Raipur), few images of Daśāvatāra are found in the Śiva temple of Deo Baloda (Durg district), ten incarnations of Viṣṇu are carved on the jambs of the door; on an heap of archaeological ruin at Tuman (Bilaspur district, around the Viṣṇu image of Dadpur (Kalahandi district), twin temples of Gandharadi (Boud-Phulbani district), in a broken temple near the Vaital temple of Bhubaneswar, on the wall of a small temple in the compound of Paramaguru family in the Jagannāth temple of Puri, in the Sikhareswar temple of Śiva-Narayanpur (Keonjhar district), in the Madhavananda temple of Niali, in the temple of Ananta-Vasudeva, in the pedestal of Kṛina-Viṣṇu preserved in the Orissa State Museum, in the Manibhadreśvara temple of Bhubaneswar and the Avatāra images in many sites of Mahānadi valley, reveal the prevalence of Daśāvatāra worship in Mahānadi valley.

Spiritual genius Śaṅkarāchārya was born in the Chera country about the year 788 A.D.[32] He had visited Puri in early part of 9th century A.D., Sringerix, Dwaraka and Jyotirdham. In order that the great wisdom of the Rishis may not be lost to posterity, Śaṅkarā established four Mathas and the four disciples at the above mentioned four places.

At Puri, Śaṅkarā established the Govardhan Matha. The teertha here, is the Mahodadhi (Bay of Bengal). The Divinity of Puri Matha is Lord Viṣṇu 'Jagannāth', also called 'Puruṣottama,' and His Sakti is Vimala. It seems, 'Jagannāth' established as the Male Deity of Govardhan Matha at Puri, by Śaṅkarā, revolutionalised Jagannāth as a Vaiṣhṇav Deity.

It is interesting to know about the Gods and Goddesses established by Śaṅkarā, at the four Mathaṣ, which he founded.

At Govardhan Matha of Puri, the divinity worshipped is Lord Viṣṇu 'Jagannāth,' also called 'Puruṣottama,' and His Sakti is Vimala.

At Sringeri Matha (now in the state of Karnataka), the divinity worshipped is Lord Śiva (Chandramouleesvara), and His Sakti is Sree Sarada.

At Kalika Matha in Dwaraka, the divinity worshipped is Lord Śiva (Siddhesvara) and His Sakti, Bhadra Kali.

At Jyotirdham Matha (now known as Joshimath), the divinity worshipped is Lord Viṣṇu (Narayana) and His Sakti is Purnagiri.

It is to be observed that Śaṅkarā observed the policy of establishing the opposite Gods of the above mentioned four sites, in installing, as Divinity to be worshipped in the Mathas, established by him. For example Dwarka is Vaiṣhṇav khetra, but Śaṅkarā installed Lord Śiva (Siddhesvara) as the Divinity of Kalika Matha in Dwaraka. Similarly, when Śankara visited Puri, it was a Śaiva kshetra, but Śaṅkarā installed a Vaiṣhṇav Deity 'Jagannāth' as the Divinity, to be worshipped at Govardhan Matha of Puri. It seems, thereby

Śaṅkarā made 'Jagannāth', fully a Viṣṇu Deity and the credit of first converting 'Jagannāth.' to a Viṣṇu-Kṛiṣṇa Deity, should be given to Ādi Śaṅkarāchārya.

Further, Śaṅkarā's commentary on the "Prasthānatrayī",[33] added fuel to the fire of Purushottama Cult, Jagannāth Cult and made them synchronised as Purușottama-Jagannāth. Śaṅkarā did not composed Hymn or Meditation verse named "Jagannātha Ashtakam",[34] (vide : Appendix). Kedarnath Mahapatra[35] came close to the observation of the author, when he stated, "The identity of the Buddhist Jagannātha with the Purushottama Viṣṇu of Brahmanism was established by the great Śaṅkarā Acharya, in the first quarter of the nineth century, whereby this place became a famous centre of Hinduism since his days." Later Rāmānuja and Chaitanya visited Puri and developed Purushottama-Jagannāth into more importance of Vaiṣhṇavism.

Sachidananda Misra[36] mentions that before Śaṅkarā, there was no worship of Purushottama-Jagannāth at Puri. Puri was a Śaiva kshetra during Śaṅkarā's visit and it seems Śaṅkarā installed Jagannāth, while establishing Govardhana Matha there.

It has been dealt earlier, how the image of Jagannāth is located at the place of Buddha, where Daśāvatāra or Ten incarnations of Viṣṇu are chiseled. Thereby, the present shape of Jagannāth Deity has been made to represent Buddha. This practice is still continuing in Orissa. The most interesting fact is that Dasā-Avatāra (Ten incarnation) are found on the inner wall of Nata-mandira of the Jagannāth temple at Puri.[37] It may be pointed out here that in the ten incarnations of Viṣṇu, inscribed on the gateway of the temple of Jagannātha in Puri, Buddha, the 9th incarnation, has been replaced by Jagannātha.[38] Here, the same ancient practice is followed and Buddha is identified as Lord Jagannāth. This practice is still continuing by the artists and sculpturos of Orissa.

The instalment of Jagannāth, as the Presiding Deity of Puri is interesting. Sōmavaṁśī King Mahāśivagupta Yayāti I whose reigning period is assigned circa 960-988 A.D.[39] or 925-955 A.D.[40] immediately after ascending the throne, followed the policy of expansion like his father. His first task was to expand the Sõmavaṁśi Kingdom in the east. According to the old tradition of the Madalapanji, K.C. Panigrahi[41] states that the re-establishment of the Shrine of Jagannāth at Puri with a temple built there, was another great work of Yayāti. In the words of H.V. Stietencron,[42] "We have seen that two important elements of the later Jagannāth Cult namely (1) the connection of Purushottama, with Narasimha and (2) the juxtaposition of Viṣṇu and Śiva on a common platform (Vedi) were possibly introduced into Central Orissa from the West along the Mahānadi river. Both elements were present in the Western hill tracts of Orissa around 900 A.D. They could advance further down into the Coastal area in the middle of the 10th century when Yayāti I established the Sõmavaṁśi rule in Utkala". Herman Kulke[43] follows the tradition of Madalapanji and states' After establishing himself as the new King of Orissa and founder of the Sõmavaṁśi dynasty, Yayāti Kesari invited the learned scholars and Priests of his Kingdom and asked them to tell him the whereabouts of Jagannāth' the Lord of the Kings of Orissa' (Odiśā rājā ra prabhu). When Yayāti came to know that Jagannātha had been taken to a secret place near Sonepur in Western Orissa, 144 years ago, after the invasion of a foreign King Raktabahu, he started on an expedition to Sonepur in order to recover the Lord of Puri. After overcoming various obstacles, Yayāti discovered the three images under a tree in the village Gapali but they were so badly decayed that he decided to have new images prepared. This sacred renewal, of the Wooden images, however, could only be performed by the Daita Priests, the descendants of the Tribal Saora Chief Bisvābasu who had been the first worshipper of Jagannātha in the hoary past. But these Daita Priests, together with the Pati priests of Puri (the descendants from, Bisvābasu's daughter Lalita and the Brahmin Vidyapati) had also fled before Raktabahu. With the help of Jagannātha Yayāti discovered the Daitas in Biribandha and the Patis in Ratanpur, places lying in Western Orissa and eastern Madhya Pradesh respectively. These priests set up new images according to the Śāstras. Yayāti, Kesari had then constructed a new temple for Jagannātha in Puri and renewed the Cult. The act of reinstalation of Jagannātha was the greatest Cultural Knit, the Sōmavaṁśi rule could give".

The above mentioned tradition of Madalapani seems to be a creation to show the ancientness of Jagannāth. Finally, the instalment of Jagannāth as the presiding Deity of Puruṣottama Khetra, i.e. Puri, by Yayati I, immortalised Jagannāth as Puruṣottama-Jagannāth.

The image of Jagannāth represented Buddha, in the lintel Daśāvatāra was chiseled one stone, in upper Mahandi valley, but when it was Hinduised as Vaiṣṇava Deity, it was made of Wood and eyes were painted round.

It has been observed above that Śaṅkarācārya was responsible for converting the Buddha Jagannāth image to a Viṣṇu-Kṛishṇa Deity. Because of this most probably, there was bearing of the Śaṅkarācārya Matha alias Govardhan Matha upon the administration of the Jagannātha temple. This bearing, finds mention in the words of K.C. Mishra[44] thus : "The priests of the Jagannātha temple learn the art of ritualistic worship from Gobardhan Matha. That is, this Matha is responsible for the education and training of the priests in respect of worship to the Deities. After obtaining sufficient training at this Matha Certificates are issued to the priests. They are then, by an order of the King, entitled to enter into the priesthood. The system is no longer in vogue in the temple. The function is now done by Muktimaṇḍapa.

For exposing of Truth or Reality, through research, sometimes old traditions has to be given up, because in the words of Swami Chinmayananda[45], "No progress in any walk of life is possible without leaving the present state and moving forward to win a new state of greater glory. No growth is possible unless there is a willingness to drop out our previous condition and accept the ampler status of the new conditions. Childhood must end in the youngster, the Youth must end in the Oldman.

"If a bud is not ready to end its present state, how can it grow and unfold itself to become a flower." The same is the system in critical research studies.

Much traditions have developed about Jagannātha, the Deity and the place of his installation in *Viṣṇu Purāṇa* (I, XV

52), *Agni Purāṇa* (chapter 63), *Padma Purāṇa* (chapter, 158, sloka 1-6 & chapter 11), *Narada Purāṇa* (chapter 52, sloka 41-93), *Brahma Purāṇa* (chapter 48), *Skanda Purāṇa* (chapter XX, slokas 35-36), and many Oriya works.[46] After much critical study on "Puruṣottama-Jagannātha," D.C. Sircar[47] also comes close to the view of the author and remarks that it is now clear that the God was enjoying the same celebrity as early as the middle of the 10th century and probably even sometime earlier.

The 'Puruṣottama Māhātmya,' a significant part of the *Skanda Purāṇa* popularised Puruṣottama-Jagannātha Cult in the whole country. R.C. Hazra,[48] informs that the *Skanda Purāṇa* is a voluminous work consisting of a very large number of parts, most of which have not yet been printed. Though, like the other Purāṇas, the Skanda also was subjected to additions and alterations more than once, there are chapters in it which were written earlier than 1000 A.D. but it seems to contain little which can be dated earlier than 700 A.D. So, in this way, the Religious Revolution of Mahānadi valley continued and its result was the evolution of Puruṣottama—Jagannātha Cult.

Reference of Śaṅkarā (SI. 105) has been made in Puruṣottama Māhātmya. So, it seems that it was composed after Śaṅkarā. King Indradyumna, the fifth King of the Solar dynasty, who ruled the earth and lived at 'Avanti' in the Country of 'Mālava,' is the main character in this Māhātmya. This shows the Western or Upper Mahānadi influence in Puruṣottama-Jagannātha Culture. Vidyāpati and Sabara Visvāvasu, are also mentioned in this Māhātmya.

The Gaṅga King Chodagaṅga left the throne in A.D. 1147 after which Kamarnavadeva sat on the Gaṅga throne in Orissa. In 1148 one Surama, daughter of Vidyāpati Pandita offered a perpetual lamp in the temple of Aniyankabhimasvara at Srikurmam. The question arises who is Vidyapati Pandita. It was quite interesting that he was famous at that time for which his daughter could divulge her identity through her father. Even the Champu Kavya notes that Vidyāpati returned with his wife Lilavati to Khimundi by the land route through Chilika. Lilavati can be equated with Lalita, the daughter of the Savara or Sailodbhava King of the Puri region who was worshipping Nilamadhava. R.N. Dash[49] after a critical study, is of opinion, that the story of Nilamadhava, Vidyapati and Lalita, which is found recorded in the 'Utkala Khanda,' of the *Skanda Purāṇa* has its roots in the Chodagaṅga period alias Gaṅga rule. So, it seems that 'Puruṣottama Māhātmya' and 'Utkala Khanda', are late additions in *Skanda Purāṇa,* about llth and 12th century A.D.

The period of the establishment of Jagannātha Trinity remains to a large extent unknown. A small relief of the Puri Trinity at the outside of the eastern prākāra of the Lingaraja temple[50] (which is Gaṅga period construction), in Bhubaneswar, further shows that Sudarsana-below the three deities of Puri is worshipped separately. Sculpture of Konarak, preserved at Konarak Museum shows King Narasimha worshipping a Liāga-Puruṣottama-Durgā Trinity. These are the works of Gaṅga ruling period.

REFERENCES

1. Satpathi, S.N. "Greater Indian conception in Orissan Culture", *AMRUTAYAVA.* (Oriya quarterly), ed. GitḌ Hota, Bhubaneswar, October 1988, p. 31.
2. Sircar, D.C. "The Avatāras of Viṣṇu", *THACOTIP,* Vol. III, The Classical Age, 1970, p. 421.
3. *Catalogue of the Brahmanical Sculptures in the State Museum,* Lucknow, Joshi, N.P. (chief editor), Part I, 1972, p. 14, vide plate I.
4. Jha, V.D. "Remarkable Brahmanical Icons in Sagar District", *PURATAN,* Vol. I, Nos. 2 & 3, 1984, Department of Archaeology and Museums, Madhya Pradesh, pp. 28-29.
5. Bandyopadhyay, P. *The Goddess of Tantra,* Punthi Pustak, Calcutta, 1987, p. 107.
6. Hunter, W.W. *ORISSA,* Vol. I, London, 1872, p. 131.
7. Cunningham, A. *The Stupa of Bharhut,* pp. 112-13, (as referred by Sah, A.P. *Life in Mediaeval Orissa, circa. A.D. 600-1200,* Chaukhambha Orientalia, Varanasi, 1976, p. 192.
8. Mathura Museum Centenary Number, June-December 1973, p. 54.
9. Pandey, S.K. "Archaeology of Chhattisgarh", *Prachya Pratibha,* Vol. V, No. 1, January 1977, Agam Kala Prakashan, Delhi, pp. 99-100.

10. *Epigrahia Indica*, Vol. XXVI, p. 49.
11. Mirashi, V.V. CII. Vol. IV, part II, Ootacamund, 1955, p. 451.
12. Thakur, Viṣṇu Singh *RAJIM* (Hindi) Madhya Pradesh Hindi Grantha Academy, Bhopal, 1972, p. 119.
13. The author observed it on 4th June 1988.
14. Cunningham, A. *Archaeological Survey of India*, Vol. XIII, plate IV.
15. *GOIMPR*, p. 568.
16. प्यारेलाल गुप्त, प्राचीन छत्तीसगढ़, रायपुर 1973, p. 165.
17. Sah, A.P. *Life in Medieval Orissa* (circa. A.D. 600-1200), Varanasi, 1976, p. 189.
18. Hazra, R.C. "The Purāṇas", *The Cultural Heritage of India*, Vol. II, Ramkrishna Mission, Calcutta, 1969, p. 246.
19. *TCOJATRTOO*, p. 61.
20. *TCOJ*, pp. 84-85.
21. Tales of Tārānāth (Quoted in 'Prajatantra' Special issue, Sunday 23-6-1973) and Datta, B.N. (Trans. into English), *MYSTIC TALES OF LĀMĀ TĀRĀNĀTHA*, Calcutta, 1944, passim.
22. *Ibid.*
23. Giri, Swami Prahad—''अवतार और जगन्नाथ'', *UNMANA*, Souvenir of Akhil Bharat Jagannāth Consciousness Conference, Cuttack, December, 1984, (Hindi section), p. 16.
24. Ray, N.R. 'Sculpture', *THACOTIP*, Vol. II, The Age of Imperial Unity, 1968, pp. 511.
25. Mahatab, H.K. *THOO*, Vol. II, Prajatantra Prachar Samiti, Cuttack, 1960, pp. 520-521.
26. *BIO*, p. 148 & pp. 144-145.
27. Published under the title "Two Vajrayāṅa Works", *Gaekwards's Oriental Series*. The opening Verse of Chapter I is as follows :-

    प्रणिपय जगन्नाथ संवेजिनवराच्चितं।
    सर्व बुद्धमयं सिद्धि व्यापिनं गगनोपमं।।

    Jagannātha is mentioned in four other verse of this work viz :--

    सः गुरूः शिष्यसंग्राहो सर्वबद्धानुकारकः।
    इत्युवाच जगन्नाथो नानये वै गुखः स्मृताः।।
    Verse 27 of Chapter I.
    तान् पयुक्तः जगन्नाथः वज्रसत्त्वविभावनैः।
    भुजवरार्ण समायुक्त मुद्रा मराडल कै स्तथा।।
    Verse 92 of Chapter I.

अतएव जगन्नाथ वालानां प्रतिबोधने।
निर्वाणं दर्शायन त्येव रुपस्यानित्य दशैकाः।।
Verse 28 of Chapter II.
सर्बज्ञः सबैदर्शी च सवैलोकायर्स कारकः।
तत्न तत्न जगन्नाथः दशितः करुणात्मभि।।
Verse 8 of Chapter V.

28. *CPOSK,* 1987, p. 299.
29. Sahu, N.K. "Ganiapali", *Interim Excavation Reports,* ed. Behers, S.C. P.G. Dept. of History, Sambalpur University, 1982, p. 15.
30. Joshi, A. *New Light on the Cultural Heritage of Orissa,* Baneeshree, Cuttack, 1980, p. 79.
31. Sahu, N.K. (State editor), *Gazetteer of India, Orissa, Balangir,* (chief editor) Senapati, N. Cuttack, 1968, pp. 492-493.
32. Mahadevan, T.M.P. "Saṅkarāchārya", *THACOTIP,* Vol. IV, The Age of Imperial Kanauj, 1964, p. 304.
33. Mohanti, P. *Concept of Purusha and Purushottama,* Gyan Publishing House, New Delhi, 1986, pp. 94-95.
34. "Compositions of Saṅkāra"; A List (Appendix), *ŚAṄKARĀ THE MISSIONARY,* Central Chinmaya Mission Trust, Bombay, 1978, p. 217.
35. Mahapatra, K.N. "Antiquity of *Jagannātha*—Puri as a place of Pilgrimage", *OHRJ,* Vol. III, No. 1, p. 21.
36. Misra,. S. "Śri Puruṣhottama Vigraha Pratistha", (Oriya), *SOUVENIR,* UGC. National Seminar, D.A.V. College, Titilagarh, 1937, pp. 27-35, passim.
37. Mishra, K.C. *op. cit.* 1971, plate No. 18.
38. Mahapatra, K.N. "Antiquity of Jagannātha—Puri as a place of Pilgrimage", *op. cit.* p. 7.
39. *PHOTSKOSKAO,* p. 204.
40. *CHOO,* p. 51 and p. 62.
41. *HOO,* p. 105.
42. Stietencron, H.V. "The Advent of Viṣṇuism in Orissa", *TCOJATRTOO,* p. 16.
43. Kulke, H. "Early Royal Patronage of the Jagannāth Cult", *Ibid.* 1978, p. 140.
44. *TCOJ,* 1971, p. 125.
45. Swami Chinmayananda, *A Manual of Self-Unfoldment,* Central Chinmaya Mission Trust, Bombay, 1985, p. 111.

46. Mishra, K.C. *op. cit.* 1971, pp. 74-78.
47. Sircar, T.C. *Studies in the Religious Life of Ancient and Medieval India,* Motilal Banarsidass, Delhi, 1971, p. 78.
48. Hazra, R.C. "The Purāṇas", *The Cultural Heritage of India,* Vol. II, The Rāmakrishna Mission, Calcutta, 1969, p. 263.
49. Dāsh, R.N. "Nilamadhava and Chodagaṅga", *UNMANA,* Souvenir of Akhil Bharat Jagannātha Consciousness Conference, Cuttack, December 28-31, 1984, Charana Gosthi, Cuttack, pp. 81-85.
50. Panigrahi, K.C. *Archaeological Remains at Bhubaneswar,* Orient Longmans, Calcutta, 1961, p. 99.

Five

Reverence and Dishonour of Śaṅkarāchārya at Jagannāth Temple of Puri

Śaṅkarāchārya was an individual of Nirvikalpa Samadhi or God Man. Nirvikalpa Samadhi[1] are of two types, viz., (i) Bhaba-pratyaya Videha Samadhi and (ii) Purna Pratyaya Samadhi.

(i) *Bhaba-pratyaya Videha Nirvikalpa Samadhi* : consists in Self-absorption without the least trace of duality in consciousness with complete Self-identification with Nature of God, without the light of consciousness. Bhaba Pratyaya Videha Samadhi has three sub-divisions viz. Prakriti Pratyaya, Aham Pratyaya and Mahat Pratyaya, i.e., Self-consciousness lost in nature and Self-consciousness lost in egotism and lost in Buddhisattva.

(ii) *Purna Pratyaya Nirvikalpa Samadhi* : Self-absorption in the secondless unique conscious Absolute Self of the Supreme Self without the least trace of duality is called Purna Pratyaya Nirvikalpa Samadhi. The Purna Pratyaya Nirvikalpa Samadhi is possible when the five waves of mind cease to function and the Sadhaka transcends the basic evolution. Purna Samadhi attained as a result of the realisation of the identity of Self with the Absolute Self of God without the least trace of duality in the Self-revealed

Consciousness liberates an individual Soul from the ills of the World and World series as he knows no other existence except the Supreme Being. The Sages say that of the varieties of Samadhi, Purna Pratyaya Samadhi alone can liberate an individual Soul.

So, when Śaṅkāra was an individual of such realisation, how can he be dishonoured ? The study done in this chapter, makes a fascinating study on this topic.

Puri is the modern name of the holy city, situated (latitude 19° 47' 55" N., longitude 85° 49' 5" E.) on the shores of Bay of Bengal. In Sanskrit literature, this Site has various names, viz. Nilachala, Nilagiri, Niladri Puruṣottama, Puruṣottama Kshetra, Sri Kshetra, Sankha Kshetra, Jagannāth Kshetra and Puruṣottama Puri. In *Māhabhāratā* (Vana parva, Ch. 114) there is description of a sacred altar on the Sea coast between Baitarani river and Mahendra mountain where Yudhistira offered oblations but it is doubtful if this site should be identified with Puri.[2]

Kedarnath Mahapatra[3] is of opinion that though Puri as a Tirtha first finds mention in the Vanaparva of the *Māhabhāratā,* and its sanctity and glory are elaborately described in the *Kūrma Purāṇa, Narada Purāṇa, Padma Purāṇa* and the "Viṣṇu khanda" of the *Skanda Purāṇa,* still its Cultural history can be definitely traced from the 7th century of the Christian era, when Indrabhūti, the founder of the Vajrayana sect of Buddhism flourished in Uḍḍiyāna or Orissa.

Scholars hold divergent views about the composition period of *Māhaohāratā,* but M.A. Mehendale[4] for all practical purposes, accepts the one expressed by Winternitz in the following words : "The *Māhabhāratā* cannot have received its present form earlier than the 4th century B.C. and later than the 4th century A.D." So, during this period, the reference of the 'Vedi,' might have come into prominence at Puri. According to the Vedic Etymology,[5] 'Vedi' means sacrificial altar or Earth where all desires are obtained ; from Vid 'to get' :

"तं वेद्यमन्वविन्दन् यद्वे द्यमन्वविन्दस्तद्वे देर्वोदित्वम्"

From the discovery of a Manuscript in the Himis monastery in Ladak; by noted Russian traveller Nicholas Notovitch,[6] and Swami Abhedananda, an apostle of Śri Rāmakrishna (Bengali book *Kashmere-o-Tibbete* it is known that Jesus Christ had visited Puri, where he was taught to read and to understand the Vedīs, to cure physical ills by means of prayers, to teach and to expound the sacred Scriptures, to drive out evil desires from man and make him again in the likeness of God. It seems, the site of modern Puri had already become popular, as a Religious centre with its Vedi, during that period.

According to the versions of the Devibhāgavata[7] and the *Kālikā Purāṇa,*[8] Daksa did not invite Śiva to his sacrifice, and this humiliation led Sati, the wife of Śiva, to destroy her body. Other sources relate that Śiva became so inconsolable at the death of his wife that he took her dead body on his shoulders and travelled aimlessly. In order to save Śiva from this madness, the Gods planned to cut off the dead body piece by piece. Parts of Sati's body thus fell at different places, and these places came to be known as Pithas.[9] At Puruṣottama site (Kshetra) in Utkala, the navel of Sati fell and is worshipped as Vimala.

Kurma Purāṇa, Narada Purāṇa, Padma Purāṇa, and *Skanda Purāṇa* are literatures of post Gupta period. According to R.C. Hazra,[10] *Kūrma Purāṇa* was composed between 500 and 650 A.D., *Narada Purāṇa* was composed about the middle of 9th century A.D. and 10th century A.D., *Padma Purāṇa* was composed not earlier than 900 A.D. and *Skanda Purāṇa* contain little which can be dated earlier than 700 A.D. and it was subject to additions and alterations more than once, which continued till late medieval period and some portions still remain unpublished.

As stated above, Kedarnath Mahapatra mentions that cultural history of Puri can be definitely traced from the 7th century of the Christian era, when Indrabhūti, the founder of the Vajrāyāna sect of Buddhism flourished in Oḍḍiyāna or Orissa. Indrabhuti was the King of Sambhala, in Uḍḍiyāna,[11] identified as the territory of modern Sambalpur region of modern Orissa, in 8th century A.D. The reference of Indrabhūti has nothing to do with Puri area. Indrabhūti opens his famous work *Jñānasiddhi* with invocation of Jagannātha. The Jagannātha, worshipped by Indrabhūti is not to be confused with the Wooden Deity of Puri. Indrabhūti has addressed Buddha, in the name of Jagannātha.

The attacks of Sasanka and Harsavardhan had an effect on the Religious background of Orissa. It finds expression in the words of H.C. Das[12] thus : "When Pravakaravardhan extended his kingdom to the west and the south, a powerful kingdom was established in Eastern India with its Capital at Karnasuvarna. The Kingdom comprised the present districts of Manbhum, Singbhum, Mayurbhanj and Midnapur. Most probably he could master over the whole of Bengal and upto Kangoda Mandal of Orissa. His conquest of Kangoda during the reign of Madhavaraja II of Sailodbhava dynasty is attested by copper plate grants, but his political sway was short-lived as the copper plates of the same monarch issued in later years used his own independent era. It is obvious that he established his supremacy, over the kingdom of Kangoda. As regards his religious outlook he was a bitter enemy of Buddhism. Being intolerant of this religion he destroyed that Bodhi tree, broke into pieces an image of Buddha worshipped in a Vihara near the Bodhi tree and in its place installed a Śivalinga. It will not be unreasonable to believe that he might have launched a mission against Buddhism in Orissa.

"Soon after his accession to the throne in A.D. 606 Harsavardhan swore vengeance at Sasanka who murdered his brother Rajyavardhan. In his first political campaign directed against Sasanka, he conquered a great part of Northern India. In his second military campaign undertaken towards the end of his reign he overran Magadha, West Bengal and Orissa upto Kangoda. Harsa's invasion took place during the reign of Madhyama Raja of Sailodbhava dynasty. But Harsa's suzerainty over Orissa was as short as that of Sasanka. Whatever be the political effect of his military conquest, his cultural campaign was very successfull. He was a great patron of learning and was encircled by a team of learned scholars of whom Banabhatta is the most well-known. The historic visit of Hiuen-Tsang, the most famous Chinese Traveller, whose accounts furnish us a vivid picture of the then socio-religious condition of India, is a memorable event in the history of India. Harsa became so much devoted to this learned scholar that in his honour he convened a special Assembly at Kanauj. Twenty tributary Kings, four thousand Buddhist monks and about three thousand Jains and Brahmins attended the Assembly organised on the bank of the Gaṅga in a specially built spacious monastery. He requested the Chancellor of Nalanda University to depute four learned Buddhist monks to Orissa for settlement of a dispute, which arose between the Hinayanists and Mahayanist over the doctrine. His attempt to settle Jayasena a learned scholar, well-versed in various subjects in Orissa, indicates his love for and respect to the scholars and scholasticism. It is known from Hiuen-Tsang's account that he introduced strong military administration in Orissa probably to prevent the inroads of foreigners from the South. His account also gives a faint picture of the socio-economic and religious condition of Kangoda."

In the post Gupta period the Vedic tradition was almost uprooted and destroyed by a host of heterodox sects like the Buddhists, Pasupatas, Jainas. Kapalikas and Vaiṣhṇavas, that Śaṅkāra was born to protect the Vedic religion (Dharma), and thus open the path of blessedness to men involved in the cycle of birth and deaths.[13]

Gazetteer authority,[14] further mention, "According to tradition, Śaṅkārachāraya (788-820 A.D.) visited Puri in the early part of the 9th century and established one of his four pithas here, the Bhogobardhan or Gobardhan Matha. Indrabhūti (8th century A.D.) mentions Jagannāth in his *Jñānasiddhi,* as an incarnation of Buddha who could be no other than Jagannāth of Puri. Since the 9th century onwards, Jagannāth and his kshetra find mention in many literary works, foremost among them being the "Anargharaghava Natakam" by Murari Mishra which was enacted on the occasion of a festival of God Puruṣottama."

It has already been explained that Jagannāth worshiped by Indrabhūti is not to be confused with the Deity of Puri. Further, the description of Puruṣottama given in Murari Mishra's work, as dealt earlier, is of Laxmi-Narayan.

Kedarnath Mahapatra[15] further enumerates, "Great Śaṅkarāchārya (788-820 A.D) who in course of his spiritual conquest of the whole of India, stayed at Puri, which was well-known by his time as a chief centre of religion and culture, and founded one of his four Pithas called 'Bhogavardhana

Pitha' here which has remained in existence till today. Śri Padmapadāchārya, one of his four disciples, who was also a Nambutiri Brāhamana like his Guru was placed as the first Jagat Guru or spiritual head of this Pitha. According to tradition Śaṅkāra defeated the Buddhist Pandits of this place by his vast learning and irrefutable arguments; converted most of them to his own faith and proclaimed Jagannātha-Buddha as identical with the great Brahmanical God Purușhottama of the Gita. This peaceful process of assimilation of a great Buddhist Deity into the pantheon of Brahmanism, strengthened its influence at Jagannātha Puri, which was a strong centre of Buddhism before his days. In commemoration of this great event, the images of Śri Śaṅkāra and Sri Padmapada were installed on the Ratnasimhasana of Jagannātha for worship. It is known from Madalapanvi, the chronicle of the Jagannātha temple written in Oriya language that their images were removed from that plate during the reign of Divyasimha Deva II (1793-1798 A.D.) Raja of Puri."[16]

It has been dealt in last chapter that the present figure or shape of Jagannāth, represented Buddha and it was Śaṅkārachārya responsible for converting this idol, figure or image of Buddha to 'Jagannātha,' a Vaiṣhṇav Deity. In 10th century A.D. a religious revolution took place, Sõmavaṁśi King Yayāti I installed this shape of Jagannāth, made of neem wood (margosa, a species of Melia), as the presiding Deity of Puruṣottama Kshetra, built a temple for it and immortalised Jagannāth as Puruṣottama-Jagannāth.

Because Śaṅkarāchārya was responsible for identifying Buddhist Jagannāth with Puruṣottama-Jagannāth or Viṣṇu, reverence was given to him and his disciple at Puri, when their images were installed on the Ratnasiṁhāsana of Jagannāth for worship, when temple was built by Yayāti I in 10th century A.D.

The removal of the images of Śri Śaṅkarā and Sri Padmapāda from the Siṁhāsana of Jagannāth temple was a great dishonour to the founder father of Lord Jagannāth Deity. Even P.K. Pattanaik[17] mentions that the idols of Śaṅkārachārya and his disciple were removed to the southern gate and many other improvements were effected in the Puri temple, during the period of Divyasingha Deva II (1793-1798 A.D.). Now, the idols of Śaṅkarāchārya and his disciple Padmāpadāchārya are no more to be found in the boundary or campus of Jagannāth temple at Puri.

REFERENCES

1. Sudhir Ranjan Sengupta, *Mother Cult,* Firma KLM Private Limited, Calcutta, 1977, pp. 106-107.
2. Kuanr, D.C. (State editor), *Gazetteer of India, Orissa, Puri,* (Chief editor) Senapati, N. Cuttack, 1977, p. 773.
3. Mahapatra K.N. "Jagannāth—Puri as a Centre of Culture through the Ages," *OHRJ,* Vol. VI, No. 4, p. 296.
4. Mehendale, M.A. "The Māhabhāratā," *THACOTIP,* Vol. II, The Age of Imperial Unity, 1968, p. 251.
5. Singh, F. *The Vedic Etymology,* National Publishing House, Delhi, (?), p. 219.
6. Connelly, J.H. and Landsberg, L. (translators), *The Unknown Life of Jesus Christ,* Nababharat Publishers, Calcutta, 1981, p. 85.
7. *Devibhāgavata* Vll, 30.
8. *Kālikā Purāṇa* XVI. 18.
9. Bhattacharyya, N.N. *The Indian Mother Goddess,* Manohar, New Delhi, 1977, p. 247.
10. Hazra, R.C. "The Purāṇas," *The Cultural Heritage of India,* Vol. II, The Rāmakrishna Mission, Calcutta, 1969, pp. 259-263.
11. *BIO,* pp. 147-148.
12. Das, H.C. *Cultural Development in Orissa,* Punthi Pustak, Calcutta, 1985, pp. 15-16.
13. Madhava-Vidyaranya, *Sankara-Dig-Vijaya (The Traditional Life of Sri Śaṅkārachārya),* Translated by Swami Tapasyananda, Sri Rāmakrishna Math, Madras, 1980, pp. 25-26.
14. *GOIOP,* p. 773.
15. Mahapatra, M.N. "Jagannātha-Puri as a Centre of Culture through the Ages," *op. cit.,* p. 297.
16. The Madala Panji published by the Prachi-Samiti, Cuttack, p. 81.
17. Pattanaik, P. K. *A Forgotten Chapter of Orissan History,* Punthi Pustak, Calcutta, 1979, p. 55.

Six
Jagannath Trinity

Opinion on the origin of Jagannāth and his Cult had become so obscure, that without going to the Reality of its beginning, S.N. Rajaguru[1] gave a partial view and stated that some believe that He was created by the Savaras, an aboriginal tribe of South Orissa, whose centre of homeland is the Mahendra mountain of Ganjam. Indrabhūti, the King of Sambhala, in Uḍḍiyāna, opens his famous work *Jñānasidhi,* with an invocation of Jagannāth. Sambhala, where Indrabhuti ruled in 8th century A.D. has been identified with Sambalpur region.[2]

S.N. Rajaguru[3] had become so unobserving in tracing the origin of Jagannāth Cult from Mahendra mountain that he went to the extent of observing thus : "The name 'Uḍḍiyāna' or 'Odyāna' still goes by the same name. A large number of Kaivartas or Kandaras settle in that part of Kalinga. They are the professional Sailors and belong to the fisherman class of that region. Since the ancient time there lived a Kaivarta dynasty to rule over that Community.

"Probably a King of that dynasty embraced Buddhism and installed the "tooth-Relic" at Dantapura. The Sacred tooth of Buddha was subsequently dispatched to Ceylone, when some cruel people attempted to destroy it. We, therefore, believe that in that royal house of the Kaivartas, there born a King named Indrabhūti who invoked Lord Jagannātha. (Buddhāvatāra) in his treatise, 'Jñānasiddhi' His son, Padmasambhava and daughter Lakshminkara are known from literature."

S.N. Rajaguru had become so blind in his conviction that though Lakshmiṅkara was the sister of Indrabhūti, he regards her, as Indrabhūti's daughter, as stated above.

These views of S.N. Rajaguru cannot be accepted, because, as already dealt, Śaṅkarāchārya was responsible for converting the Image of Buddha to Purusottam-Jagannāth, a Vaiṣhṇav Deity, in 9th century A.D. and Yayāti I installed Puruṣottam-Jagannāth as Presiding Deity of Puri in 10th century A.D. Now the problem arises about the period, when the worship of Jagannāth, Subhadra and Balabhadra Trinity started.

K.N. Mahapatra[4] states, "But the question which still awaits solution is the depiction of the images of Jagannāth, Balabhadra and Subhadra in wood without hands and feet. They may be taken as symbolical representation of the famous Triad, the worship of which was well-established in India at least since the first century of the Christian era."

The earliest Trinity trace is found in the Pre-historic Cave painting Yogimath Donger, discovered by the author, dated to neolithic period and assigned to about 10 millennium B.C.[5] in Upper Mahānadi valley. The problem of the depiction or origin of the image of Jagannāth is solved.

It was Yayāti I, the Sōmavaṁśī King, who installed Jagannāth as the Presiding Deity of Puri in 10th century A.D. and had built a temple for it. The Mādala Pānji credits Yayāti I with the establishment of the Shrine of Jagannāth at Puri. Therefore K.C. Panigrahi has rightly stated that Yayāti's work at Puri was both political and religious, meant to be spectacular.[6]

It was Anantavarman Chodagaṅga, who began the erection of the present Jagannāth temple at Puri in 12th century A.D. Even more surprising is the fact that during the two centuries following Chodagaṅga upto the 14th century, there is no mention of Jagannāth and no trace of today's Trinity. All the inscriptions of the Gaṅgas only ever praise Puruṣottama, and not until the time about A.D. 1310 do we find Jagannāth being praised in an inscription by Bhānudeva II.[7]

Rāmānuja had visited Puri, during the reigning period of

Choḍagaṅga. It was Rāmānuja who established the worship of Lakshmi-Narayan in the Puri temple. According to 'Prapannamrita' by Anantacharya, Rāmānuja replaced the Smarta form of worship that prevailed in the Puri temple by the Pancharātra rite. One of the Jagannāth temple Servitors, Bhitarchhu Mahapatra, belongs to the Śrī Sect of Vaiṣhṇavism. Choḍagaṅga probably came in contact with Rāmānuja and built a new Temple of Puruṣottama. The only structure of the same date as the Vimana of the Jagannāth temple is the temple of Lakshmi (Banerjee, R.D. *History of Orissa,* Vol. II, p. 376). A small image of Lakshmi is still kept on the dais of Jagannāth.[8]

It was the formative period of Trinity. P. Mukherjee puts it thus: "'Trayee' (Triad) conception prevailed in 13th century. At Konarak we find a Triad image consisting of Jagannāth, Śiva and Durgā. The Ananta Vasudeva temple inscription of the 13th century refers to 'Bala-Kṛishṇa-Subhadra.' The Puri inscription of Anangabhima III dated 1225 A.D. mentions 'Halin, Chakrin and Subhadra.' Thus even in the 13th century the names Jagannāth, Balarama and Subhadra were in formative stage."[9]

P.N. Mahanti[10] remarks, "The three deities Balabhadra, Subhadra and Jagannāth round whose worship Jagannāth Dharma has grown up represent the three Gods of Hindu Trinity (Brahmā, Viṣṇu and Maheśwara), the three attributes of Nature (Sattwa, Rajas and Tamas), and the Triratna (three Jewels) of Buddhism namely, Buddha, Saṁgha and Dharma."

It has already been known that the image of Buddha was converted to Viṣṇu-Kṛishṇa alias Puruṣhottama-Jagannāth. So, it should be accepted that the original conception of Trinity of Hinduism merged with Triratna (three Jewels) of Buddhism namely Buddha, Saṁgha and Dharma. Sudar-sana was added to the Trinity in due course and Jagannāth was identified with Viṣṇu and Kṛishṇa.

With the visit of Rāmānuja, to Puri and his influence, Lakshmi had become associated with Jagannāth in 12th century A.D. The Gaṅga period was therefore the formative phase of Jagannāth Trinity and must have happened at a definite moment of the development of the Cult. This has been proved by the discovery of inscriptions, on Jagannāth temple, after the removal of line plaster in recent years. Most of the inscriptions belong to Gaṅga period.

The worship of the Trinity of the Hindus goes back to early Christian century. It has been traced in two reliefs of Kushan period (Ist century A.D.). now preserved at the Government Museum of Karachi in Pakistan. One relief is carved in red sandstone, containing the standing figures of Balarama, Ekanamsa and Kṛishṇa. The two-armed figure of Balarama holds a plough in the right hand and has no hood of serpent over his head. The two-armed Ekanamsa, standing in the middle, has her right hand raised while her left hand is placed akimbo. Kṛishṇa has got four hands holding a gada in his upper right hand, Chakra in his upper left hand, padma in his lower left hand, while the lower right hand is shown in the pose of Abhaya-mudra. The other relief of the same period has the figure of Kṛishṇa, killing the demon Keshi. These two reliefs were discovered from Mathura.

In 'Brihatsamhita,' the Indian astronomical work of Varahamihira, dated to 5th century A.D., reference to Ekanamsa as a Deity worshipped with Rāma or Balarama on its right side and Kṛishṇa on its left side is found in the 58th chapter. This is the earliest literary evidence of Balarama, Ekanamsa and Kṛishṇa worship.

A relief of this Triad was discovered at Imadpur of Bihar, with an inscription of Pala King Mahipala and is preserved at London Museum. In this relief Balarama is four-armed under a canopy of seven hooded serpent. Ekanamsa stands on a full blown lotus, right hand stretching below, is in Varada-mudra, while She holds a mirror in her left hand. The four armed Kṛishṇa is to the left of Ekanamsa.

Figures of Balarama, Ekanamsa and Kṛishṇa are found in a relief (3'34" × 2'4") preserved at Museum of Lucknow. Ekanamsa is standing over a full blown lotus with a lotus nimbus over her head, flanked by two Vidyadharas on both sides. There are two female attendants on both the sides of Ekanamsa deity. She holds a full blown lotus in her left hand and her right hand is stretched below. Balarama to the right of Ekanamsa stands under the seven hooded canopy and has four arms. Kṛishṇa standing on the right is also four-armed holding the attributes of Viṣṇu.

A small brass plaque (measuring 3" × 3") with the images of Balarama, Ekanamsa and Kṛishṇa is preserved in Orissa State Museum at Bhubaneswar. The figures are two-armed. Balarama is shown wearing kirita and mukuta, holding a mushala in the right hand and hala in the left hand, and standing under a canopy of three-hooded snake. Ekanamsa stands in the middle, with kirita on her head, holds a full blown lotus in her right hand, while her left hand is shown in varada-mudra. Kṛishṇa stands to the left of Ekanamsa by wearing kirita and mukuta over the head, right hand holds a gada and left hand holds a padma (lotus). This brass plaque is dated 8th or 9th century, by K.N. Mahapatra.[11] The same author, dates the sculptures, brought to light from Turintiari village of Puri district to 12th or 13th century A.D.

Excellent relief of Baladeva, Ekanamsa and Krṣṇa Trinity are found in a side temple of the Lingaraja temple at Bhubaneswar, dating from the Gaṅga time.[12]

A small relief of the Puri Trinity at the outside of the eastern prakara of the Liṅgarāja temple at Bhubaneswar, shows that Sudarsanaṁ below the three Deities of Puriṁis worshipped separately. Though the Liṅgarāja temple was built by Sõmavaṁśi King in 11th century A.D. the Natamandira and the Bhogamandapa were added to it, during the Gaṅga period.[13] Therefore, the above-mentioned Trinity relief of this temple, might have been chiseled, during Gaṅga period. Sculpture of Konarak, preserved at Konarak Museum, shows King Narasimha worshipping a Liṅga-Puruṣottama -Durgā Trinity.

All these arts of Trinity, shows the popularity of Trinity worship. The construction of another temple named "Ananta-Vasudeva temple," at Bhubaneswar in 1278 A.D. by Chandrika Devi, the daughter of Anangabhima Deva, shows the popularity of Trinity worship. The images, in this Viṣṇu temple are known as Ananta, Vasudeva and Subhadra, while in the inscription of Chandrika Devi, they are called Bala, Kṛishṇa and Subhadra.

Sculptural relief with three icons in a bullock cart, believed to be the three Deities of the Jagannāth temple, is preserved in the Orissa State Museum.[14] This relief should be dated to the formation period of Trinity worship.

It has already been mentioned that Rāmānuja popularised the Pāncarātra rites, at Puri. The Pāncarātra system emphasized Krṣṇa in his relations to his sister Ekānaṁśā and his brother Balarāma-Saṁkarṣana. Ekānaṁśā was interpreted as a form of Durga, and Balarāma as a form of Śiva. Moreover the worship of Sudarsāna was emphasized as well.—Thus the Pāncarātra system was almost ideally able to take up the most important elements of the Jagannāth Cult.[15] In Pāncarātra philosophy Śiva came to be known as Balabhadra.[16] So, it can be said that Jagannāth Cult in its final phase brought the synthesis of the three main Cults of Hinduism, Vaisnavism, Śaivism and Śaktism. In the dilapidated brick temple of Turintiara village under Balipatna Police station of Puri district, images of Balabhadra, Subhadra and Kṛishṇa are found carved in chlorite stone. They are assigned to 12th or 13th century A.D. and proves the popularity of Triad worship in Orissa, during that period.

A. Echmann, H. Kulke and G.C. Tripathi,[17] consider the year 1230, to have been the appropriate period for the establishment of the Triad. It is their hypothesis and there is probability of finding new results, if research is continued in this topic.

It can be said that there were two religious revolutions in Mahānadi river valley. The first revolution was the evolution of Lord Jagannāth and the second revolution was the establishment of Trinity worship. Noticeable are the almond shaped eyes of Balabhadra and Subhadra, while Jagannāth has circular eyes.

Definite period of the establishment of Jagannāth Trinity is not yet known. It seems the Trinity worship developed within 12th -13th century, in Gaṅga period and the worship of Jagannāth Trinity was well established when the Suryavaṁśi Gajapati Kings began to rule.

This work does not solve the 'mystery' of the establishment of Jagannāth Trinity. It is a hypothesis only. Further findings, datas and detail studies in future will lead to the study of the development of the present-day Jagannāth Trinity at Puri. Jagannāth Cult has become purely Bhrahminical, during its development and is shrouded in legends, traditions, mythology, superstitions and blind faiths, being in the clutch of Mukti Mandapa. The images worshiped on the Ratnavedi are of Jagannāth, Balabhadra, Subhadra, Sudarśana ard miniature image of Lakshmi, Saraswati and Madhab, with the main Deities. Originally Jagannāth Culture has developed with cosmopolitan outlook, therefore being propagated by His Divine Grace A.C. Bhaktivedanta Swami Prabhupada, it has practically entered to most past of the Globe, through International Society for Kṛishṇa Consciousness.

REFERENCES

1. Rajaguru, S.N. "The Origin of Lord Jagannāth and His Cult," *Shree Jagannāth Smarika,* Vol. I, Sri Neelachala Seva Sangha, New Delhi, 19th December, 1969, p. 53.
2. *BIO,* p. 148.
3. Rajaguru, S.N. "Religious Evolution in the Medieval History of Orissa," *OHRJ,* Vol. XXIX, No. 1, p. 98.
4. Mahapatra, K.N. "The Worship of Jagannāth, Balabhadra and Subhadra," *Shree Jagannāth Smarika,* Vol. I, Sri Neelachala Seva Sangha, New Delhi, 19th December, 1969, p. 50.
5. (i) *CPOSK,* p. 20.
   (ii) Kuanr, D.C. (State editor), *Orissa District Gazetteers, Kalahandi,* (Chief editor) Senapati, N. Cuttack, 1980, p. 36.
6. (i) Mohanty, A.B. (ed.) *Madala Panji,* pp. 4-6. and Acharya, P.M. *Odisar Itihasa* (Oriya), Cuttack, 1975, p. 49.
   (ii) Panigrahi K.C. *Chronology of the Bhauma Kara and the* Sōmavaṁśi *of Orissa,* Bhopal, 1961, p. 33.
7. Kulke, Hermann, "Some Remarks about the Jagannāth Trinity," *Sudīsien-Institut, Der Universitat Heidelberg* (South Asia Institute of Heidelberg University), Reprints of Publications of Staff Members, 147, p. 127.
8. Mukherjee, P. "History of the Conception of Jagannāth," *Shree Jagannāth Smarika,* Vol. I, Sri Neelachala Seva Sangha, New Delhi, 19 December, 1969, p. 14.
9. *Ibid.,* 19 December, 1969, p. 14.

10. Mahanti, P.N. "Message of Jagannātha Dharma," *Ibid.* 19 December, 1969, p. 8.
11. Mahapatra, K.N. "The Worship of Jagannāth, Balabhadra and Subhadra," *op. cit.* 1969, p. 50.
12. Kulke, Herman-"Some Remarks about the Jagannātha Trinity," *op. cit.* p. 131.
13. *HOO,* p. 342.
14. *TCOJ,* plate No. 5.
15. Echmann, A.; Kulke, H. and Tripathi, G.C. "The Formation of the Jagannāth Triad," *TCOJATRTOO,* p. 185.
16. *Ibid.,* pp. 187-189.
17. *Ibid.,* p. 194.

Seven

Evolution of Dadhibaban, Patitapabana and Trutiya Deities

Rāmānuja visited Puri in the 12th century A.D. According to Prabhat Mukherjee[1] a reasonable conjecture will be that Rāmānuja visited Orissa between 1122 and 1137 A.D. While dealing with the conquest of Rāmānuja, Swami Rāmakrishnananda[2] informs that reaching Śripurushottama-Kshetra (Puri) after a few days, he took rest for some time. He founded a Monastery there and called it Embar Math after the name of Govinda, his own disciple. Out of fear of defeat the scholars of the place did not meet Rāmānuja in any discussion, though the latter invited them. Rāmānuja grew all the more eager to establish his doctrine there. He requested the priests of Lord Jagannātha to worship the Deity according to the Pāncharātra Agama. When they refused to adopt any new doctrine, he applied to the King for arranging a discussion. Being frightened at this, the priests took refuge in Śri Purushottama. It is said that, on that night, Rāmānuja while asleep, was thrown by Jagannātha to Kurma Kshetra, a hundred *yojanas* (a measure of distance equal to about nine miles) away from that place. When he woke up Rāmānuja saw that he had come to a different place, where none of his numberless disciples was near him. On enquiry, he came to know that he was in Kurma Kshetra. Knowing for certain that it was an artifice of God, after his morning duties, Rāmānuja went to the temple of Śri Kurmadeva, and with deep devotion worshipped that image of the incarnation. Pleased with him, the Deity recommanded him through His priest to wait there for some time for his disciples and Rāmānuja complied. Reunited with his disciples after a few days, he went to Simhachala.

P. Mukherjee[3] surmises Rāmānuja's visit to Puri and narrates, "Rāmānuja, like Śaṅkarāchārya, started on a mission to preach his faith. At Puri, he established two Maths-one in his own name and the other in the name of his cousin and disciple Govinda. Rāmānuja was known to his disciples as "Mannāth,". He wanted to confer that name on Govinda, but the latter hesitated to accept the designation of his GURU.

"Rāmānuja then translated Mannāth into Tamil as "Emperu-Man-ar." Shortening it into 'Embar' he gave the designation to Govinda, and named the second Math after him. Later on, he met the Raja of Orissa who was impressed by his exposition of Vedanta.

"Rāmānuja's work in the Puri Temple has been described by Anantācharya in Prapannāmrita.Winning the Raja over, he next sought to alter the Smart a from of worship that prevailed in the temple of Jagannāth. But he encountered stiff opposition from the Servitors of the temple. Rāmānuja had the divine Service performed by other Brahmins according to the Pancharātra rite, which was observed in the Śri-Raṅgam temple. Consternation and disgrace started at the face of the priests and at nightfall they assembled before the altar of Jagannāth. "Hark three, O Lord" they cried. "The Yatindra seeketh to introduce changes in the form of Thy worship.We belong to the old school and we abhor such changes. Sare us we beseech Thee, from this imperious Sannyasi. Otherwise we will die before Thee." The deity was moved at this supplication and he appeared before the Yatindra in a vision and advised him not to insist on changes. But Rāmānuja was adamant. Jagannāth then got him removed overnight to a distance of hundred Yojanas-to Kurmakshetra."

The *Gitāgovinda* of the celebrated poet Jayadeva (circa. 12th century A.D.) popularised the Rādhā-Kṛishna Cult in Orissa.[4] Since that time up-to-date Rādhā-Kṛishṇa Cult has always been predominant at Puri. Jayadeva[5] sings of Joyful Kṛishṇa, careless Kṛishṇa, bewildered Kṛishṇa, tender Kṛishṇa, lotuseyed Kṛishṇa longing for love, indolent Kṛishṇa, cunning Kṛishṇa, abashed Kṛishṇa, languishing Kṛishṇa, four quickening Arms, Blissful Kṛishṇa and Ecstatic Kṛishṇa.

It has already been stated that Śaṅkarāchārya established the Govardhan Matha at Puri in 9th century A.D. and the Divinity of Puri Matha is Lord Viṣṇu 'Jagannātha,' also called 'Puruṣhottama.' It has been emphasised that 'Jagannātha' established as the Male Deity of Govardhan Matha at Puri by Śaṅkāra, revolutionised the image of Buddha as Jagannātha, a Vaiṣhṇav Deity, i.e., Viṣṇu-Kṛishṇa. During the period of Sõmavaṁśi King Yayāti I, a religious revolution took place in 10th century A.D. and Jagannātha was made the presiding Deity of Puri. Further in 12th century A.D. after Rāmānuja's visit to Puri and composition of *Gitāgovinda* by Jayadeva, the image of Jagannāth was altered to be of Kṛishṇa. Gradually Trinïty worship developed and Sudarsana was added. This Religious composite unfoldment, growth or evolution of Jagannātha, influenced the popularisation of unique image of Viṣṇu-Kṛishṇa in Coastal belt.

The Viṣṇu-Kṛishṇa image discovered from Dharmasālā in Çuttack district and preserved at Orissa State Museum in Bhubaneswar, is of interest.

The figure is a unique one on account of the fact that, it represents both Kṛishṇa and Viṣṇu.[6] It is a four-armed image. The upper left hand holds a Sankha, while the upper right hand has a Chakra. The image stands in 'Tribhanga' pose. The legs are portrayed in the conventional pose of Kṛiṣṇa. A flute is held in lower hands in the pose in which Kṛiṣṇa is usually portrayed in picture. The two female figures stand on either side of the main image. Another female figure is squatting in front of the image in pose of prayer with hands in anjali pose and face upturned towards the image. The flute of a tiny Anantaśayana-Viṣṇu is also to be found on the right hand side of the pedestal of double lotus. The figure of ten incarnations of Viṣṇu are carved at the bottom of the pedestal and also on the two sides of the main image. Since Kṛiṣṇa is associated with cows, the figure of cows are turned up towards the image in the bottom of the pedestal.

"The flying Vidyādharas with wreaths in their hands are to be found on either side at the top. There is a long necklace of champakmāla hanging down from the neck to the knees of the image. The yajnapavita or the sacred thread is worn by this image. The figure of Garuda, the vehicle of Viṣṇu is not to be found here. Similarly Ashṭagopis always associated with Kṛisṇa are not portrayed here."

From above description it is clear that it is an image of both Viṣṇu and Kṛisṇa. P.K. Ray[7] informs that no such composite image of Viṣṇu-Kṛisṇa has, probably, been found anywhere in India. It is for this reason that the image is of great iconographic importance. The image may be ascribed to about 13th century A.D.

So, it can be said that frorn 12th century A.D. tne image of Jagannāth at Puri, consciously was recognised as Kṛisṇa and Kṛisṇa and Viṣṇu began to be looked upon as identical. When this conception developed, fresh attempt was made for assertion of the Kṛisṇa aspect and this was the cause of the origin of Dadhibaban worship.

H.V. Stietencron[8] is of opnion that the Wooden God was also installed in temples without his brother and sister, all by himself and this was probably an earlier aspect of the Wooden God, as we shall presently see. His name, when alone was Dadhivāmana. The origin and meaning of this name are as yet unknown. Speculations connecting it with the child Kṛsṇa (vamana) stealing curds (dadhi), or with Balarāma who Krsna (vamana) in white colour (dadhi), are equally unconvincing. Nor does the correlation with an ancient King named Dahivāhana[9] seem to be helpful. It is more likely that Dadhivāmana is a distorted Sanskrit adaptation of the original name of the Wooden God and that its original form must be sought for in the languages of the tribals of Orissa and northern Andhra Pradesh.

The hypothesis of H.V. Stietencron that the single image of Jagannātha, worshipped as Dadhivāmana, probably is an earlier aspect of the Wooden God, cannot be accepted. It has already been observed that when the single image of Jagannātha was asserted to be an aspect of Kṛishṇa in 12th century A.D. it came to be known as Dadhivāmana. To popularise Jagannāth as Kṛishṇa, the single image known as Dadhivāmana worship started.

The earliest temple of Dadhivamana was built at Tekkali in 1150 A.D. after the death of Anantavarman Codagangadeva, by his wife Kasturikāmodini.[10] H.V. Stietencron's[11] survey has registered 344 Dadhibāmana temples in Orissa. Most of them are in the Puri, Cuttack, Ganjam and Sambalpur districts, the centre of the Cult being in the rural midlands of the Western Puri district. There is possibility of many more temples of Dadhibāmana to have been existing.

Patitapābana

"Patitapābana 'The Purifier of the Fallen-ones,' is an aspect of Jagannātha which originated as late as the 18th century. The name refers primarily to a painting inside the main (eastern) gate of the Jagannātha temple precincts. This painting faces east and is visible from outside the gate. It shows Jagannātha alone, without the two other members of the triad. He is there to be seen by those who are not allowed into the temple; the impure ones whom he, mercifully, is ready to purify if they strive for purification.

"We have two slightly different accounts of the origin of this image. Both connect the image with Rajạ Rāmacandradeva II of Khurda, who was taken prisoner by Taqi Khan in 1730 A.D. The King who remained imprisoned in Cuttack for about 6 months is said to have fallen in love with the Nawab's daughter. His alleged love affair with the Moslem girl, or a rumour about his conversion to Islam, induced the priests of Puri to declare the King as outcaste. He was 'fallen' (patita) from caste and as such was no more allowed to enter the temple until fully purified from the stains of his contact with non-Hindus. But since he was still King, the image of Patitapabana was painted in order to give him a chance to see the God from outside.[12]

Trutiya Deba (Tṛtiy Deva)

The single image of Jagannātha is worshipped as Trutiya Deva by the rural people. Like Patitapavana, he is recognized as the only one of the triad who really belongs to the low class people. Temples of Trutiya Deba are found in Cuttack, Dhenkanal and Puri districts.[13]

REFERENCES

1. Mukherjee, P. *The History of Medieval Vaiṣhṇavism in Orissa,* Asian Educational Services, New Delhi, 1981, p. 28.
2. Swami Rāmakrishnananda, *Life of Śri Rāmānuja,* Śri Rāmakrishna Math, Madras, 1965, passim.
3. Mukherjee, P. *op. cit.* pp. 27-28.
4. Ray, P.K. "A Unique Image of Viṣṇu-Kṛishṇa in the Orissa State Museum." *OHRJ,* Vol. 4, p. 259.
5. Miller, B.S. *Gitāgovinda of Jayadeva,* Motilal Banarsidass, Delhi, 1984, pp. 69-123.
6. Ray, P.K. *op. cit.* p. 255.
7. *Ibid.,* p. 257.
8. Stietencron, H.V. "Early Temples of Jagannātha in Orissa : The Formative Phase," *TCOJATRTOO,* p. 63.
9. For the Jain King Dahivāhana of Campa see Abhidhāna Rajendra Kosa, Vol. IV. s.v. According to tradition there was also a Jain King Dahivāhana in Kalinga. About King Dadhivāhana of Kāṣi see the Dadhivāhan Jātāka.
10. The Inscription of Queen Kasturikāmodini, vide : Rath, T.C. *Utkala Sahitya,* Vol. 21, No. 10, Sal 1325, p. 473 and Jagadeva, Raja L N.H. *Bhañja Pradipa,* Oriya quarterly, Vol. XT/3, Sal 1349.
11. Stietencron, H.V. "The Jagannātha Temples in contemporary Orissa," *op. cit.* Manohar, New Delhi, 1978, p. 473.
12. *Ibid.,* pp. 470-71.
13. *Ibid.,* pp. 471-72.

Eight

A Critical Review of K.C. Mishra's View

Institute of Oriental and Orissan Studies, held an International Seminar on 'Buddhism and Jainism,' at Cuttack from 11th to 16th January, 1976. In this seminar B. Panda contributed a paper named "Jagannāth the Incarnation of Buddha," G. Mahapatra contributed the paper, "The Buddhavatāra of Jagannāth," and K.C. Misra contributed paper named, "Is Jagannātha Buddhistic ?"[1]

Even though G. Mahapatra submitted a paper named, "The Buddhavatāra of Jagannātha," in this above mentioned seminar, in his (Ph. D). Thesis, "The Land of Viṣṇu (A Study on Jagannāth Cult)"[2] 'he has followed the literary Purāṇic Tradition of Puruṣottama Māhātmya, which is a significant part of the *Skanda Purāṇa.* It has already been observed in Chapter III, that the story of Nilamadhava, Vidyapati and Lalita, which is found recorded in the 'Utkala Khanda,' of the *Skanda Purāṇa,* has its root in the Chodagaṅga period alias Gaṅga rule (12th century A.D.).

So, it has been ascertained that 'Puruṣottama Māhātmya' and 'Utkala Khand,' are late additions in *Skanda Purāṇa,* about 11th and 12th century A.D. Because of such literary prevailing traditional approach of Gopinath Mahapatra, he has missed the right approach to the study of Jagannātha Cult.

K.C. Misra[3] is also a literary scholar and deals the topic 'Is Jagannāth Buddhistic ?' It will be interesting to discuss this work fully.

K.C. Misra states, "It is a perplexing problem to find out the degree of Buddhistic influence on Lord Jagannāth. Authorities are of different opinions on the subject and scholars view that Jagannātha originally was a Buddhist deity, the idol of Jagannātha containing tooth of Buddha, the Rathayatra of Jagannātha is in the line of Buddhist traditions and the three deities of Jagannāth, Balabhadra and Subhadra stand for the three Ratnas of Buddhism. In addition to these contentions it is also argued that the bathing festival of Lord Jagannātha, the making of half finished images are in line with the Buddhist rituality.[4]

"These are the reasons why many scholars believe that Jagannātha is another projection of the Buddha. The confusion arises because of the flexible nature of Buddhism in its long course of history. In fact Buddhism was never an established religion in the conventional use of the term. Professor A.L. Basham[5] has pointed out that what Ashok preached Buddhism was actually a simple Indian Sect. Asoka did not preach even Buddhism, the Dharma was only a system of morals, consistent with the tenets of the Sects of the empire and calculated to lead to peace and fellowship in this World and heaven in the next.

"Lack of definite outlines both in quality and extent led Buddhism to be flexible and to be capable of being absorbed in any other religion. At the highest point of its growth, it became over dominating and extended its influence on other deities including that of Jagannātha."

The authorities quoted by K.C. Misra had perceived that the idol of Jagannātha contained the tooth of Buddha. It cannot be accepted, because it is known that in the ninth year of the reign of King Śrimeghavarna, Buddha's tooth-relic was said to have been brought from Kalinga and consecrated in a temple in Ceylon[6] (present Sri Lanka). The Hindus do not worship relic. Tradition grows and usually is handed over through a tale, belief or practice and to the traditional minded people, it acts powerfully. One such traditional scholar is

Kailash Chandra Rath,[7] who mentions that if Buddha is no more, if Buddhist Vihara with its sweet philosophic fragrance has disappeared and buried, and if Buddhist monks no more move about in their yellow robes, certain aspects of Buddhism still prevail in the culture of Orissa, unnoticed to the naked eye. The Cult of Jagannāth and the concept of Trimurti as Buddha, Dharma and Sangha are the brilliant instances of it.

It is already observed in Chapter IV about the installation of Jagannāth as a Deity. It is studied in Chapter VI, that Subhadra and Balabhadra were added as trinity Gods, during Gaṅga period. So, the views of Kailash Chandra Rath and above mentioned authorities, holds no more good.

K.C. Misra[8] writes, "Pandit Nilakantha Das[9] has gone to the extent of telling that Buddhism through Jainism might have influenced the Cult of Jagannātha. Festivals rituals, writings, traditions and other religious influences of Jainism, Buddhism and Hinduism intermingled themselves to such an extent that it becomes difficult to point to what extent Jagannātha belongs to what religion. According to Wilkin, Jagannātha possibly had connections with Buddhism but the local influence was overwhelming. It could be just possible that Jagannātha was an aboriginal deity engrafted into Buddhistic influence and in course of time was known as a Hindu God.[10]

"It may be possible that Jagannātha contains influence of Buddhism and Jainism but it is purely a Hindu deity. Because there are some Buddhistic influences on Jagannātha we cannot say that Jagannātha is Buddhistic. There are many instances of Hindu influences on Jaina and Buddhist shrines but this does not justify to superimpose Hinduism on these religions. Similarly we cannot say that Jagannāth is non-Hindu."

Pandit Nilakanatha Das did a pioneer study on Jagannāth, so there is every possibility of some mistake cropping up in such research. But, what about K.C. Misra? He has done D. Phil Calcutta University, in the topic. 'The Cult of Jagannātha.' Because of his literary bent of research, he is unable to grasp or expose more reality, by comparative genuine careful systematic investigation, towards increasing the sum of knowledge. It has already being, studied in Chapter IV, that there was no aboriginal influence on Jagannāth Cult and the Tribal elements are an ethos, which developed in 12th century A.D.

K.C. Misra mentions, "The idea that Jagannātha consists of three images is not correct. Actually they are four. They represent Chaturbhyas of Parovoratra Agam namely—Vasudev, Sankarsan, Pradyumna and Anirudha. They are regarded as four padīs or mantras of pranva, which is the root of World sound i.e., Paraparyanti, Madhyana and Vhaikari,[11] The Agni, Padma and Brahmanand purāṇas bears witness to it. In Buddhism there is no caste system whereas is the Jagannāth temple, the Caste system is accepted. Again the idea of a Buddha's tooth being worshipped is not acceptable by the Hindus. It may be mentioned here that the tooth of Buddha was taken away by Guasiva to Ceylon. Therefore, there was no chance that Jagannātha would have contain the tooth of Buddha or resembled as miniature charity.[12]

"Again the argument that certain Buddhistic traditions are accepted by Jagannātha temple may be a matter of coincidence and are not sufficient to prove that Jagannātha is a Buddhistic deity. The Rathayatra of Jagannātha has no comparison in Buddhism. It is open to people of all classes and castes, some of whom have no entrance to the Jagannātha temple. Had Jagannātha been a Buddhist deity, then such an annual open show of the God should have been unnecessary. Similarly the bathing festival of Jagannātha is held on the Jyestha Purnima (full-moon day of Jyestha (June)) whereas Buddhist observe Buddha Jayanti on Vaisakh Purnima (full-moon day of Vaisakha (May)).

"Jagannātha is essentially a Hindu deity and at its beginning phase it was very simple without much rituals and worshipped by the Sabaras. It is important to note that Buddhism was also at its initial stage simple and ritual-less and adopted by the lower rank of society. This striking similarity of Buddhism and Jagannāthaism is a historical fact not much noted of. This may be the most important reason for the Buddhist scholars to claim that Jagannātha is a Buddhist deity."

It is emphatically proved in Chapter IV that there was no Sabara influence at the beginning of Jagannāth Deity, it is a development or evolution of 12th century A.D. By dealing with Rathayatra and rituals, K.C. Misra has tried to deal his paper, which has no genuine argument, because rituals are created by the Priest class, becomes traditional at last. This proves that K.C. Misra is unable to break the literary traditions and therefore is gropming in ignorance, so far as the topic on Origin of Jagannāth Deity is concerned.

K.C. Misra observes, "Historically Buddhism did not have great influence on Orissa. On the other hand the Jainism during the time of Kharavela had tremendous influence on Orissa. If Jagannāth could be a Buddhist deity, then there should have been many more Buddhist shrines at Puri or near about Puri. Strikingly we have no evidence of such deities of any degree or number near about the locality or at the Sea-shore. On the other hand the period of Jagannātha temple was busy in building some of the finest temples of country, including that of the immortal Bhubaneswar and Konarka, why then such builders of Orissa did not erect any Buddhist temples following that of Jagannātha or even earlier ? We cannot say that the Buddhist did not want this because at the same period in Bihar and Central provinces significant and sufficient Buddhist shrines and monuments were erected. Even the relics of Khajuraho which has significant parallel comparison with that of Konark has Buddhist images.[13] These are pertinent questions which sufficiently prove that influence of Buddhism or Jagannātha was either nil or very minor. Whatever little influence is alleged that Jagannātha has Buddhist influences as a result of historical growth which is an inevitable consequence of different religions, leaving close to each other, surviving for centuries.

"For common observer the images of Buddha and Jaina throughout the World wherever they are found are an object of beauty. The image of Tathagata has been both poetic and spiritual. But the image of Jagannātha stands no comparison to this. Moreover, there is a comparison between the stories of the creation of the Jagannātha images and that of Buddha.

That Maitraya Buddhisattava came in the guise of a Brahmin and created the deity is questionable.[14] The story of Brahma appearing in the guise of a Divine Carpenter (Viswakarma) remained confined in the temple is found in the Purāṇas.[15] The Buddhist scholars might have heard about this and it could be just possible that the stories were twisted to suit to their design."

The above mentioned view of K.C. Misra that historically Buddhism did not have great influence on Orissa, is a great misnomer. To make a resume here, it may be said that Tapassu and Bhallika, the two merchants of Utkala are regarded as the first lay disciples of the Buddha by the Mahāvāgga of Vinaya text, the Añguttara Nikāya, as well as, by the Jātaka. while the Nikāya literature points out that the Vassa and the Vañña tribes of Utkala recognised the teachings of the Blessed one and repudiated their earlier beliefs in Ahetuvāda, Akiriavāda and Natthikavāda. It is further learnt from the Jataka story that King Kālinga of Dantapura paid reverential honour to the Bodhi tree for seven days and nights, and the Dāṭhāvaṁśa (Dāthā dhātuvaṁśa) and the Buddhavamṁa would have us believe that after the Parinirvāna of the Buddha, one of his tooth relics was brought to Kalinga to be enshrined at Dantapura.[16]

It is universally known a fact that the Kalinga war was the turning point in the life of the Mauryan King Ashoka and it drew him directly to the teachings of the Buddha images which resembles the shape of Jagannātha have been found at Sanchi, Mathura Museum, Banaras and Bodh-Gaya, dating to early historical period. Harekrushna Mahtab[17] is also of the view, "There is no doubt that at one time the symbols of Buddha, Dharma and Sangha were being worshipped all over India. Recently a stone of Asokan polish with the symbols of Buddha. Dharma and Sangha at the top has been found out at Bhubaneswar and it is now preserved in the Ashutosh Museum of Calcutta. The Symbols are a little different from those found out at Sanchi and other places but the Bhubaneswar symbols are exactly like the images of Jagannātha, Balabhadra and Subhadra. The Bhubaneswara discovery proves that in Orissa the worship of the symbols was prevalent since the Ashokan period."

The able reviewer of Mr. Fergussion's "Tree and Serpent Worship," remarks that "One of the General Cunningham's happiest hits is his derivation of the three fetish-like figures of Jagannātha and his sister and brother, from three of the combined emblems of the Buddhistic Trinity, placed side by side as at Sanchi." "The resemblance" he adds, "is rude but unmistakable."[18]

In Upper Mahānadi valley, such images of Buddha has been found also, the earliest one, being at Rajim, which is dealt in Chapter VI. So, the discussion of K.C. Misra is nullified, as he has done no serious search or laboured in the large sense, at National level.

The story of the creation of Buddha and Jagannāth images might have been twisted in literature, but it is definite that such images representing Buddha were created in Ashokan period and at Sanchi, Buddha Gaya etc. in 1st century B.C. and they are the earliest shape of this form.

K.C. Misra finally is of the opinion thus : "The Navakalevar ceremony of Jagannātha is a unique ritual the parallel of which is not found in any religion of the globe, less so in the Buddhism. Jagannāth's wooden images usually change every twelve years particularly when there shall be two months of Asara in one year. The Buddhist images does not undergo any change. 'The Buddhist images are all either made of Metal or Stone. They are never made of wood or any special type of wood.[19]

"Buddhism is essentially a humanistic religion and Buddha never believed in rituals. On the other hand, Jagannāth is based on elaborate rituals the kind of which is not found anywhere in the world. The idea of wooden images as in Jagannātha and the name of the deity have references in the *Rigveda* and *Atharvaveda*, the *Rāmayana* and *Mahabharata*[20]. This is significantly unique for Jagannātha.

"Though there are certain influences on Jagannātha and His rituals which are usually associated with Buddhism they are the results of historical process and coincidence. This would never prove that Jagannātha was Buddhistic in origin, as pointed out by some historians."

K.C. Misra speaks of rituals and discusses. This is no

method of examining, in scholarly debate. Rituals are the nature of rites, manner of performing Divine Services or Ceremonies. Rituals are recorded and the usually the product of Priest classes of every religion. These have nothing to do with the investigation or the study of the Origin of Jagannāth Deity. Tree worship in ancient India was common and popular. In the Gitā, Lord Kṛishṇa tells Arjuna : "Among the trees, I am the Peepal," by saying so, he indicated the high position of the Peepal occupies among trees. Hence, the Hindus worship it and never cut it. Even Prince Siddhartha who later became the Buddha, roamed about from place to place, but enlightenment dawned upon him only, when he reached Gaya (in the Kingdom of Magadha) and sat for several days in meditation under a Peepal tree. Since then, he has been called the Buddha, the Enlightened one.

The place where the tree stood is today known as Bodh-Gaya. The tree still exists. Many saplings of this tree have been planted in different Buddhist countries, to Ceylon, a sapling was carried by Sanghamitra, the daughter of Ashoka the Great. It was through her that Buddhism came to Ceylon (present Sri Lanka). That tree, planted there in 288 B.C. still exists and is an object of great veneration.

The Peepal tree has earned a place in the field of art also. In the Bharhut sculptures, the tree is shown being worshipped by devotees and being garlanded by 'apsaras' or heavenly maidens.[21]

According to Nalinaksha Dutt[22], Gautama Buddha took his seat under a Peepal tree at Uruvelā, when he was offered milk by a milkmaid named Sujāta, who took him to be the tree Spirit (Vṛikshaka). Whatever might have been the site of Buddha's Enlightenment, it is sure that he attained it, while meditating under a Peepal tree.

It has already been studied in this work that the word 'Jagannātha', has been used for the first time of Sanskrit literature in 'Devi Mahatyama' of *Markandeya Purāṇa,* whose composition period was late Gupta period 5th century A.D. K.C. Misra has not been able to differentiate the designations 'Purushottam,' and 'Jagannāth,' therefore this confusion. The present shape of Jagannāth was at first, one of the icon of

Buddha image, as found in Sanchi, Budha Gaya, Mathura Museum, Banaras and many other places. This Image was installed as the Image of Jagannāth, ascribed as Viṣṇu- Kṛishṇa by Ādi Śaṅkarāchārya, at Govardhan Math of Puri. In 10th century A.D. a religious revolution took place, the image of Jagannāth was made of Neem wood and installed as the Presiding Deity of Puri. In 12th century A.D. this Jagannāth was ascribed as Kṛishṇa and in Gaṅga period (i.e., 12th-13th centuries), the images of Subhadra and Balabhadra were added, with Sudarsana. Brahmanism has finally taken over the 'Jagannāth Cult', into its fold. Therefore, much interpolations have been done and the wooden images are said to have references in the Vedīs. What is referred in the Vedīs, is 'Purushottama' and not 'Jagannāth'. The whole work has made the effort in revealing the reality of Jagannāth Deity, which had been lost, due to Human action or mechanism.

REFERENCES

1. Das, H.C., Das, C. and Pal, S.R. (ed.) *Buddhism and Jainism,* Institute of Oriental and Orissan Studies, Cuttack, 1976, pp. 33-37, pp. 178-179 and pp. 274-276.
2. Mahapatra, G. *The Land of Viṣṇu (A Study on Jagannātha Cult,* B.R. Publishing Corporation, Delhi, 1979, passim.
3. Misra, K.C. "Is Jagannātha Buddhistic?, *Buddhism and Jainism, op. cit.,* Cuttack, 1976, pp. 274-276.
4. (a) Mahatab, H.K. *THOO,* Vol. II, Cuttack, 1960, p. 522.
   (b) Mitra, R.L. *Antiquities of Orissa,* Vol. II, Calcutta, 1882, p. 135.
   (c) Hunter, W.W. Orissa, Vol. I, London, 1872, pp. 131-132.
   (d) 'The Festival in Ceylone,' *Indian Antiquiry,* Vol. Ill, 1874, pp. 253-254.
5. Basham, A.L. *The Wonder that was India,* pp. 56-57.
6. Sircar, D.C. 'Ceylon,' *THACOTIP,* Vol. Ill, The Classical Age, 1970, p. 284.
7. Rath, K.C. "Buddhism and Orissa", *Sidelights on History and Culture of Orissa,* ed. Das, M.N. Vidyapuri, Cuttack, 1977, p. 325.
8. Misra, K.C. "Is Jagannātha Buddhistic ?" *op. cit.,* pp. 274-275.
9. "Hints on the Significance and History of Jagannātha," *OHRJ,* Vol. VII, No. 1, pp. 2-3.
10. *TCOJ,* p. 25.
11. *Ibid.* Chapter on Theology.

12. Ganguli, M.M. *Orissa and Her Remains—Ancient and Mediaeval (District Puri),* Thacker Spink & Cy. Calcutta, 1912, p. 405.
13. Agarwalla, Urmele, *Khajuraho Sculptures.*
14. Mitra, R.L. Budda Gaya, Chapter I, pp. 10-12.
15. *TCOJ,* pp. 31-71.
16. *BIO,* p. 13.
17. *THOO,* Vol. II, Prajatantra Prachar Samiti, Cuttack, 1950, pp. 520-521.
18. *Ibid.,* p. 520.
19. *TCOJ,* Chapter on Tradition, pp. 71-100.
20. *Ibid.,* pp. 71-74.
21. Sinha, R.P.N. *Our Trees,* Publication Division, Govt. of India, Delhi, January 1968, p. 76.
22. Dutt, Nalinaksha, "Buddhism", *THACOTIP,* Vol. II, The Age of Imperial Unity, 1968, p. 367.

Nine

Overall Study and New Archaeological Discoveries, Prove the Theology of Lord Jagannāth Correct

While giving the Ganesh Chaturthi discourse Bhagvan Śrī Satya Sai Baba[1] informs that everything is Divine vibration—the walls, the roof and this mike. Sage Saraswatha could listen to these vibrations and taught them to the other sages. What is the source of the Vedas? Who gave them to man? The Vedas were present everywhere in the form of vibrations. The Vedas were thus heard through sound, through vibrations. If you sit down and listen with a pure heart, you too can listen to it. Why go so far? Just close your ears and you can hear Omkar from within. Om is the source of the Vedas. Om Ityakaksharam Brahma (the sacred syllable Om is Brahman). Everything originated from Omkar. The same air produces seven different notes through different reeds in the harmonium. Similarly, Omkar is one, all other sounds are Vikaras (modifications of Omkar). Vinayaka is the source of all these vibrations. You may listen to any sound but the most sacred is Omkar.

The genius in the Vedic Masters therefore gave us 'OM' as an idea—idol for the intellect to worship in the inner temple.[2] In Mandukopanishad, Prasnopanishad, Mandukya Karika,

Kaivalyaopanishad and Mundakopanishad 'OMKAR' is dealt in details.

According to S.K. Ramachandra Rao,[3] "The Mantra is invariably preceeded by the articulation (or rather ejaculation): 'OM', which has the significance of submission, acceptance (of the Deity) and inviting the attention of the Deity. It is said that the expression 'OM' is like unto the head of the Deity, while the 'shoot' (Pallava) of the Deity's feen. The expression 'OM' is followed by the seed—syllable specific to the Deity. Which in turn may be followed by the chosen name of the Deity. Thus, 'OM' and the Pallava are common to all the Mantras; the Mantras differ only with regard to the particular form of the Divinity visualized. The central point in a Yantra is usually taken as the position of the expression 'OM' and the outer most figure (square or circle) as the Pallava. In between these two limits, the Deity is projected in terms of the body of the Yantra."

While dealing with the Theology of Lord Jagannath, K.C. Mishra[4] states, "With this tradition behind them the poet—Sages of Jagannāth cult, not only presented the cosmic picture of Jagannāth by their Supernormal vision, but also they looked upon. Him as the Buddha and burst out into rapturous songs in praise of His Glory. Sāraḷādāsa in the Sabhāparva of his 'Mahābhārata' prays:—"Jagannātha,you are present here as the Buddha for the deliverance of the people of the world." The same devotional expression is found in various places of the Ādi, B Vana, Musali and the Śalya parvas of his famous work. Jagannātha Dāsa while narrating the legendary origin of Jagannātha in his "Dāru Brahma Gita" and "Deula Tola", asserts the identification of the Deity with the Buddha. In the "Daru Brahma Gita," for instance, he writes, "After the sixth day (in the course of his formation), His hands and feet became feeble and He then discarded them in order to be the Buddha. Acyutānanda Dāsa, in many places of 'sūnya-Samhita' declares in clear terms that Jagannātha is no other than the Buddha. Addressing him, he says: "Lord, you will enjoy as the Buddha in the Kaliyuga the oblations of the devotees on the shore of Mahodadhi (the great Sea).

Elsewhere in the same book Jagannātha himself is supposed to have said "Hearken to us, Oh, Acyutā, in this Kaliyuga we have again appeared as Buddha, and thus disguising ourselves as Buddha, we have incurred the curse, the curse of the Munis. Even Pratapa Ray, the writer of "Śasisena" declares "Hari Himself is present in sanctuary of Śrī Nilagiri (the Jagannātha temple, Puri) in the form of the Buddha." "Examples of this kind abound in the writings of these Vaiṣṇavas, who as worshippers of Visnu and Krishna, are attracted at the same time towards the Buddha and Buddhism. It may be said that Krishna is born in Mathura, is brought up at Gopa and subsequently becomes the ruler of Dvārakā, is regarded by these philosophers as a part of Jagannātha. Jagannātha to them, is the embodiment of sixteenth Divine attributes, and Krishna, as incarnation of Jagannātha and as the son of Nanda, possesses only one attribute (Kaḷā). Acyutānanda has rightly said that the Jagannātha is the possessor of 16 Kaḷās and he is responsible for the creations of ten incarnations. All these incarnations are completely lost in Him. This is also supported by unbroken tradition current in Orissa. At other places worship is made to the Avatāras only but in Jagannātha Kshetra Pūrṇa Brahma is worshipped. This is the unique feature in the conception of Pañchasakhas of Orissa.——— An illuminating suggestion[5] revealing the mystery of Pranava was made by Acyutānanda Dāsa. According to him the Ratnavedi (Simhāsana), Sudarśana and the three icons, Jagannātha, Balabhadra and Subhadra all are mounted in the figure called Oṁkār Yantra. This Yantra is constituted of Five Mātrās or marks which have been termed by the poet as Nāda, Vindu, Daṇḍaka, Tāraka and Kuṇḍaḷa. When these marks are conjoined, they form the letter "OM" of the Indian, especially alphabet of Oriya which again is the outline of the image of Jagannātha himself. The five matras symbolise the original Divine principles, their image forms in the Jagannātha cult and also the bija mantras as shown in the table below.

Mātrās	*Divine Principles*	*Image*	*Bija mantra*
1. Nāda	Mūla Prakrti (Basic principle)	Simhāsana	Pḷiṁ
2. Vindu	Mūla Brahma	Sudarśana	Dhḷiṁ
3. Danḍaka	Viṣṇu	Jagannātha	Kḷiṁ
4. Tāraka	Brahmā	Subhadra	Sḷiṁ
5. Kuṇḍaḷi	Śiva	Balabhadra	Hḷiṁ

''Further the following diagrammatic presentation of ''OM'' in the five mātras will show that five is an elemental number and the five matras symbolise the entire world of existance resolved in terms of five. Thus, Jagannātha as manifested in the form of Oṁkāra, stands for the summation of all things and the Oṁkāra yantra is the most defitting form for the image of Jagannātha. In this tradition, it is worth noting that Jagannātha is represented by a part of Yantra (Danḍaka) and also as the entire Yantra itself. This accounts for the predominance of Jagannātha.''

In the Religious literatures, the author has noticed that mythology, yoga and Atmagyan (self knowledge) are found. much mysteries are surrounding Lord Jagannātha and His Cult. Mahānadi river valley is the land where quest for co-existence among the Hindus and Tribals took place and Tribal absorption with much traditional accounts have developed.[6] In recent years Ruprect Geib's excellent work on '' Indradyumna legend,'' though a pioneering work in the field is virtually unknown in Orissa, as it is written in German.[7] The Nila Mādhava-Jagannātha tradition is also studied by G.N. Dash,[8] which goes thus:-

''A Chief of an aboriginal Tribe, the Savaras (the corresponding Oriya term is Sabara) worshipped a Deity named Nila Mādhava, a form of God Viṣṇu, secretely in a hilly area named Nilagiri geographically supposd to be located in or near present day Puri. The name of the Savara chief is Visva Vasu (the corresponding Oriya form is Bisva Basu) according to most of the versions put Jara alias Basu according to "Sarala Mahābhārata." A Hindu king of north India sent a Brahmna explorer in search of the Deity whom he wanted to worship. According to most of the versions the Brahmana explorer is named Vidyapati (the corresponding Oriya form is Bidyapati), but according to "Sarala Mahābhārata" his name was Basu (the corresponding Sanskrit form is Vasu). The name of Hindu king is Indradyumna according to most of the versions but according to the "Bana Parba" of "Sarala Mahābhārata." His name is Gala or Galaba. The Hindu King having been informed of the secret existence of Nila Mādhava by the Brahmana explorer Vidyapati came with an army to worship the Deity. But the Deity vanished miraculously and the Savara Chief was deprived of worshipping the Deity. Later the Deity reappeared but in the form of a holy log (daru) out of which the king got the images of Jagannātha, Balabhadra and Subhadra (and also Sudarsana) carved. The king then consecrated the images according to the Brahmanic scripture, worshipped them and thus founded the Cult of Jagannātha at Puri.

"This story structure has some resemblance with the family histories of many of the Feudal Chiefs (the Feudatory Rajas) of Orissa which has not escaped Hunter's notice.[9] According to these family histories—a Ksatriya Prince/Chieftain/Scion of a Royal family of north India comes to Orissa either as a fugitive or as an adventurer or on a pilgrimage to Puri, the abode of Lord Jagannātha, then ceremonially kills a (tyrannous) tribal chief of a locality and finally established /lays foundation of a kingdom making the killed or martyred tribal Chief the ista devata or the presiding deity of the newly established/ founded kingdom of that locality becoming its first king."[10]

G.N. Dash[11] concludes his study by stating : "To sun up in medieval period in Orissa, as well as in the other parts of India, aboriginal Tribes were continuously getting Hinduized and absorbed into the Hindu Society. Of the many channels of Hinduization like Ksatriyaization open to them one was through the Hinduizations of the Tribal Shrine or Deity.

"Thus a thorough study of the medieval social dynamics

and particularly the process of the Pujakaization type of Kṣetra-centred-Hinduization of the Tribals and Jati mobility and also the interesting and significant roles played by the "Ksetra mahatmya" or 'Sthala Purāṇa' type of traditional account in the same processes can explain satisfactorily the apparently unbelievable and paradoxical phenomenon that the priests of Triba; origin have been functioning for centuries at one of the most famous Hindu Shrines, the temple of Lord Jagannātha at Puri, where the untouchables were denied entrance till 1948."

II

The Nile-Mādhava Jagannātha tradition has developed, which gives the Tribal connection of Lord Jagannātha. The different versions of the traditional account of "Stala Purāṇa" or "Ksetra Mahatmya" type, referred to here as the Nila–Madhava Jagannātha tradition and accepted as the major source material for this study are to be found in two inter-related groups of texts: (1) Sanskrit texts like the Brahma Purāṇa, the Puruṣottama Mahatmya of the Skanda Purāṇa, Niladrimahodaya etc. which to use Redfields's terminology, are parts of the great tradition and may be called as Brahmanic versions and (2) Oriya texts like the Mahābhārata by Sarala Das and the Deula Tola texts by Sisu Krsna Das, etc. which, again in Redfield's terminology, are parts of the little tradition and may be called here as non-Brahmanic or folk versions. The traditional account purports to tell how Lord Jagannātha came to be worshipped in Puri.[12] This shows that both in Great tradition and Little tradition, the Nila-Madhava Jagannātha tradition is rampant or high spirited. Hence, it is commonly accepted and believed.

The story element of different Purāṇas has been well dealt by Gopinath Mohapatra.[13] Brahma Purāṇa is entirely a new work and consists mainly of chapters taken from the Mahābhārata, Harivamsa, Viṣṇu Purāṇa, Markandeya Purāṇa and Vayu Purāṇa. These chapters of this spurious work which have not been traced anywhere else, deal chiefly with the praise of the shrines and holy places in Puruṣottama-Kṣetra (Puri), Koṇārka, Ekāmra- Kṣhetra (Bhubaneswar) and Viraja-

Kṣetra (Jajpur), which lie in Orissa and belong respectively on the Vaiṣṇavas, Sauras, Śaivas and Śāktas, As the chapters on Koṇārka, Ekāmra-Kṣetra and Viraja Kṣetra must have been written by different hands and inserted at comparatively late dates, it is probable that the present Brahma Purāṇa owed its origin to those Vaisnavaś of Orissa who wanted to popularize Puruṣottama- Kṣhetra as great Vaiṣṇava holy place. There is evidence to show that this work was compiled between A.D. 900 and 1200.[14]

The story element of Brahma Purāṇa is given by Gopinath Mohapatra[15] thus :-

"In the 'Satya Yuga' or the age of truth, there lived at Avanti a pious King named Indradyumna. Once, possessed by curiosity to see the four-armed Viṣṇu, he sent out for Puruṣottama kṣetra. But before his arrival there, the God buried the image of the Deity in sand. (This according to Skanda Purāṇa, he did on the request of Yama). Indradyumna thus having failed to see the Image carved in azure blue stone, decided to construct a temple and installed another image of the Deity. He collected stones from the "Vindhya mountain" with the help of the kings of "Kalinga", "Utkal" and "Kosala," and so on completed the temple. Thereafter, following God's command (conveyed to him in dream), regarding the installation of the Idol, he went to the sea shore and cut a great tree with an aze. Just then, Viṣṇu and Viswakarmā reached there in disguise and made the four images, namely those of Balabhadra. Subhadra, Jagannātha and Sudarśan. Indradyumna celebrated the installation of these idols.

"Although the Brahma Purāṇa and the Skanda Purāṇa, broadly present the same version of the story, the two differ in treatings the detail. While the Skanda Purāṇa is more descriptive than Brahma Purāṇa, the latter makes no reference to Nilagiri. Nila Madhava, Vidyapāti, Viswāvasu and Mahāvedi. It alludes to the Deity merely as an image made of Sapphire, rather than name it as Nilamādhava. Then, instead of making a pointed reference to Mahāvedi, the writer speaks of it only as "as suspicious place." The most interesting feature of this

Purāṇa as also like Nārada Purāṇa is that there is no reference to Śavara worship at all.

"It can, therefore, be presumed that in the early stages, of the Aryāns, Nilamādhava was a deity and that in course of time, when the place became densely forested and inaccesible to others, the worship of God fell in to the hands of the forest dwellers, i.e., the Śavaras. But by the time of Brahma and Skanda Purāṇas, it once again gained popularity with the Aryāns. However, the image by then was lost, and in its place the present Trinity came into being. The sandstorm referred to in the Skanda Purāṇa is symbolic of the deeper religious storm passing over the Mādhava Cult. It alludes to the burial of the Mādhava Cult and the emergence of the Trinity. And it is Brahma Purāṇa that offers, for the first time, the concept of the Trinity."

According to Rajendra Chandra Hazra,[16] "The Skanda Purāṇa is a voluminous work consisting of a very large number of parts, most of which have not yet printed. Though, like the other Purāṇas, the Skanda also was subjected to addition and alternations more than once, there are chapters in it which were written earlier than A.D. 1,000, but it seems to contain little which can be dated earlier than A.D. 700."

The story element of Skanda Purāṇa, in which Puruṣottama Māhātmya is found is also given by Gopinath Mohapatra[17] thus :-

"This Purāṇa projects the Cult of Jagannāth with such crystalline clarity as dispels the darkness around it. Currently regarded as the most authentic source of the Cult, Skanda Purāṇa is widely quoted by Acholars. The story briefly related, runs as follows :

"Seeing in this Kṣhetra the direct Salvation of the people, Yama requested Viṣṇu to disappear from the Scene. Viṣṇu (Niḷamādhava) agreed.

"Indradyumna, the King of Avanti, having once heard about the unique power of Niḷamādhava, sent his priest Vidyapati to locate the dwelling place of Niḷamādhava.

Vidyapati thus came to Puruṣottama Kshetra and saw Niḷamādhava, worshipped by a Śavara, named Visvāvasu. But when he was on way back to his Country, a fierce storm rose and Niḷamādhava disappeared under sand.

"Indradyumna, on receiving the awaited message set out with all his men for Nilagiri, but could not see the God, since he had disappeared before the King's arrival there. Then, following Narada's advice, Indradyumna built a temple to honour the God and offered a thousand horse sacrifice at the place. In the meantime, there appeared a massive tree floating on the Sea. The King had three images, namely, those of Jagannātha, Balabhadra and Subhadra carved out from the tree with the help of an old Carpenter (God in disguise), who appeared there on his won, as it by the grace of the God.

"Indradyumna went to 'Brahma Loka' to invite Brahma to preside over the inaugural ceremony of the temple and the installation of the Deity–images therein. His journey to the distant, Divine Loka took many years, during which a certain King Gāla, who happened to be a worshipper of Mādhava idol on that temple, claimed the temple as his own property. However, when Indradyumna came back to the Kshetra, Gāla was so impressed by his spiritual power that he did not protest. Soon, after Brahmā descended from the 'Brahma Loka' inaugurated the temple. Indradyumna finally went to Brahma Loka entrusting the temple to King Gāla.

"Ostensibly, the Purāṇa, in its narrative, makes several innovations Unlike the 'Padma Purāṇa' suggesting that the God Puruṣottama was worshipped by the Bhils, the Puruṣottama Māhātmya tells that it was the Śavara Visvāvasu, who worshipped the God. It substitutes the term 'Mahāvedi-Antarvedi' for 'Vedi' (used in the Mahābhārata). It also introduces the concept of the Chaturddhā Mūrti (four images) by detailing the manner in which the four idols were installed in the temple at Mahāvedi. Again, 'Skanda purāṇa' is the first to bring out the idea of three–deity–worship and also to suggest how each Deity was invoked by a separate mantra or hymn. It thus lays Purusasūkta for Jagannātha, Dvādasāksara mantra for Balabhadra and Devi Sūkta for Subhadra. The specification of the colour and dress of the three Deities is also another novel feature of this Purāṇa.

"In this way 'Skanda Purāṇa' presents a vivid picture of the Cult. Then, the works, like 'Kapila Samhita, Bārhaspatya Sūtra', 'Nilādri Mahodaya', 'Tirṭha Chintamni, 'Kalika purāṇa', 'Puruṣottama Chāndrika', 'Tantra Yāmala', 'Rudra Yāmala', etc. treat the subject in more or less the same way in the Skanda Purāṇa."

The story element in different Purāṇas like, 'Narada Purāṇa,' 'Kapila Saṁhita,' 'Vana Parva and Muṣali Parva in Sārala Mahābhārata,' 'Deula Tola of Nilāmbara Das, Deula Tola of Śiśu Kṛṣna Dāsa,' and others have been well dealt by Gopinath Mohapatra.[18]

III

Many traditions have developed in glorifying Lord Puruṣottama Jagannātha and the Gajapati Kings of Orissa, one of such tradition is of Kanchi–Maveri Though it is connected with later period of the origin of Purusottama Jagannātha Deity and its trinity, during Suryavansi King Puruṣottamadev (reigning period A.D. 1467-1497), it shows the development of romanticism and how reality gets lost in this Culture. Therefore, it is worth narrating it. Krishna Chandra Panigrahi[19] deals with the Kanchi–Kaveri tradition thus :-

"Orissan traditions persistently refer to the conquest of Kanchi by Puruṣottama. Although they differ in details, the main story as presented by them, is as follows :

"Purushottama wanted to marry the daughter of the King of Kanchi, but the latter refused to give his daughter in marriage to a King who performed the menial duty of a Sweeper on the occasion of the Car Festival of Lord Jagannātha every year. The Orissan King took it to be an insult to Lord Jagannātha and himself and promised to capture the Kanchi princess Padmavati or Padmini by force. Accordingly, he led two expeditions to Kanchi, but the first one proved to be a failure. Then he propitiated Lord Jagannātha who promised in a dream to help him in the War. It is stated that in his second expedition Lord Jagannātha and his brother Balabhadra proceeded ahead to Kanchi in the guise of two horsemen and therefore, the second expedition of the devotee and the servant Purusottama proved successful. The King succeeded in capturing Padmini or Padmavati and bringing her down to Orissa. To avenge the insult hurled at Lord Jagannātha, he wanted to give her in marriage to a Sweeper, but his clever Minister saved the situation by presenting her to him when he was doing the duty of a Sweeper at the time of the Car Festival at Puri. The King then agreed to marry her and the incident thus ended in comedy.

"The story with some variations occurs in the Madalapanji and a work named 'Kanchi-Kaveri.' It also migrated to Assam and Koraput in Orissa, where the stories on the lines of the Kanchi-Kaveri traditions of Orissa can be traced. The Sculptured representations of Lord Jagannātha and his brother Balabhadra in the guise of horsemen proceeding ahead to Kanchi, are to be found on the wall of the Jagamohana of the Jagannātha temple at Puri. These representations have been referred to the 'Vedhaparikrama,' an Oriya work by Balarama Dāsa, a contemporary of Puruṣottama's son and successor Prataparudra, and therefore cannot be taken to be later creations. The work was meant as pilgrim's guide and it states that, 'After visiting this you will find the representations of the two brothers galloping valiantly towards Kanchi, on the wall of the Jagamohana. The two brothers are without doubt, Jagannātha and Balabhadra.

"It is also stated in the above story that Purusottama brought from Kanchi an image of Ganesa, an image of Saksigopala now to be found in the temple of Saksigopala in the Puri district, and a jewelled Throne which is identified with the present Ratna Singhasana on which the images Jagannātha, Balabhadra and Subhadrā are now installed. The identification of these objects has been a matter of controversy. In the 'Chaitanya-chariamrita' of Krishnadasa Kaviraja it is stated that the image of Saksigopala was brought by Puruṣottama from Vidyanagara. It may be noted that the Capital of Vijayanagara and also Rajahmundry were both known as Vidyanagara. In the Gaudiya Vaiṣnava literature Vidyanagara always meant present Rajahmundry which is sometimes mentioned as Mahendradesa or Mahendranagara. Not only in the above literature, but also in the Oriya Mahābhārata by Sarala Dāsa the present Rajahmundry is described as both Vidyanagara and Mahendranagara. Most of the scholars discussing the story now think that the image of Saksigopala was brought by Puruṣottama not from the Vijayanagara Capital but from Rajahmundry. He never conquered Vidyanagara, the Capital of Vijayanagara. There is still an image of Genesa in the compound of thc Jagannātha temple which is taken to have been brought by Puruṣottama from Kanchi. The jewelled throne; as already observed, still serves as the pedestal of Lord Jagannātha.

"Prof. R.D. Banerjee considers the story as a mere romance, but Dr. Subrahmanyan and Mr. Mukherjee recognize its historicity. It may be pointed out that a historical tradition in course of time gathers round it a lot of embellishments and for that matter its historicity is not completely rejected. The Kanchi-Kaveri tradition should not be rejected as completely unhistorical. As Scholars have identified the Kanchi King of the tradition with Saluva Narasimha who was a contemporary of Puruṣottama. There are ample historical evidences that there were wars between the two Kings. The name of the Capital of Saluva Narasimha was not Kanchi, but Chandragiri, but the former has the most sacred and important place of his Kingdom. Kanchi was the capital of the famous Pallava dynasty and as such, had become famous as a political and cultural centre. We may mention in this connection that Kalilendra actually invaded Bidar, the new Capital of the Bahamani Kingdom, but in the Orissan inscriptions he has been represented as Kalavargesvara. Kalavarga has been identified with Gulbarga, the old Capital of the Bahamani kingdom by all Scholars. In a similar manner Kanchi has taken the place of Chandragiri in the Kanchi–Kaveri tradition.

"In the 'Sarasvativilasam,' the name of the mother of Prataparudra, son and successor of Puruṣottama, appears as Rupamvika. We know from the Southern sources that the name of Saluva Narasimha's mother was Mallamvika and his wife's name was Tippamvika. It is not unlikely that the original name of Saluva Narasimha's daughter was Rupamvika which was changed into Padmini or Padmavati after Puruṣottama's marriage with her. The custom of changing the name of the bride after marriage was prevalent in Orissa and in other parts of India. The name of Prataparudra's daughter was changed into Tukka after her marriage with Krisnadeva Raya. So, it is not surprising that in the Kanchi-Kaveri tradition the original name Rupamvika appears as Padmini or Padmavati.

"Puruṣottama's marriage with the daughter of Saluva Narasimha has not been referred to in any of the contemporary records of the South. The marriage of Prataparudra's daughter does not also find mention in any of the Orissan documents even though it was a historical fact. Political marriage under compelling circumstances were being considered as disgraces to the King and the Country and therefore, no references were made to such marriages in the records of the Countries concerned. So, it is not surprising that we do not find any evidence of Puruṣottama's marriage with Saluva's daughter in any Southern record.

"The date of the Kanchi–Kaveri tradition, which resulted in the marriage of Padmavati by Puruṣottama, has been a matter of controversy. Mr. P. Mukherji thinks that it took place in A.D. 1469 in the early part of Purusottama's reign. This does not appear to be improbable though Purusottam's expedition to Kanchi at this stage of his reign is not attested to by inscriptions. The expedition seems to have been dashing raid and therefore, no record is available of it. Rupamvika's (Padmavati's) son Prataparudra succeeded his father in A.D. 1497, when he was sufficiently old. If we identify Puruṣottama's Queen Rupamvika with the daughter of Saluva Narasimha, we should presume that the marriage had taken place in the early part of his reign and not in the later part when he defeated the Saluva King and humiliated him by capturing Udayagiri.

"The Madalapanji states that Kapilendra invaded

Kondameru shortly before his death and brought–Chandravati Dei as prisoner. Kondameru can be identified with Kondavidu and Chandravati with Padmavati of the Kanchi-Kaveri tradition. If these identifications are accepted, then it has to be admitted that the marriage of Puruṣottama with Saluva Narasimha's daughter would have taken place before the death of Kapilendra. Before his death he had actually led an expedition to the South to supress the revolt of his son Hamvira, in course of which he might have also reconquered Kondavindu and defeated Saluva Narasimha who seems to have been in league with his son, and forced him to give his daughter in marriage to Puruṣottama. The peculiar circumstances under which the marrriage was performed appears to have given rise to the romantic story of the Kanchi-Kaveri tradition.

"Although we accept the historicity of the tradition, we do not accept the supernatural and romantic elements that have got into it. All that we intend to say is that Puruṣottama married the daughter of Saluva Narasimha under peculiar and pressing circumstances and the Kanchi-Kaveri tradition is based on this historical facts."

Kanchi is the head piṭha (site) of Ādi Sankaracharya Matha. So, the Kanchi-Kaveri tradition also proves that Lord Puruṣottama-Jagannath is connected with Ādi Sankaracharya, who revolutionised the spiritual outlook of men, during this time in India, i.e., Bharatavarsha.

IV

It is worth to know the opinion of K.C. Panigrahi,[20] on the Cult of Jagannāth, which goes thus :-

"The origin of the Jagannātha Shrine and his Cult are shrouded in obscurity. One great difficulty is that for the early history of Jagannātha we have only some legends and no other evidences. The legends again vary from source to source and make the task of extricating history from them almost impossible. What is true to the faithful is not true to the historian. The faithful take the legends as the true history of Jagannātha notwithstanding their Supernatural and variable character. We need not relate here the story which states how the dead body of Śrī Krisṇa came floating from Dwarka to Puri turned into Wood and was ultimately carved into the image of Jagannātha and his associates. The earlier details of the story given in the Purāṇas do not tally with those of the same story given by Sarala Dāsa in his Oriya Mahābhārata composed in the fifteenth century A.D. The story of the origin of Jagannātha given in the Vana Parva of Sarala Dasa's Mahābhārata relates that Śrī Krishna's dead body came floating from Dwarika to Puri and turned into Wood. This fact was known to Jara Śavara and his wife Lalita and they were instructed by Indra to keep it secret. Accordingly Jara Śavara kept the sacred object in the dense forest and worshipped it for several years. In the meanwhile the King Indradyumna, son of King Galamadhava of Somavamsa, came to know of it. The name of Indradyumna's wife was Gundakeri and he was the ruler of Sakalya Dvipa. Indradyumna became eager to trace out the dead body of Śrī Krishna turned into Wood and therefore to trace it out he sent a Gauda Brahmin named Yadu who was the son of Vedasravana Vasukara and grandson of Chandakara. The rest of the story relates how the Brahmin Yadu came to Puri, lived in the village of Jara Śavara and ultimately traced out the sacred object worshipped by the Śavara Chief. After that Indradyumna came to Puri, got the sacred Wood carved into three images of Jagannātha, Balabhadra and Subhadra and enshrined them in a temple built by him. This story of the origin of Jagannātha widely differs from the same story given in the Puranas and in an Oriya work named 'Deulatola.' In these versions of the story Indradyumna has been represented as the King of Malava. Galamadhava was not his father, but was an altogether different later King who falsely claimed to be the builder of the first Jagannātha temple built by Indradyumna. According to these versions the name of the Śavara who worshipped Niḷamādhava or the sacred Wood was Visvavasu and his daughter's name was Lalita who was ultimately married to Vidyapati.

"It will thus be seen that the legends which have come down to us about the origin of Jagannātha are of highly conflicting character. They can give us no true history of Jagannātha The matter-of-fact of history of Lord Jagannātha can be reconstructed only when some corroborating evidences are obtained from the more reliable sources like epigraphic records and Coins or from the objects obtained from a systematic Excavation somewhere at Puri. Till then the history of the Origin of this great Hindu Shrine will continue to be a guess work.

"The institution Lord Jagannātha at Puri, however, seems to be of great antiquity with its history going back to the pre-Christian era. In Chapter-114, of the Vana Parva of Mahābhārata the Sage Lomasa acquaints Yudhisthir with the sacred places of Kalinga. He first acquaints him with the Shrine of Viraja, situated on the river Baitarani. Yudhisthira after having taken a plunge into the river Baitarani heard a voice, which Lomasa explained to be that of the dwellers of the forest reciting Mantras. Then he explained to Yudhisthira the sacredness of the Spot from which the Voice came. He said that once the Self-existent (Svayambhu) performed a sacrifice here and gave the entire earth to Kasyapa. The earth was angry and sank into the Netherland. Kasyapa propitiated her and she uprose and showed herself in the form of an altar. The bottom of the altar reached the Sea. Yudhisthira was advised by Lomasa to ride upon the altar and then to bathe in the Sea. Yudhisthira followed the advice of Lomasa and rode upon the altar and took a plunge in the Sea. The sacred place described in this passage evidently refers to a Shrine other than the Shrine of Viraja situated on the river Baitaraṇi. This sacred place, as its description indicates, was situated on the Seashore. In all likelihood the sacred spot referred to in the Mahābhārata was Puri situated on the Sea coast. If this interpretation is accepted, the origin of the Sacred Shrine of Jagannātha goes back to the pre-Christian era and should therefore be considered as old as the origin of Viraja at Jajpur. The Mahābhārata has distinctly stated the name of the Shrine of Viraja, but it has not given the name of the sacred spot mentioned immediately after it. The unnamed Sacred spot was evidently Puri.

"Indradyumna, who prominently figures in all the legends as the builder of the first temple of Jagannātha, still remains a legendary person and his historicity has not yet been established. Had it been possible to prove his historicity, it would have possible to throw some light on the early history of the Shrine. the numerous Copper plate grants and stone inscriptions of the ruling dynasties of Orissa do not refer to Lord Jagannātha. The absence of reference however, does not prove that he did not exist in Orissa. It only shows that the Deity had not become so famous as he came to be later. There is a reference in the Khurda plates of Mādhava Raja II of the Sailodbhava dynasty to Lord Mādhava, the holder of the disc and this Mādhava is identified by some Scholars with Niḷamādhava, which was the earlier name of Jagannātha, but the identification seems to be far-fetched.

"The word Puruṣottama which is another name of Jagannātha and also of the sacred city of Puri, occurs in the Hindol plate of Subhakaradeva III, but it is capable of yielding two meanings. The relevant passage in which this word is found, has been translated as 'it was heard that being an overlord, he was deserted by the Soldiers (lit. horsemen), but his glory was never impaired by his adversaries and he was the best of man.' This verse like many other verses of the Bhauma Copper plate inscriptions, is capable of yielding two meanings. The word Visadi means 'one who was deserted by his horsemen' and it also means one who was Sad (Visali).' Similarly the word Puruṣottama means 'the best of men' and it also means' 'the City of Puruṣottama' which is another name of Puri. The reference is thus ambiguous and we are not sure whether it means the city of Puruṣottama or the King Subhakaradeva I of the Bhauma dynasty.

"We have already referred to the story of Raktavahu invasion recorded in the Madalapanji in Chapter VI, which is probably an echo of the Rastrakuta invasion of Orissa under Govinda III in the reign of Subhakaradeva I of the Bhauma dynasty. If this interpretation is accepted, we may be sure that the sacred City Puruṣottama (Puri) and the temple of Jagannātha, Balabhadra and Subhadra existed in the early Bhauma period of the eighth century A.D. We have also stated earlier that the Bhaumas came from Assam. Both Kamarupa and Uḍḍiyana (identified by many with Orissa) were the primary piṭhas of Vajrayana, and Jagannātha and Kamaksya, respectively of Orissa and Assam (Kamarupa) were established on the spots bearing identical name Nilachala and this name Nilachala is still attached to both the great Shrines of both the States. It is not therefore, improbable that the Bhaumas built a temple at Puri for Lord Jagannātha and worshipped him as a Buddhist Tantrik deity. The name Nilachala of the Jagannātha shrine seems to have originated from the Bhauma period.

"The indubitable references to Lord Jagannātha and his temple are however found in the later Gaṅga copper plate records in which Choda Gaṅga, the founder of the Gaṅga dynasty in Orissa, is represented as the builder of the present Jagannātha temple at Puri. We have already observed in Chapter VII that Yayati I also built a temple at Puri for Lord Jagannātha. Both Yayati I and Choda Gaṅga were actuated by political motives for paying a greater attention to the shrine of Jagannātha, which must have acquired a great sanctity by the time they ruled in Orissa. Both these Monarchs did not possess any legal claim to the Throne of Orissa, and, therefore, they wanted to placate the public opinion of this Country by building the spectacular temple of Jagannātha whose Cult had a great significance in the national life of the Oriyas, and who was considered to be the unquestioned Supreme Deity of their Country.

"The probable course of the history of Jagannātha seem to be that in the earliest times of his existence he was a Brahmanical Deity worshipped as an altar as described in the Vana Parva of the Mahābhārata. The altar was probably a Wooden one and like the image of Jagannātha, liable to be renovated every twelve years. It next came to the custody of the Śavaras who seem to have been the rulers of the region. Then the Bhaumas came from Assam in the first part of the eighth century A.D., ruled over Orissa, obtained the Shrine from the Śavaras, got the Wooden alter carved into three images, enshrined them in a temple built on the spot and gave it the name Nilachala which was the name of the famous shrine of Kamaksya in their homeland of Assam. Since the early Bhauma rulers of Orissa were Mahayana Buddhists, it is most likely that the three images carved represented tri-ratna as suggested by General Cunningham and explained by Dr. Harekrishna Mahatab. In the next two political periods Yayati I of the Sõmavanśi dynasty and Choda Gaṅga of the Gaṅga dynasty built spectacular temples in the Shrine which gradually became famous as a great religious centre of the Hindus. The survival of the first two temples built in the Bhauma and Sõmavanśi periods, might still be lying in different parts of Puri, used as later fixations. Puri has not yet been archaeologically surveyed.

"References to Lord Jagannātha or his shrine at Puri in the medieval Sanskrit works, are many. The Sanskrit work 'Jnana-Siddhi,' assigned to the eighth century A.D. and attributed to Indrabhuti opens with a salute to Jagannātha worshipped by 'all Sages who have conquered all their desires.' The word 'Jagannātha' in this sense also occurs in several other verses of the same work. In these references the word has been used in its etymological sense meaning 'the Lord of the Universe,' but some Scholars through a forced interpretation maintain that the Jagannātha of the verses refer to Lord Jagannātha of Puri. This interpretation cannot be accepted. A definite reference to Lord Jagannātha of Puri occurs in the Sanskrit drama 'Anangha Raghava Natakam,' by Murari, assigned to the medieval period. The Sutradhara of the drama clearly states that it was meant to be staged in festival of Lord Puruṣottama of the Sea shore studded with the Tamala trees. The famous astronomer Satananda clearly states that he was a resident of Puruṣottama and that his famous work 'Bhasvati', was completed in the Kaliyuga year 4200 or 1099 A.D., which falls in the closing part of the

Sōmavanśi rule. Dr. H.K. Mahatab cites a number of other Sanskrit works composed before the Gaṅga rule in Orissa, in which Lord Jagannātha or his Shrine at Puri has been referred to (Odisa Itihasa, Part I, pp. 186-190). From the beginning of the Gaṅga rule in Orissa, the mention of Lord Jagannātha and his shrine in the Sanskrit and Oriya works become a rule rather than an exception.

"For several reasons the Shrine of Jagannātha became most famous from the beginning of the Gaṅga rule in Orissa in the early part of the twelfth century A.D. The spectacular great temple built by Chodagaṅga on the charming seashore, attracted notice of all Hindus. The great antiquity of the Deity enshrined in it also enhanced to Sanctity. The political conditions of India after the Turkish invasion in the closing part of the twelfth century A.D., also enhanced the sacredness of Jagannātha's Shrine. The Muslims rapidly occupied the neighbouring regions of Orissa but Orissa itself remained a strong independent Hindu Kingdom upto 1568 A.D. The faithful flocked to Puri to follow their religious performances unmolested.

"The Cult of Lord Jagannātha is composite one and the diverse elements that compose it, have got into it at various stages of its development. Its composite character became well marked in the Gaṅga period. It is really surprising how the diverse Cults, so different in conception and origin and sometimes even antagonistic to each other, could be welded together into a cosmopolitan form of religion that became the order of the age. Before the commencement of the Gaṅga period Śaivism, Śāktism and Vaisnavism were the three main Cults which existed side by side in Orissa, each preaching its own Superiority, but at no time either in theory or practice, losing its separate entity. In the Gaṅga period there was attempts to amalgamate them into one form of religion that contained the principles of each, but yet exclusively represented none. The Pithas or Shrines continued to bear distinct names in accordance with the Cults of their origin. Puri, Bhubaneswar, Konark, Mahavinayaka and Viraja or Jajpur, the traditional five piṭhas representing five distinct Cults, continued to be respectively termed as Vaiṣnava, Śaiva Saura, Ganapatya and Śākta centres, but the form of worship that came into vogue in them became essentially a cosmopolitan one. The movement aimed at a synthesis of Cults and Sects by adopting principles not merely from the different Cults of Hinduism, but from Buddhism, Jainism and from the primitive Cults that were practised by the primitive people of Orissa. The Cult of Jagannātha embodies all these diverse elements and affords the best example of this synthesis.

"It is, therefore, no wonder that different Scholars would put different interpretations on the origin and the development of the Jagannātha Cult. It is maintained by some Scholars that the images, now known as Jagannātha, Subhadra and Balabhadra, were originally Triratna symbols worshipped by the primitive Śavaras, and the Śavara origin of the Cult is further sought to be supported by the existence in the Jagannātha temple of a Class of Servants known as Daitapatis (Devata-Vatis on the custodians of the Deity), who claim their descent from the Brahmin Vidyapati through the Śavara daughter Lalita. It is also suggested by some that these three images represent an Ananta, Vasudeva and Ekanamsa as given in the Brihatsamhita. Some Scholars also think that they represent Buddha, Dharmma and Sangha and one Scholar would like to trace their origin to Jainism. The views of the different Scholars on the subject are, no doubt, partially right, for in reality Jagannātha grew into an institution embodying the principles of all the Sects and Cults known to India. The Shrine of Jagannātha was much earlier than the period of the Gaṅgas, but the character of the Cult in its earlier phases is not definitely known. During the Gaṅga period the final shape of Jagannātha Cult embodying the principles and ideas of various Sects had been reached and the theory of its Brahmanical origin emphasized and given wide publicity. Brahmanism was a great unifying factor in the history of Indian Civilization and in its gradual development one may recognize the assimilation of various heterogenous ideas and beliefs, all synthesized into the larger concept of Hinduism. The emphasis on the Brahmanical origin of the Jagannātha

Cult is nothing but an attempt to endour the various strains, that went to the formation of this Cult, with an authoritiative sanction. The orthodox interpretation of the three images as current in the Gaṅga period and the subsequent period of the Suryavansis, the last independent Hindu dynasty of Orissa, came down to the early British period when Stirling wrote his 'An Account of Orissa,' in 1822. It has been recorded by Stirling that according to the orthodox interpretation, the three images of Jagannātha, Balabhadra and Subhadra respectively represent Vishnu, Śiva and Durga. The Jagannātha religion in its final phase thus sought to synthesize the three main cults of Hinduism, viz : Vaisnavism, Śaivism and Śāktism, but at the same time it also retained some practices of the older Cults and religions to which it owed its origin.

"Although the Cult originated and developed at Puri, it did not really remain confined to that place, but it gradually spread to other Shrines of Orissa. As a matter of fact, it became the religion of Orissa, and not of the Jagannātha temple alone. The Spirit of the age in which the synthesis of the Cults took place manifested itself in art, architecture and literature of the period, of which enough materials are now available. The Cult as well as the principles which formed it, influenced the religious history of Orissa. The great Temple at Konarka which, to judge from the presiding Deity, was purely a Saura Shrine, bore the stamp of this cosmopolitanism. It is difficult to ascertain the form of worship that was in vogue in that great Temple, for worship had long been abandoned there; but among its innumerable sculptures, there are still to be found several panels in which the representations of a Śiva lingam, Jagannātha and Durga are depicted side by side, with a worshipper paying homage to them all. The worshipper is a royal personage who most likely represents the Gaṅga King Narasimha I, the builder of the temple.

"The great Temple of Lingaraja which, unlike the temple of Konarka, is still under worship, affords ample evidence to show how this Śaiva Shrine was influenced by the Jagannātha Cult. The influences of the Jagannātha Cults are to be discerned in the daily worship of the Deity, in the mantras with which he is invoked, in the offerings which are given to him, in the surroundings in which he is worshipped, in the festivals which are held in his honour and in the orthodox literature in which he has been extolled and the modes and merits of his worship propounded. It is now an accepted fact with the priests here that the Lingaraja is a combination of both Vishnu and Śiva. In other words, he is Harihara and not Hara alone. A natural line that exists in that Swayambhu lingam (Lingaraja) is pointed out by them as the line demarcating the Śiva and Vishnu portions of the same Deity which is invoked as Harihara. Hemlock and hemlock leaves which are generally given to a Śiva-lingam are not allowed in the Lingaraja temple. The leaves of Vilva and Tulasi, which are favourites respectively of Śiva and Vishnu are used in daily worship.

"The temple and the surroundings in which the Lingaraja is now worshipped underwent important changes and modifications to fit in with the new conception about the Presiding Deity. During the Gaṅga period the Natamandira and the Bhogamandapa were added to the Lingaraj temple and so the Vrisa-Stambha which now stands in front of the Bhogamandapa, would have been a work of that period. This Stambha bears at the top not only a Vrisa (bull) the mount of Śiva, but also a Garuda, the mount of Vishnu, which having been placed side by side in front of the temple, have evidently been meant to make the synthesis of the two Cults visual to a visitor at his first approach to the Shrine. The crowning members of the great Lingaraja can be seen from a distance and the top most two of them, as in other temples, are an ayudha (Weapon) and a pataka (Flag). In order to bring home to the general public that the Shrine belongs to both the Sects, the ayudha which must have originally been a trisula, was replaced by one consisting of half a disc and a trident. It is said that this change was brought about by a daring man who climbed to the top of the spire in the dead of night under the orders of a Gaṅga King, pulled down the original ayudha, replaced it by this new and composite device. This man is said to have been granted rent-free lands and given the title 'Nihsanka-malla' (the fearless hero) which is still borne by the descendants living in the Nuapalli village near Bhubaneswar. Some orthodox Śaivas explain the disc as the pinaka, the bow of Śiva, but this explanation is untenable in view of the fact that the pinaka or bow is never used as a crowning member in any Śaiva temple.

"In remodelling the Lingaraj temple the Gaṅga Kings also introduced some Vaiṣnavite features which are not to be found in any Śaiva Shrine. In the southern door-jambs of the Natamandira are to be found the images of the Vaiṣnava dwarapalas Jaya and Vijaya in place of Chanda and Prachanda. These images holding in the upper two hands Sankha and Chakra and in the lower two a Gada stuck to the ground, are close prototypes of the dwarapalas of the Ananta-Vasudev temple built in A.D. 1278 and they furnish us with the further evidence that the Natamandira was erected during Gaṅga period. The interior of the Natamandira also contained arrangements for the Jhulana festival which is observed in the Jagannātha temple at Puri, but which has now been somehow discontinued in the Lingaraja temple. On the western side of the main temple of Lingaraja and on the northern side of its Bhoga-mandapa the images of Jagannātha and Laxmi-Narayana have been enshrined so that a devotee while making a circumambulation will first meet these Vaiṣnavite deities before he enters the main Shrine to pay homage to the Swayambhu lingam. Among the subsidiary temples standing within the compound of the Lingaraja, there are two to the south of the main shrine of which one contains the image of the Varaha incarnation of Vishnu and the others, the three images of Ananta, Vasudeva and Ekanamsa. No Śākta influence can be traced in the worship of the Lingaraja, but provision exists for the worship of Parvati enshrined in a beautiful temple with a three-chambered porch, which stands to the north of the main shrine and which was erected in the Gaṅga period. On the day of Lord Tribhuvaneswara (Lingaraja) returns to the temple after completing the Car festival of Asokaśtami, a mock quarrel is staged between two parties of priests respectively of Lingaraja and of Parvati, because during the Car festival the former takes with him Laxmi, wife of Viṣṇu and not Parvati.

"The cumulative effects of the influence of the Jagannātha Cult on the Lingaraja temple have been that it has lost its distinctive character of a Śiva Shrine and has adopted the cosmopolitanism of the Jagannātha at Puri. The Sudra priests, known as Vadus, who have been described in the sixty-second chapter of the Eklamra Purāṇa as the descendants of a Śavara mother by a Śaiva Saint known as Siddhabhuti, are, like the Daitapatis of the Jagannātha temple, still the custodians of the Lingaraja shrine, although the Brahmins have also taken a share in the worship in recent times. Notwithstanding the well-known orthodox dictum that the offerings given to Śiva are not to be partaken of by any Hindu, even the cooked rice offered to Ligaraja, is now eaten by all caste Hindus including the Brahmins. The custom is certainly analogous to the one prevalent in the Jagannātha temple where, while partaking of the cooked rice offered to the God, no caste distinction is observed.

"That those influences of the Jagannātha Cult are not of recent origin in the Lingaraja temple, is proved by the Ekamra purāṇa and the allied works. They are unanimous in their assertion that no real distinction exists between the Śaiva and the Vaiṣṇava Cults and that it is only superficial people who find a distinction in them. Thus says the Ekamra Purāṇa:-

"There is no distinction between Vishnu and Śiva. This is the eternal Dharmma and the man who observes this Dharmma attains Mukti."

"In another place the same authority seeks to synthesize the four main Cults, viz. Vaisṇavism, Śaivism, Śaktism and Saurism:-

"O Goddess (Parvati), you and Viṣṇu, and Surya and Achyuta are my emanations. The intelligent people say that there is no distinction between them (i.e., between Viṣṇu and Surya). So Viṣṇu and Śiva split the one body into two. The God (thus became) Ardhanarisvara and (in him) the female portion is really Janardana. O Goddess (Parvati), do not see any distinction (for) he who is Viṣṇu, is also Maheswara. The vicious fool who makes a distinction goes to hell."

"Instances can be multiplied from the same work to show that it takes all the main Cults to be one and the same Cult. It also utters warnings against the followers of Viṣṇu who want to vilify Śaivism. It says :-

"In the Kali age those persons who having been Vaiṣṇavas became the vilifiers of Śiva, will certainly go to hell. There is no doubt about it."

"On the ground that the Lingaraja is the combination of Viṣṇu and Śiva, it also justifies the partaking of the offerings made to him.

"Bhubaneswar is no Lingam; (he) is the image of Parama Brahma. (So) the partaking of the offerings made to him leads to the merits that accrue from a great sacrifice."

"The 'Svarnnadri-mahodaya,' in its sixty chapter further explains the reasons why the offerings given to Bhubanesvara are not to be tabooed. It says :-

"This Lingam is neither God, nor Rudra, nor Mādhava. Since half of each exists there, it is Swayambhu. The offerings given to a Lingam are not to be partaken of, (but), Bhubanesvara is not a Lingam. So, O Son, eat the offerings with the Gods and Demons."

"The same work in the same Chapter also asserts that offerings given to Lingaraja are not polluted by touch. In other words, it sanctions that the lower-castes can take the offerings in the company of the higher Castes. The sanction still exists and it is now a common custom that the lower-caste people carry even the cooked rice offered to Lingaraja to distant places where it is served to the people of all castes and ceremonial occasions.

"Culturally the Suryavamsi period merges into the Gaṅga epoch, but towards the end of this period Vaiṣnavism became predominant in Orissa on account of the visit of Śrī Chaitanya to this country, his long sojourn at Puri and his great influence on Prataparudradeva (A.D. 1497-1541), the last great King of the dynasty. So the ascendancy of the Jagannātha Cult popularly affiliated to the Vaiṣnava Cult, was more in evidence at Bhubaneswar. The earlier work, "Ekamra Purāṇa," while describing in its 18th and 22nd Chapters the procedure of visiting the main shrine, enjoins that, a pilgrim after having a dip in the Vindusarovara, must first see Ananta Vasudeva and then go to the Shrine of Lingaraja. Though the procedure gave the first precedence to a Vaiṣnava Shrine, nonetheless Ananta-Vasudeva was never conceived as the Supreme Deity of the place. On the other hand, the work has consistently maintained that at the request of Śiva, Vasudeva with his brother Ananta agreed to fix his abode at Ekamra, and to serve as the 'Ksetrapala' or the protection of the place. It thus maintains that Bhubaneswar was mainly a Śaiva Shrine and Vaiṣnavism was allowed to exist here on equal terms. But this position was soon to change alongwith the growing popularity of Vaiṣnavism as a result of Śri Chaitanya's activities and the patronage of Vaiṣnavism by Prataprudradeva under the former's Spiritual guidance. The 'Kapila-Samhita' which would have been compiled in or after the reign of Prataparudradeva, propounds just the opposite view of the 'Ekamra Purāṇa.' The eleventh chapter of the 'Kapila-Samhita,' gives an account of Śiva's coming to Ekamra which, on account of its historical significance, is worth quoting here in its main outline :-

"In the age of Treta Śiva once told Narada that since Baranasi had become over crowded, he would not like to stay there any longer and would choose a solitary place for his abode. Narada told him that there was a beautiful place known as Ekamra, situated to the north of Nilachala on the Sea-coast and that Vasudeva with his brother had been living there (at Ekamra). If he wanted to fix his abode there he should first go to Vasudeva, practice penance to propitiate him and obtain his permission to stay there. According to the advice of Narada Śiva went to Ekamra and at his first meeting with Vasudeva, fell at his feet and propitiated him with various prayers. Vasudeva at last agreed to assign him a place in Ekamra, but not without a condition. The condition was that he must not try to go back to Banaras again. Śiva agreed to the condition and was therefore given a place in Ekamra.

"The inner significance of the story is that Ekamra was originally a Vaiṣnava Shrine and that Śaivism was allowed to exist there after a compromise and on certain conditions. This, however, is just contrary to the archaeological evidence that we find with regard to its origin. It is evident that, in the last part of the Suryavansi period, the Cult of Jagannātha, popularly representing Vaiṣnavism, became the predominant form of religion in Orissa and all other Cults were made subserviant to it. This Jagannātha Cult, as we have already seen, is in reality an amalgam of different Cults and religions, and even of the practices and faiths followed by the primitive tribes. There was therefore a grand experiment in the field of religion in this eastern coast of India to reduce heterogeneity of a sort of homogeneity.

"The Shrine of Lord Jagannātha was visited by the great Saints like Sankara, Ramananda, Ramanuja, Mādhava Tirtha, Narahasi Tirtha, Kavira, Nanaka and Chaitanya, each of whom contributed to the growth of its catholocity and many of whom left some institutions at Puri which are still named after them. The process of the growth of the Jagannātha Cult marked by changes, modifications and innovations, reached its zenith by the end of the Gaṅga period and after that it ceased to have any growth whatsoever. Admittance of the Ḥarijans and Adivasis into the Jagannātha temple would have been the logical sequence of its liberality, had the process of its growth been allowed to continue unhindered. Stagnation of this great Shrine started from the Suryavansi period and it was enhanced in the Muslim period when Orissa became a benighted Country with but little contribution either to the body politic of India or to the general Indian culture.

"The laudable aim of providing a common religious institution to all Hindus, irrespective of their Castes and Sects, conceived by the Oriyas of the early periods, was scarcely understood or appreciated by their later descendants who set their face against any reform or innovation in the Shrine of Jagannātha. Certain ritualistic elements quite foreign to the earlier conception of the Jagannātha Cult, were also introduced into the Shrine. We have been that Pratarudradeva made the signing of the 'Gitagovinda' in the presence of Lord Jagannātha by dancing girls, a compulsory ritualistic performance. In the last phase of the development of the Cult. Jagannātha was no doubt conceived to be identical with Śrīkrisṇa, but Śrīkrisṇa of this conception was a Sahajiya type as depicted in the 'Gitagovinda,' Sex never played any part in the Cult of Jagannātha in its earlier existence. He was conceived as Yogesvara far above all carnal desires. He always appears with his elder brother Balarama and younger sister Subhadra and therefore nothing of amorous or obscence nature was to be sung or talked of in their presence. While allowing the 'Gitagovinda' to be sung by the dancing girls in the presence of Lord Jagannātha, the original import of the Jagannātha Cult was scarcely understood. Jagannātha was the sole source of inspiration to the earlier Oriyas, but as we have already observed, the Oriyas from the sixteenth century A.D. developed a diversified religious interest and started to be the followers of all sorts of Sects and Saints. The debasement of the Jagannātha Cult and the diversification of the religious interest synchronized the gradual decline of the moral and the military Spirits of the Oriyas."

V

As mentioned earlier by K.C. Panigrahi, "What is true to the faithful is not true to the historian." Analysis of blind faiths will not do. Realisation and revelation comes to the Yogic individuals through intuition. Lord Jagannātha has been kind enough and blessed the author with Self disclosure of Divine Supernatural communication through archaeological discoveries. The whole difficulty is that the Historians and History Congress of India are following the historical political Chronological era alias period, as established by foreign English Historians so far, as the study of ancient history chronology is concerned. "THE POLITICS OF HISTORY," is not understood. One of the principal findings of recent research is that the whole of the ancient Indian civilization, from the remotest antiquity to the ending of the Harappans in the 2,200-1,900 B.C. span was a continuum.[21]

After independence of India the Scholars of India, for the first time compiled their own history named "The History and Culture of the Indian People," under the general editorship of R.C. Majumdar, published by Bharatiya Vidya Bhavan, Mumbai. The Chronological dating of the early period of the History of India, in these series, was not free from the pressure and acceptence of the British Yoke.

Indian elite in general and the Scholars in particular are so much under the influence of the writings of Western Scholars, that any fresh and independent conclusion about Indian history becomes jarring to them if it goes beyond the ambit of Western writings. Very few Indian Scholars have shown courage to deviate from the general guidelines of Indian History provided by their Western counterparts. The isolated efforts of these Indian Scholars concern only one or the other aspect of Indian history. But, in general it has been proved beyond an iota of doubt that facts in our history have been twisted, mischieveous interpretations have been put on them and wrong conclusions have been drawn by most of the Western writers to suit their individual motive or whim. Under the general editorship of S.D. Kulkarni, eighteen volumes of "Bhishma's study of Indian History and Culture," have been published in recent years.[22] It is perhaps the first comprehensive attempt to present a matter of fact History of India, based on original sources inclouding the Vedas, the Puranas, the Epics and the mass of Secular literatures in

Sanskrit and other Indian languages. While interpreting facts, due cognizance of ancient Indian traditions has been taken. In so doing the modern research methodology has been followed and each issue has been critically examined from all possible angles. These series of Books are receiving wide acceptances, appreciations and favourable estimations of the deep serious thinkers, writers and Scholars of the Orient. Deep thinking Western Scholars,[23] are now in Search of the Cradle of Civilization. Ram Swarup[24] states,''A fateful thing has been happening. The East is waking up from its slumber. The Wisdom of Hinduism, Buddhism, Taoism and Confucianism is becoming available to the World. Already, it is having a transforming effect on the minds of the people, particularly in countries where there is freedom to seek and express. Dogmas are under a cloud; claims on behalf of Last Prophethood and Only Sonship, hitherto enforced through great intellectual conditioning, brow-beating, and the big stick, are becoming unacceptable. Religions of proxy are in retreat. More and more men now seek authentic experience. Borrowed creed will not do. Men and Women are ceasing to be obedient believers and are becoming seekers. They no longer want to be anybody's sheep, now that they know that they can be their own shepherds. An exteral authority, even when it is called God in certain scriptures, threatening and promising alternately, is increasingly making less and less impression; people now realize that Godhead is their own true, secret status and they seek it in the depth of their own being. All this is keeping with the Wisdom of the East.''

With this abckground, it is worth knowing the date of Lord Buddha[25], which is assigned to 1885-1805 B.C. and Ādi Shankaracarya, assigned to 509 B.C. to 476 B.C., as they are concerned with the evolution of Lord Jagannatha Deity. S.D. Kulkarni[26] states that in determining the period of Ādi Shankara, as 509 B.C. to 476 B.C. we have collected all possible evidence in favour of this date. The currently held view about Ādi Shankara's period, at 788 A.D. to 820 A.D. is not backed by any record of any of the Peethas (Mutts) founded by Ādi Shankara.

VI

Tantra (vide : Appendix-II) is the backbone of Spiritual religious Culture of Mankind, because "Kundalini," is the gift of Tantra to Mankind.[27] Only with the rise of Kundalini, different types of Samadhis or observation in different types of Consciousness takes place. Though no social sanction was received, the people continued to practise Tantra in the rituals and continued to attach to it a philosophical content. Tantra was a parallel Cultural current alongwith the philosophical one in the Indian Culture.[28]

The earliest conception of Female and Male principals in union has been discovered in Mahanadi river valley. Stone Sockets, with a Socket on the lower part and has component on the upper part, which fits into the lower Socket. the shape of this Socket owes its shape origin to the rock shelter painting of Yogimath Donder (hill), (vide : photo plate), which was discovered by the author on 21st December, 1970. Such a Stone Socket was collected by the author from Mohangiri site of Kalahandi district, which is now preserved at Manikyapur Museum of Bhawanipatna. It can be interpreted as union of Śiva and Śākti, which represents the Yoga of Sexual transformation. Such a Socket set is collected by Pradeep Mohanty and Baba Mishra jointly from Kharligarh site of Balangir district and exhibited at Manikyapur museum of Bhawanipatana. One set of such Sockets is traced at the temple ruin, on the left bank of Udanti river, within Bargaon village area in Nuapada district of Orissa. One half of such Socket is found at Patalgaṅga site of Nuapada district. Such an object has been found from layer-III (Early historic phase), from Veerapuram of Andhra Pradesh, where it is interpreted as a votive Linga.[29] The shape of such Stone Sockets has been utilised for the shape of Lord Buddha, in Amaravati Cross bar railing, which shows the presentation of Rahula (Vide : photo plate).

Because of this background and archaeological discoveries, the author[30] had reported that the latest study of S.D. Kulkarni informs, "In determining the period of Ādi Śankara, as 509

B.C. to 476 B.C. we have collected all possible evidence in favour of this date. The currently held view about Ādi Śankara's period at 788 A.D. to 820 A.D. is not backed by any record of any of the Peeṭhas (Matts) founded by Ādi Śankara.'' During his digvijaya he visited Puri, Sringeri, Dwaraka and Jyotirdham. In order that the great Wisdom of the Rishis may not be lost to prosterity, Śankara established four Maths and the four disciples at the above mentioned four places.

''ŚRĪ YANTRA,'' a diagrammatic embodiment of the creative Sexual activity of the Universe is placed till today in all the Mathas founded by Śankaracarya. It is the most important of all Tāntric Yantras, each of the other triangles is occupied by the Devatas which represent the Sub-divided energy.- Self of the Goddess. This is the very image of the process of creation, metaphysically Sexual. To a Tāntric, Creation is a continuous process. So the form, the desire (KĀMA) assumes is that of his female identity by making the World for one to enjoy as Bliss, Consciousness and ultimately the Being. So, it can be said that the whole Creation is pleasure garden of the Creator, which operates through the Kamadeva, the God of Desire.

''In Puruṣottama Puri, Śankaracarya defeated the Buddhists and established one of the icon of Buddha as Divinity of Govardhan Matha as Lord Viṣhṇu Jagannātha and his Śākti is Vimala. It seems 'Jagannātha', established as the male Deity of Govardhan Matha in Puruṣottama Puri by Śankara, revolutionalised Jagannātha as a Viṣhṇav Deity. further Sankara's commentary on the ''Praṣthānatray,'' added fuel to the fire of Puruṣottama Cult, Jagannāth Cult and made them synchronised as Puruṣottama Jagannatha. Lord Puruṣottama Jagannātha was made the Presiding Deity of Puruṣottama Kṣetra during the period of Sōmavanśi King Mahasivagupta Yayati-I in early part of 10th century A.D.

''With the development of Śākta tantra and Śaiva tantra, about the 9th century A.D. Buddhism in Orissa was suppressed, though its influence in literary works continued in Orissa till 16th century A.D. Sexo-Yogic system of Buddhism and Nāthism had become very popular and had influenced the social flow. Conversion of one of the image of Buddha as Lord Viṣṇu Jagannātha Deity by Ādi Śankaracarya was a great blow, a sudden misfortune or calamity to Buddhism. Because of such hostility, gradually there was decline of Buddhism. Even Śankaracarya is known to have founded his Sringeri Matha on the site of a Buddhist monastery.''

Though Tantra had early origin, from the dawn of Civilization period, by following the established British made historical chronology, H.D. Bhattacharya[31] states that it is only in later literature, from about the fifth or sixth century A.D. that Tantra as a special religious or philosophical concept gradually came into use.

Puri, from remotest past, was the site of Lord Puruṣottama. While dealing with antiquity of Jagannātha Puri as a place of Pilgrimage, K.N. Mahapatra[32] states,'' We now turn to the ''Anargharaghava Nātakam,'' by Murari Misra, written half a century of Sankar's visit to Puri. This drama was presented at the time of a festival (Yatra) of God Puruṣottama, who was being worshipped on the Sea-shore :-

"नान्द्यन्ते सू त्रधारः–अलमतिबिस्तरेण। भो भो लबणोद–वेला–वनाली नमालतुर कन्दलस्य त्रिभुवनमौलि–मण्डन–महानीलमणेः कमला कुच–कलश केलि कस्तूरिका पत्राड्क रस्य भागबत8 पुरूषोतमस्य यात्रायां मु पस्थानीया सभासद8''[33]

''This World famous God, Puruṣottama, the consort of Kamala, worshipped on the Sea-shore, in whose Yatra, this great drama was presented before an audience of learned people, can be no other than Jagannātha in Puri, who must have been well known throughout India, by the time of Murāri, who is assigned to the 9th century A.D.[34] Murāri, who wrote his drama 'Anangha Rāghava' in imitation of 'Mahavira charita' of Bhababhuti, got it performed, at the time of the Yatrā (perhaps Car festival) of god Puruṣottama in Puri, who must have been the family-deity of his royal patron, whose name is not given.''

Kedarnath Mahapatra has confused the names ''Puruṣottama' and ''Jagannātha'' to be the same. By that time 'Puruṣottama Jagannātha' deity had not yet developed as the presiding

Deity of Puruṣottama kshetra Puri. It is a great misnomer of K.N. Mahapatra's understanding, therefore a misunderstanding.

The information of Puruṣottama and his consort Kamalā, in 'Anargha Rāghava Nātakam' of Murāri Misra, dated to 9th century A.D. is of importance. The name 'Kamalā'' is used both for Goddess Parvati and Goddess Laxmi. So, it seems that during that period the image of Puruṣottama was Uma-Mahesvara or Laxmi-Narayana. This shape represents 'LATA MUDRA,' a Hatha Yoga practice, a premier mudra before the sexual act for pleasure or for Yoga of Sexual transformation. Interaction between man and woman.' Tantra-wise are three purposes—pleasure, procreation and Samadha.[35] In Yogic conception, when man and woman come together, they should first perform Hatha yogic 'Lata mudra,' and after its practice, they can use their Sexual energy for Pleasure, Pro-creation and Samadhi. So, it is worth knowing details about LATA MUDRA.

About ''LATA MUDRA'', 'B. Bhattacharya[36] says,' This is the ultimate secret of LATA Sādhana, the female entwines the body of the male like a Creeper, as do these Snakes. The erotic in the Human body creeps through the body and becomes love and understanding. That is Sankara's burning of Kāma with the third eye. You know the legend. That is the end of Sādhana. Let the Serpent lie tame as a friend clinging to the body.

''Didn't you seek the Secrets of the Lata-Sādhana? The male-female āsanas clinging over long hours are parts of this Sādhana. The (Cadavar) Śava āsana too is another type of Lata Sādhana. Did you not want to know?

''Watch them, the two, the male and the female, 'O' they lie quiet on you as two earthwoems, like two hands joined in prayer, yet how powerful they are. Death in life, life in death.''

When Lata mudra is practiced by Śiva-Parvati, it is called Śiva Lata mudra. Robert E. Svoboda and his Guru (Master)

Vimalananda describe this Mudra (literally means 'gesture,' physical, mental and psychic attitude which expresses and channelizes Cosmic energy within the mind and body. Also means 'grain,' one of the elements of the Pancha makara Sadhana in Tantra), thus[37] :-

"When a man and a woman come together for Śiva Lata mudra, the woman must sit on the man's left thigh and hold his penis with her right hand. He must cup her left breast with his left hand. Like a Creeper She drapes herself around him, clinging tightly like a delicate vine; and he permits himself to be clung to, offering her support.

"There are three types of Śiva Lata mudra, mundane, spiritual and one which is beyond both the mundane and the spiritual. The mundane gives maximum Sexual excitement, the Spiritual is for Sadhana, and 'beyond' is too advanced to be dealth with here. In all types the female counts Japa with her left hand, the male with his right. The Mantras are specific for each type. He forgets who he is, and she forgets who she is. He thinks, 'I am Lofd Śiva in the form of Bhairava (the Fearful Lord), and this is my Śākti, my Bhairavi.' She thinks, 'This is my Lord Śiva, and I am His Grand Consort. His Bhairavi (the Fearful Goddess).'

"If the couple is doing it for mundane purposes they must concentrate on exciting each other. Without realizing it She will begin to breathe through her left nostril and will direct that Śākti to him. His right nostril will be working and that Śākti of his will be directed to her. Hypersecretion of all the glands will result, and at the moment of greatest excitation cessation of breathing occurs for a moment. Then the male mounts and discharges his semen convulsively. Because of hypersecretion he will now eject three teaspoonful of semen as opposed to his normal one teaspoonful. Because the vagina and cervix have become utterly loose and dilated the sperm will go directly to the mouth of the cervix. The result is a child, if this is done at the right time of the month. This is the Brahmacharya appropriate to the ordinary householder because by such Sex, satiation occurs for a month or more and ojas is not wasted by frequent orgasms.

"The Spiritual Śiva Lata mudra is quite different. The Śiva must control his Śākti very carefully to ensure that She does not become Sexually excited. The couple should be able to sit together for at least three hours without the least exeitation, no twitching or oozing. The girl must understand that She will not get an ordinary orgasm this way. If She waits patiently She will eventually get a super orgasm which will make her forget Sex for ever. If this Mudra is done properly She will go into Bhava Samādhi. Her emotions will crescendo until her mind became totally one-pointed directed towards Śiva, and she will partly forget her Worldly existence for a While. Even Mahabhavasamādhi, which I call emotional highlights, is possible-total immersion in Śiva but with retained awareness of the Bliss. Wonderful:"

With this Spiritual and Yogic description of "LATA MUDRA," It is worth knowing the Conclusions reached by K.N. Mahapatra[38], which is given thus :

"Thus, Puri had become a stronghold of Hinduism in India before the establishment of the Muslim power in Northern India. From the discussion made above, the following conclusions may be arrived at :-

(a) The Uḍḍiyana Piṭha of the Vajrayāna, which was the centre of activity of the famous Indrabhuti existed some where in Orissa near Puri and became known as Oḍra Piṭha in the age of revival of Brahmanism.

(b) God Jagannātha, the manifestation of Buddha, who was propitiated by Indrabhuti can be identified with the Jagannātha of Puri, who was all through these centuries regarded as an incarnation of Buddha and as such Jagannātha-Puri was famous as a sacred place of the Buddhists, before the days of Indrabhuti (first quarter of the eighth century).

(c) The identity of the Buddhist Jagannātha with the Puruṣottama Viṣhnu of Brāhmanism was, established by the great Sankara Ācharya, in the first quarter of the ninth century, whereby this place became a famous centre of Hinduism since his days.

(d) There had existed a temple of Puruṣottama where the drama of Murari was presented, (circa. 850 A.D.) which finds mention in the Prabodha Chandrodaya Natakaṃ of Krishna Misra. Chodagaṅga Deva built the present temple after demolishing the old temple built probably by Yayati-I which was in a dilapidated condition, having been neglected by the former rulers of Utkala.

(e) Puruṣottama Ksetra had become a famous centre of Hinduism long before the beginning of the Muslim-rule in Northern India.

VII

The whole narrations needs an overall critical research narration, to know the Origin of Jagannātha Deity and its Theology. As mentioned K.C. Panigrahi had stated that the matter-of-fact of history of Lord Jagannātha can be reconstructed only when some corroborating evidences are obtained from the more reliable sources like epigraphic records and coins or from the objects obtained from a systematic excavation somewhere in Puri. Why only Puri? The whole Mahanadi river valley should be searched of its archaeological remains.

The pre-historic rock shelter painting of Yogimath donger (hill) was discovered by the author[39] on 21st December 1970 and assigned to neolithic period. The Gazetteer[40] authority assign this rock art to 10th millennium B.C. This art has line drawings with three figures semi circles meeting together, in red-tint colour alias archil or orchel. When the use of iron came to be known, the early human beings chiseled stone sockets of those shapes, with sockets on the lower parts, which fits into the upper parts. The sets of such Sockets, when exposed, can be identified as the union of Male and Female principals. (Vide : Appendix-II).

Nine chiseled marks are found at the bottom of the art, on the edge of the rock. These nine chiseled marks shows that they were ment for wooden fixation, for protecting the rock art. Because of this finding, it can be claimed that use of iron had already started during neolithic period, when this rock art of Yogimatha donger was painted. Bulls and one Cow with calf are painted on this rock art. This proves that domestication of animals and agriculture had begun, when this rock art was painted.

According to T.N. Mishra[41], "Archaeological materials from the Indus Valley Civilization also point to the existence of a fertility Cult in India from the proto-historic period. The discovery of numerous phallic stones and ring stones, the figure of a male ithypallic horned God (probably the prototype of Śiva) and the figure of a Mother Goddess are ample to indicate the prevalence of the said Cults. However, no representation of the Sexual act has been reported in the art and ritual objects yielded by the Indus Civilization. The earliest depiction of the Sexual act among the objects excavated so far in India, is found on a pot of the chalcolithic period at Dāmābad. Another early representation of Sex has been noted in the Kupgallu Cave in Mysore."

So, it can be confered that the earliest conception of union of Male and Female principals originated in peninsular India, south of Vindhya mountains. Vedic Arya Rishi Agastya was the first to cross the range of the Vindhya mountain.[42] He is the first Aryan explorer and originator of the art of Colonisation. A great missionary, as he appears to have been, his influence can be traced across the Seas to the distant lands of Cambodia, Bornee and Java, in the Indo-Javanese heirarchy of Gods, highest rank is given to Agastya.[43]

It seems Sage Agastya came in contact with the Yogic principals of the Union of Male and Female principals alias the Yoga of Sexual transformation from peninsular India and with his influence, this principal finds literary first expression in Brhadaranyaka upanisad of the Sukla Yajurveda.[44] This finds expression in the words of K.P. Sinha[45] thus :-

"The role of Sex-elements in connection with religious rites is also found in the Vedic literature. In the description of Goddess Uṣas, there are elements which are prone to arouse

Sex-feelings. In the Vājasaneyi-Saṁhita of the Yajur-Veda, there occurs a hymn (23, 22-31) which seems to indicate that Sexual Union was employed for the promotion of agricultural products. The description of the horse-sacrifice occurring in the Satapatha Brahmana (1. 1., 18, 20, 21) bears some Sex elements. The description goes thus : The horse to be sacrificed is covered with a garment and slain. The Queens go round it thrice from left to right and thrice from right to left. The Chief Queen goes near the horse. The Queen and the horse are then covered with a garment and are given to lie together. In the meantime, the priest, the maidens and other Queens indulge in vulgar and Sexual talks. This part of the horse-sacrifice has thus a clear reference to Sex and hence may be interpreted as having something to do with the fertility-Cult. Further, in the 'śatapatha Brahmana,' we come across numbrous passage in which Sexual union is identified with Sacrifice (2, 4, 4.21 ; 2.5. 1. 11; 5. 1. 3. 19; 5. 2. 5. 8; 6. 3. 1. 30 ; 6. 3. 3. 38; 7. 5. 1. 6). The 'Atiareya Aranyaka (2.1. 1. ; 2. 3. 7.) also refers to Sex-element when it describes Seed and Woman-blood as Ādiya and Agni, respectively.

"In a number of Upanisadic passages, Woman is conceived as the sacrificial fire, her lower private portion as the sacrificial wood, the generative organ as the flame, and so on (Chhandogya Upanisad of Sama Veda, 5. 18. 1-12), (Brhaddranyaka Upanisad of Sukla Yajur Veda, 6.2.13). The Brhaddranyaka Upanishad (6. 4. 3) describes the lower private part of Woman as the sacrificial altar and the smaller parts of the same as representing different parts or materials of sacrifice. It is added that one who remembers this during copulation gets the result of the Vajapeya sacrifice. This means that sex enjoyment should be regarded as sacrifice and that it should be done without any attachment. In the 'Vamadeva-Upasana', of the Chandogya Upanisad (2. 13. 1-2), it is said that the sign made by a man to a woman is him-kāra (the sound 'him'), his lying with her is Udgitha (the Sound 'aum'), his facing towards her is pratihāra (inspiration) and so on. The Taitiriya Upanisad and the Taittiriya Aranyaka say that Prajapati in the form of immortal Bliss exists in the generative organ. The Brhadāranyaka Upanisad also says that all the elements of Bliss culminate in the Bliss of the generative organ.

"Thus, all the elements of the Tāntric practices with the five Makaras can be traced to the sacrifical rites of the Vedas and the philosophical discources of the Upanisads."

The study proves that there are archaeological findings, which prove that the earliest conception of Female and Male principals in union, found was utilised to represent Lord Buddha at Crossbat-railing of Amaravati Buddhist Stupa.[46] Originally the shape of the two Sockets having components, which fits into each other, have their origin in Pre-historic period and early historic period. This shape was utilised to represent Lord Buddha in Amaravati Stupa. Ādi Sankaracharya had defeated the Buddhists at Puruṣottama Puri and had established this Buddha icon as Lord Viṣhnu Jagannātha, the Divinity of Govardhan Matha in Puri.

As observed Puruṣottama was worshipped separately from remote period in Puri. A religious Spiritual revolution took place, further Śankara's commentary on the "Praṣthānatraya,' added fuel to the fire of Puruṣottam Cult, Jagannāth Cult and made them synchronised as Puruṣottam Jagannātha, which was made the presiding Deity of Puruṣhottama Kṣetra (Site), during the ruling period of Sõmavaṁśi King Mahasivagupta Yayati-I in early or medieval period of 10th century A.D.[47]

This religious Spiritual revolution act during Mahasivagupta Yayati-I period, whose reigning period is circa. A.D. 925-955, according to B.K. Rath,[48] and A.D. 963 to 991, according to Bina Kumari,[49] was the greatest Cultural Knit, the Sõmavanśi rule could give, to the Spiritual mundane World.

Recent archaeological discoveries as dealt and the image of Jagannatha, prove the Theology of Lord Jagannatha, as the symbol of "OM KAR," is a Yantra. According to Swami Paramahansa Satyananda Saraswati,[50] "The Sanskrit word Yantra is such a descriptive word and is perfectly apt for the name of this form of Mandala. According to the dictionary it means an instrument, a machine, an apparatus, an implement. And this exactly sums up the mystical diagram in all ways. It is indeed an implement, a machine (though not an electrical or mechanical one) because it acts as an instrument for turning in with Consciousness. It is indeed a machine—a machine to induce states of meditation. It is a Spiritual machine. - - - - - Without them Tantra would fail to give the result that it does. We are not asking you to believe in the power of Mandalas and Yantras, but at least keep an open mind and in the future practice for yourself, that you can know from your own experiences.''

Though Tantra had earliest origin, all are lost in mystery, from the post Gupta period in history of India. Tantra as a special religious or philosophical concept gradually came into use. So, our present period is the age or centuries of Tantra. Hence Tantra should be well understood.

Paramahansa Satyananada Saraswati[51] may again be quoted, when he states :-

''Tantra encompasses all aspects of life. Its philosophical basis reaches the loftiest heights of comprehension, yet at the same time is amenable to practical application. It has different levels of meaning and significance which only unfold themselves gradually through personal experience.

''Modern man is looking for something, but does not know what it is. We feel that Tantra, including Yoga, is the answer that you are looking for. It is based on the Wisdom and experiences of thousands of tuned in enlightened Sages, throughout the ages. It is tested by time.

''Without joy and experience of higher awareness, life is dull, frustrating and often purposeless. Even one small glimpse of a transcendental experience will inject new aspiration, new joy into even the most unemotional person. Tantra promises just this higher awareness, happiness and knowledge. Tantra is a method of instructing and leading you to material and Spiritual fulfillment. Cosmic awareness can come through participation in the World, it is not necessary to reject life and become an ascetic. This is the way of Tantra.''

VIII

In the great Mahanadi river valley, from archaeological discoveries of the author, it is known that the earliest conception of the Union of Male and Female principals has been discovered. During the whole medieval period from 600 A.D. to 1200 A.D. the whole Valley, which includes the new Provinces of Chhattisgarh and Orissa had passed through Religious Eclecticism.[52] Twelveth century A.D. saw a new illuminary and that is Jayadeva the author of ''Gitagovinda''. In the words of Chittaranjan Das,[53] ''Whatever the great poet Jayadeva's actual birth place may be and even if we assume that there have been more than one Jayadevas, it has to be admitted that Jayadeva, the poet of the 'Gitagovinda,' fame was very much associated with the temple of Puri and that the book has been traditionally sung before the Deity of this temple as a part of its regular Schedule. There have been translations of the 'Gitagovinda,'' into Oriya during the subsequent centuries, sometimes faithfully following the original in its erotic elabration and also sometimes making some departure in the interpretation to give the whole thing a predominantly metaphysical look. But as explorations made up till now indicate, though 'Gitagovinda,' as a single work in erotic adoration has occupied so much place in the literary tradition of Orissa, through the centuries after the poet, one does not find another work of the same category in Orissa which could prove that Jayadeva really represented a whole trend or something of the sort. Yet more strange is the fact that the main temples of Orissa which were built after Jayadeva's time do not have a Sculpture that depicts the theme of Radha and Krishna.''

Though the theme of Radha and Krishna as depicted in Jayadeva's ''Gitagovinda,'' are not found in temple sculptures of Orissa, it should not be forgotten that Uma-Maheswar, Laxmi-Narayan and plenty erotic sculptures with different Lilas of Lord Krishna are found on the Sculptural arts of temple architectures of Orissa from 12th century onwards.

It was Jayadeva who emphasized the importance of the

worship of Rādha along with Kṛishna in the Vaiṣnava pantheon, in his immortal lyric Gitagovinda.' Recent archaeological discoveries have given more realistic approach. Therefore P.K. Ray[54] states, "The Prachi valley is famous for the finding of Dasavatara images in different places. The finding of Dasavatara images had great influence in the mind of Sri Jayadeva, echo propagated the doctrine giving top most place to Śri Kṛishna as an Avatara. In the theory of Śrī Jayadeva Krishna has been given the place of an Avatara and round him the other incarnations have started. Thus it appears that the Prachi valley was famous for the worship of Dasavatara images in various forms. There is every possibility that the celebrated Sanskrit poet Jayadeva was born in Kenduli at Prachi valley when the worship of such images were already prevalent in this Valley. Though he was a great devotee of Mādhava, yet his depiction of the theory of ten incarnations suggest that he gave top most priority to Śrī Krishna, who is taken as Avataree by him not as Avatara. There is every possibility that he was influenced by the Vasudeva Krishna Cult prevalent much earlier to that of other forms of Vaiṣnavism in Orissa. We have already discussed that the four handed image of Viṣhnu holding Chakra, Sankha, Gada and Padma may be identified as Vasudeva on the basis of various iconographical texts. So it appears that, the four handed image of Vishnu known as Mādhava (Vasudeva) was subsequently converted to two handed image, known as Krishna-Gopinatha, which became the favourite Deity of Śrī Jayadeva."

In the words of Barbare Stoler Miller,[55] "The lyrical religious eroticism of the Gitagovinda earned Sainthood for Jayadeva and a wide audience for his poem. All versions of the legend that sanctifices Jayadeva's life say that he was born in a Brahman family and that he became an accomplished student of Sanskrit and a skilled poet. However, he abandoned Scholarship at a young age and adopted an ascetic life, devoting himself to God. As a wandering mendicant, he would not rest under one tree for more than a night for fear that attachment to the place would violate his Vow. His ascetic life ended when a Brahman of Puri insisted that Jagannātha, "Lord of the World," himself had ordained the marriage of Jayadeva with the Brahman's daughter–Padmavati, who was dedicated as a dancing girl in the temple. Padmavati served her husband and he shared her devotion to Jagannātha. As Jayadeva composed, She danced–thus the Gitagovinda. In the process of writing the poem, Jayadeva conceived the climax of Krishna's supplication to Rādhā as a command for Rādhā to place her foot on Krishna's head in a symbolic gesture of Victory (Gitagovinda, X.). But the poet hesitated to complete the couplet, in deference to Krishna. He went to bathe and in his absence Krishna appeared in his guise to write the couple, then Krishna ate the food. Padmāvati had prepared for Jayadeva and left. When Jayadeva returned, he realized that he had received Divine Grace in exalting Krishna's loving relation to Radha."

This is nothing but the highest form of Tantra, i.e., Vaiṣṇav Tantra, because it is the Chief peculiarity of the Tantras, is that it gives prominence they give to the Female energy of the Deity. Śākti (Kāli) of the Śākti cult is the Mother or the Supreme Being. Similarly, Śiva of the Śiva Cult is the father or the Supreme Being. The Tantras attempt to blend these concepts, the Motherhood and the Fatherhood of God. Motherhood of God is supreme in Tantra, because Mother's love is deep and pure, for the children.

Jayadeva's language for Love, has been described beautifully by B.S. Millar[56] thus :-

"Poetry is distinguished from ordinary modes of speech by the controlled and stylized ways it strives to transcend the limits of ordinary language. The lyrical techniques of Jayadeva's songs combine with the conventional language of Sanskrit erotic poetry to express the intimate power of Divine love. As Jayadeva's elaborates the passion of Rādhā and Krishna, he creates an esthetic atmosphere of erotic mood (śṛngararasa) that is Bliss for devotees of Krishna. The poet's aim is implied in an opening verse of the Gitagovinda (1.4):

"If remembering Hari enriches your heart,

If his arts of seduction arouse you,

Listen to Jayadeva's speech,

In these sweet soft lyrical songs.

The relation between esthetic and spiritual experience is made explicit in the signature verse of the final song of the poem (xii. 19) :

> "Make your heart sympathetic to
> Jayadeva's splendid speech!
> Recalling Hari's feet is elixir
> Against fevers of this dark time.
> She told the joyful Yadu hero,
> Playing no delight her heart.'

The concept of mood, rasa, is at the heart of all Indian artistic expression. Rasa is literally the taste or favour of something. The rasa of a verse, song, dramatic scene, or musical performance is the flavour of a pervading emotion (sthāyibhāva). Sanskrit poets and critics came to realize the unique power and the esthetic potential of sexual passion (ratibhāva) in its aspects of pain and pleasure. The erotic mood that emerges from passion was expressed in the antithetical modes of 'separation' (vipralambhaśṛṅgara) and 'consummation' (saṁbhogaśṛṇgara). To experience this mood in the interplay of its two modes was considered the height of esthetic joy. Jayadeva created the religiously potent atmosphere of the Gitagovinda by exploring the poignant mood of separation within the broader play of Divine passion in consummation.

"Passion is transformed into erotic mood when a poet distills essential qualities from the confusion of spontaneous emotion and then patterns them according to universalizing rules of composition. Passion is made palpable through sensuous descriptions of movements and physical forms. Seasonal changes in nature and bodily signs of inner feeling are coloured richly to create a dense atmosphere of passion. The theorists dictated that the gestures exposing a character's mental states must be subtle expressive enough to arouse a sensitive audience but never so crudely detailed that they stimulate wanton desire. In the Gitagovinda this restraint functions to make potentially pornographic subject matter the material of esthetic and religious experience.

"In Jayadeva's environment of springtime (sarasavasanta, I 27,) Rādhā and Krishna are vehicles (Vibhava) for the universalization of erotic emotion. These youthful figures with gleaming flesh and lotus-petal eyes manifest signs of emotion (vyabhicāribhāva, sāttvikabhāva) to communicate the passion of their separation. For Jayadeva, their longing and reunion is the concrete example of religious experience in which the disquieting distination between "I" and "Mine" versus "you" and "yours" is claimed. The esthetic experience of their love is the means for breaking the imaginary barrier dividing human from Divine.

"The poet's direct presence throughout the poem dramatizes his view that the discipline of esthetic perception is a way to enjoy Krishna's graceful love. Each signature verse is a variation on the idea that the emotional states of Rādhā and Krishna have religious power through the medium of the poet's lyric presentation.

"In sight into Jayadeva's conception is found by following the way he presents his characters through the movement of the poem's twelve parts. After evoking Rādhā and Krishna in their secret erotic relationship and stating his own aim, Jayadeva invokes the ten cosmic incarnations of Krishna. He proceeds to present increasingly intimate aspects of Krishna's relation to existence, focusing on the suffering he shares with Rādhā in the frustration of their love. Krishna's ecstatic reunion with Rādhā within the forest thicket in spring time allows the poet's audience to witness the centre of existence. The vision (darśana) of Krishna revealed through Rādhā at the end of the poem is a vision of the soul of his erotic mood (ekarasa xi, 24-31, song 22). Its effect is comparable with Krishna's manifestation to Arjuna is the eleventh chapter of the Bhagavad Gita. Rādhā's heart, strengthened by the long, trial of their separation and by the force of Krishna's suffering, is filled with erotic mood (sarasmanas,xii,1) that is the consummation (sanbhogaśṛṅgāra) of the erotic, esthetic, religious experience Jayadeva creates for himself and his audience. This vision is contained within the structure of the poem, like the vision that climaxes a worshipper's controlled approach to the Deity in the womb of a Hindu temple. On another level, the poetic perspective follows the movement of Rādhā's friend's (sakhī), who goes between the parted lovers to describe the condition of each of the other. This perspective begins on Rādhā's side, but it subtly shifts to mediate between Rādhā and Krishna and bring them into union. The friend, the poet, and the audience share the experience of secretly participating in the play of Divine Love.

"The Gitagovinda begins with a classical verse indicating the subject of the poem.

'Clouds thicken the sky,

Tamala trees darken the forest,

The night frightens him,

Rādhā, you take him home:

They leave at Nanda's order,

Passing trees in thickets on the way,

Until secret passions of Rādhā and Mādhava

Triumph on the Jamuna river bank.'

"The place, the time, the characters, and their relationship in the poem are superficially clear in this verse. But details of the episode are rich in symbolism and have encouraged complicated interpretations of Jayadeva's meaning. Most interpretations turn on the identification of the speaker of the first half of the verse and on the reference to Krishna's 'fear' and Rādhā's role as his guide through to dark forest. The opening speech is variously attributed to Krishna, Rādhā, Nanda, or even the friend of Rādhā. Jayadeva is characteristically ambiguous here—the many voices that are possible in the verse all direct the sexual energies of Krishna towards Rādhā, but each voice slightly shifts the quality of the darkness and of Krishna's fear. When we hear Krishna's youthful fear of the dark is suggested. When we hear Rādhā speaking to herself, the words suggest a woman sensing the sexual fear of her adolescent lover. When we hear Krishna himself speaking he is courting Rādhā in the veiled language of love, where feigned fear is a device of seduction. The composite voice further suggests that fear may relate to the cosmic age of darkness, the Kaliyuga for which the union of

Rādhā and Krishna is the cure.

"The darkness of the night in the forest is described in voluptuous sounds and imagery that echo through the entire poem. It is in this secret, sexually stimulating environment that Krishna and Rādhā enact the initial triumph of their Divine love and then suffer the long night of separation that ends on their reunion. They follow the path through the forest as a pair, which Jayadeva calls Rādhā-Mādhava. The triumph of their possions occurs in this dual state, which is the defining structure of their relationship in the Gitagovinda. The 'home' of which Rādhā brings Krishna is a forest thicket (kuñja), the secret place of their Divine love, in which they meet again at the end of their journey.

"The erotic mysticism of the Gitagovinda, which inspired the Vaiṣhnava Saint Chitanya was interpreted allegorically by chitanya's followers in terms of the Sahajiya-doctrine of devotional esthetics (Bhaktirasa): they used love as a metaphor whose primary reference was a metaphysical conceptions. Although many elements in the Gitagovinda are codified in the Sahajiyā doctrine of love, this reading seems artificial. Jayadeva's verses nowhere praise unbodied joy : they explicitly sensual, and celebrate the sensual joy of Divine lone. Though imagery, tone color, and rythm. Jayadeva inter weaves levels of physical and metaphysical associations, and the cosmic energy of Krishna's love with Rādhā is condensed into a religious ecstasy."

With this background, the author[57] had stated that from the time of Codagaṅga, the Vaiṣnavism of the Rāmanuja school pushed its way to Orissa and ultimately the Vaiṣhnava of Mādhava sect received Royal patronage in the time of the imperial Gaṅgas. Twelfth century A D. indeed is significant with the history of Vaiṣṇavism in Orissa. Middle of this century_witnessed the rise of Jayadeva as a great Saintly luminary inthe herizon of Orissa. Jayadeva conceived the Supreme God in the form of Mādhava. It was Jayadeva who emphasised the importance of the worship of Rādhā along with Krishna in the Vaiṣṇava pantheon in his immortal lyric 'Gitagovinda'. The conception of 'Gitagovinda' influenced the later sahajiya Vaisnava sect. Like the worship of Laksmi-Nārāyana and Rādhā -Krishna, worship or Sita-Rama and also started and it had attained celebrity during the reign of the Imperial Gaṅgas.

With the conception of "Gitagovinda" and "Vaiṣṇava tantra", Lakṣhmi-Narayana imagea like Uma-Mahesvara were made during Gaṅga period in Orissa, which traces can be found in Lakṣmi-Narayana images at (1) Inside Lingaraj temple of Bhubaneswar, (2) Lakṣmi-Narayana temple at Lakṣmi sagar, in the vicinity of Bhubaneswar, (3) Lakṣmi-Narayana temple at Chaurasi, (4) Laksmi-Narayana in the Math of Thakurpatna in Prachi valley, (5) Pratapnagari, (6) Konduli, (7) Cuttack town and (8) Belkhandi.

These prove that two forms of Vaiṣṇavism are followed in Orissa. They are right hand Vaiṣṇavism and left hand Vaiṣṇavism.

The right hand Vaiṣṇavism is the Prema-Bhakti Cult started by Jayadeva. In the words of Sarat Chandra Behera[58], "All religious faiths in Orissa ultimately converged in the great institute of Jagannātha. The Cult of Jagannātha assimilated in its fold different creeds which evolve through centuries in Orissa. Under the Suryavami-Gajapatis Jagannātha Consciousness was the greatest religious force of the people. Kapilendradeva having inflicted a defeat on Mālik Pārisa (sultan Sasiruddin) presented a Sari called "pandarika Gopa" to Lord Jagannātha. In Matukapalle inscription purusottama Deva is described as "Jagannātha vara Prasada." Prataparudra was equally devoted to Lord Jagannātha.

"The reign of Prataparudra marks the climax in the growth of Vaisnavism in Orissa. Before the arrival of Śrī Chaitanya Bhakti movement had already dawned over Orissa. Jagannātha, Balarama, Achyutananda, Yasovanta and Ananta were the Five Associates who had absorbed in their writings the essence of Tantra, Buddhism, Vedanta and the Cult of Prema-Bhakti. The most famous of these Five Associates, Jagannātha Das, has composed Srimad Bhagavata, which is considered to be the most representative work of Oriya literature. In this magnum opus he in corporated all the different faiths which evolved in orissa and identified Śrī Krishna with Lord Jagannatha. Śrī Krishna of the Five Associates is the personal God of Purāna as well as the Impersonal Being of the Upanisads. Rāi Rāmānanda, who was the Governor of Rajhmahendri under Prataparudra was an exponent of the Prema-Bhakti Cult. Before the arrival of Śhī Chaitanya he had expounded the chief tenets of this Cult and composed the great work "Jagannātha Vallabha" when Śhī Chaitanya came to Orissa in 1510 A.D. he was anxious to meet Rāi Rāmānanda. The meeting of these two stalwarts of Neo-Vaisnavism has been graphically narrated by Krishnadas Kaviraj in his famous Bengali book "Chaitanya Charitammta". In course of the dialogue Śhī Chaitanya is reported to have commented that Rai Rāmānanda was already well versed in Prema-Bhakti Cult. After this meeting Rai Rāmānanda relinquished his services and devoted to rest of his life in the service of the Lord. Śhī Chaitanya in the company of the Five Associates, Rai Rāmānada and Sarva Bhauma spent eighteen years it Puri. He identified Sri Krishna with Jagannatha and consequently Krishna consciousness and Jagannatha Consciousness were rolled into one. In the words of Sir Jadunaht Sarkar[59], "The diverse religions of Orissa in all ages have tended to gravitate towards and finally merged into the Jagannātha worship at least in theory."

The presence of Laksmi-Narayana images alias sculptures in Orissa, are the examples of "LARA MUDRA HATHA YOGA" practice of yoga of sexual transformation,which is left hand Tāntric Vaisnavism. These show that pravṛti-mārga (manu-smriti,12-88) or the path of enjoyment (lefthand vaiṣṇavism) was once prevalent in Vaisnavism of Jagannātha Cult and 'PREM-BHAKTI' of Vaiṣṇavism in Jagannātha Cult is still prevalent, which is right hand path of Vaiṣṇavism Spirituality (nivṛtti-mārga).

Religious eclecticism is in its highest form in Jagannātha Cult and Orissa province in general. Therefore there was no Cultural-Spiritual differences between different Religious Sects, and that is why the rulers of Orissa in different periods found it possible to support all sects.

Now the world is moving towards Globalisation,which will pave the way for further evolution for "ONE WORLD, ONE MANKIND" and "HUMAN BROTHERHOOD AND SISTERHOOD" .. Pravṛti-mārga and nivṛtti-mārga of Jagannatha Spiritual Culture and Orissa province in general has much to offer in this century, which is going to be the century of "YOGA" because only Yogic path leads to "ALTRUISM"

References

1. Baba, Śrī Satya Sai -"Selfless Service earns Divine Grace," *SANATHANA SARATHI*, Vol. 44, September 2001, no. 9, Prasanthi Nilayam, Andhra Pradesh, pp. 278-279.
2. Chinmayananda, Swami- *Vedanta the Science of Life, part-III*, Central Chinmaya Mission Trust, Bombay, 1982, p. 1039.
3. Ramachandra Rao, S.K. *YANTRAS*, Śhī Satguru Publications Delhi,1988, p. 35.
4. Mishra, K.C. *The Cult of Jagannatha*, Firma K.L.Mukhopadhyay, Calcutta 1977, pp. 168-175.
5. A Palm-leaf manuscript of "SAYANTRASUNYA SAMHITA," was traced by K.C. Mishra and collected by him, which was presented to Orissa State Museum, Bhubaneswar for preservation.
6. Dash, G.N. *Hindus and Tribals-Quest for co-existence*, Decent Books, New Delhi, 1998, passim.
7. *Ibid.*, 1998, Preface, p. xi.
8. *Ibid.*, 1998, pp. 39-40.
9. Hunter, W.W. *Orissa, Vol.I*, Smith Elder&Co., London,1872, p.94.
10. Kulke, Hermann, "Kshatriyaization and social change, a Study in Orissan setting." *Aspects of Change in India : Studies in Honour of Prof. G.S. Ghurye* ed. Pillai, S.D., Bombay, 1996, pp. 398-409.
11. Dash, G.N. *op. cit.* 1998, p. 101 and pp. 107-108.
12. *Ibid.*,1998, p. 35.
13. Mohapatra, G. *The Land of Vishnu (A Study of Jagannatha Cult)*, B.R. Publishing Corporation, Delhi, 1979, pp. 21-38.
14. Hazra, Rajendrachandra-"The Purāṇas," *The Cultural Heritage of India*, Vol. II. The Ramakrishna Mission, Institute of Culture, Calcutta, 1969, pp. 262-263.
15. Mohapatra,Gopinath -*op. cit*, Delhi, 1979, pp. 21-22.
16. Hazra, R.C. *op. cit*, Calcutta, 1969, p. 263.
17. Mohapatra, G. *op. cit*,1979, pp. 23-24.
18. *Ibid.*, Delhi, 1979, pp. 22-38.
19. Panigrahi, K.C. *History of Orissa (Hindu Period)*, Kitab Mahal: Cuttack, 1981, p. 208 and pp. 215-219.
20. *Ibid.*, Cuttack, 1981, pp. 325-347.
21. Rajaram, Navaratna S. THE POLITICS OF HISTORY, Voice of India, New Delhi, 1995, Preface, P. xv.
22. Kulkarni, S.D. (General editor) *Bhishma's Study of Indian History and Culture*, (XVIII), 18 volumes, Shri Bhagavan Vedavyasa Itihasa Samshodhana Mandira, (BHISHMA), Thane,

Bombay, 1998-1997, passim.

23. Feuerstery. Kal, S. and Frawley, D. *In Search of the Cradle of Civilization,* Motilal Banarsidass, Delhi, 1999, passim.
24. Swarup, Ram-"Introduction to the reprint," *Mohammed and the Rise of Islam,* by Margoliouth, D.S., Voice of India, New Delhi, 1985, p. XX.
25. Kulkarni, S.D. (General editor), *Bhishma's Study of Indian History and Culture,* Vol. I, Shri Bhagavan Vedavyasa Itihasa Samashodhana Mandir, (BHISHMA), (Thane), Bombay, 1988, p. 375.
26. Kulkarni, S.D. (General Editor), *Ibid,* Vol. IV 1994, Introduction, p. 1 and vol. XI, Ādi Shankaracarya- The Saviour of Mankind, 1987, passim.
27. Saraswati, Swami Paramahamsa Satyananda, *KUNDALINI TANTRA,* Bihar School of Yoga, Mungar, 1992, passim.
28. Kulkarni, S.D. (General Editor), *op. cit.,* Vol. I, (Thane), Bombay, 1997, p. 462.
29. Sastri; T.V.G., Bai; K.M.& Rao, J.V.P. VEERAPURAM, Bhavani Printers, Hyderabad, 1984, passim.
30. Singh Deo, J.P. *TĀNTRIC ART OF ORISSA,* Kalpaz Publications, Delhi, 2001, pp. 111-112.
31. Bhattacharya, H. D. "Tantric Religion," *The History and Culture of the Indian People , Vol. IV, (The Age of Imperial Kanauj)* ed. Majumdar, R.C. Bharatiya Vidya Bhavan, Bombay, 1964, pp. 315-316.
32. Mahapatra, K.N. "Antiquity of Jagannātha-Puri as a place of Pilgrimage," *O.H.R.J.,* Vol. III. No.1, June 1954, pp. 9-10.
33. Anargha Raghava Natakam, Act. I, P. 8, Published in Nirnaya Sagara Press.
34. *History of Sanskrit Literature,* by Dr. Dasgupta and Dr. De, Vol. I, Classical period, p. 449.
35. Singh Deo, J.P. *Tāntric Art of Orissa,* Kalpaz Publications, Delhi, 2001, p. 31.
36. Bhattacharya, B. *THE WORLD OF TANTRA,* Munshiram Manoharlal Publishers Pvt. Ltd., New Delhi, 1992, pp. 447-448.
37. Svoboda, Robert E. *AGHORA (AT THE LEFT HAND OF GOD),* Rupa & Co., New Delhi, 1993, pp. 271-272.
38. Mahapatra, K.N. *O.H.R.J.,* Vol. III, No.1, June 1954, p. 21.
39. (i) Singh Deo, J.P. "Pre-historic Cave Painting of Jogimath Donger," *O.H.R.J.* Vol. XXII, No. 2, pp. 21-22.
    (ii) Singh Deo, J.P. *Cultural Profile of South Kōsála,* Gyan Publishing House, New Delhi, 1987, p. 20.
40. *Orissa District Gazetteers, KALAHANDI,* Cuttack, 1980, p. 36.
41. Mishra, T.N. *Impact of Tantra on Religion and Art,* D.K. Printworld (P) Ltd., New Delhi, 1997, p. 101.
42. Singh Deo, J.P. *Cultural Profile of South Kōsala,* Gyan

Publishing House, New Delhi, 1987, p. 58.

43. Kulkarni, S.D. (General Editor). *Bhishma's Study of Indian History and Cultural, Vol. I, (Beginning of Life, Culture and History)*, Shri Bhagavan Vedavyasa Itihasa Samshodhana Mandira (Thane), Bombay, 1997, p. 218.
44. Nathan, R.S. *OUR HERITAGE, Book-I.* Central Chinmaya Mission Trust, Bombay, 1986, p. 120, (appendix).
45. Sinha, K.P. *Thoughts on Tantra and Vaisnavism*, Punthi-Pustak, Calcutta,1993, pp. 30-31.
46. Stone, E.R. *The Buddhist Art of Nagarjunakonda*, Motilal Banarsidass, Delhi, 1994, Vide : Illustration No. 32, Presentation of Rahula, Crossbar from Amaravati railing, Archaeological Museum, Amaravati.
47. Singh Deo, J.P. *Tantric Art of Orissa*, Kalpaz Publications, Delhi, 2001, p. 112.
48. Rath, B.K. *Cultural History of Orissa*, Sundeep Prakashan, Delhi, 1983, p. 62.
49. Sharma, Bina Kumari-*The History of Sōmavaṁśī Rule in Orissa*, Punthi-Pustak, Calcutta, 1983, p. 29.
50. Saraswati, Swami Paramahansa Satyananda-*A SYSTEMATIC COURSE IN THE ANCIENT TĀNTRIC TECHNIQUES OF YOGA AND KRIYA*, Bihar School of Yoga, Munger, Second edition, 1989, p. 336.
51. *Ibid*, Munger, 1989, p. 339.
52. (i) Sah, A.P. *Life in Mediaeval Orissa Cir. A.D. 600-1200*, Chaukhambha Orientalia, Varanasi, 1976, pp. 203-205.
    (ii) Nema, S.R. *Political History of the Sōmavaṁśī Kings of South Kōśala and Orissa*, Oriental Publishers, New Delhi, 1978, pp. 128-139.
    (iii) Chakravarty, M. *Religious Life in the Kalachuri Empire*, Punthi-Pustak, Calcutta, 1999, passim.
53. Das, Chittaranjan-*A Glimpse into Oriya Literature*, Orissa Sahitya Akademi, Bhubaneswar, 1982, pp. 84-85.
54. Ray, P.K. *PRACHI VALLEY (Archaeological Survey Report)*, Orissa State Archaeology, Bhubaneswar, 1975, pp. 69-70.
55. Miller, B.S. *GITAGOVINDA OF JAYADEVA*, Motilal Banarsidass, Delhi, 1984, pp. Introduction, 3-4.
56. Miller, B.S. *Ibid*, 1984, pp. Introduction 14-17.
57. Singh Deo, J.P. *Tantric Art of Orissa*, Kalpaz Publications, Delhi, 2001, pp. 142-143.
58. Behera, S.C. "Rise and Growth of Vaisnavism in Orissa," *Sidelights on History and Culture of Orissa*, ed. Das, M.N. Vidyapuri, Cuttack, 1997, pp. 375-376.
59. Mukherji, Prabhat- *History of Medieval Vaisnavism in Orissa*, Asian Educational Services, New Delhi, 1981, passim.

Ten

Conclusion

In the mundane World there are prevalent many cults and religions, which are the product of Intuitive knowledge. Cult is a system of religious belief or worship. In the remote past, when the sense of Human weakness and dependence has inspired to hold communion with a higher power, there religion has made its appearance. There had been Great Teachers of the World. The diverse religious beliefs and practices of mankind are not a mere medley, not a mere outburst of indiscretion and want of reason, but they form a Cosmos and may be known as a part of human life from which prudence and reason have never been absent and in which a growing purpose has fulfilled and still fulfils itself.

In the true sense :

ONLY ONE TRUTH

There is only One Caste--

the Caste of Humanity.

There is only One Religion--

the Religion of Love.

There is only One Language--

the Language of Heart,

or the Language of Silence.

There is only One God--

the Omnipresent, Omnipotent

and Omniscient Lord,

—Sadguru Swami Śivananda

Cosmos means the World or Universe as an orderly or systematic whole. *Rigveda* the earliest literature of India contains the most ancient traces of cosmogonic speculation.[2] Cosmological values of India are the religious, philosophical and legal writings dating from hoary antiquity. These may be grouped as the Vedās, the Aranyakas, Upanishads, the Sutras, Dharma Sastras, the epics, the Purāṇas and the Agamas, in India. In these literatures Nārāyana, is conceived as a Cosmic God resting on the Serpent Sesa, later arises another aspect of Viṣṇu; he appears as Kṛishṇa, Chief of a Clan and hero of innumerable exploits. The worship of Kṛishṇa seems to have given stimulus to the Bhakti movement.[3]

According to D.C. Sircar,[4] Vaiṣhṇavism, as the name implies, means the particular theistic religion of which Viṣṇu is the object of worship and devotion as the Supreme God. Finally it progressed as a religious sect. The earliest reference to devotion to, and worship of, a personal God, out of which Vaiṣhṇavism arose, may be traced to the 'Ashṭādhyāyi' of Panini of Gandhara (5th century B.C.). As early as 4th century B.C. Vasudeva was the object of devotion, is proved by the statement of Megasthenes that the Sourasenoi, i.e., the people of the Mathura region, held Herakles in special honour; for there is no doubt that Herakles was the Greek analogue of Vāsudeva-Kṛishṇa. Vaiṣhṇavism alias Bhāgavata religion, which originated with the Yādava-Sātvata-Vṛishni people of the Mathura area, appears to have spread to Western India and the northern Deccan with the migration of the numerous Yādava tribes.

The author[5] had expressed the view that the site of Śabarinārāyaṇa on the upstream of the Mahānadi is the earliest trace of Vaiṣhṇav worship in eastern India. The legend is that here Sabari worshipped Rāma, and as a boon asked that her name should precede his, hence the name of the place Śabari-nārāyaṇa (shortened to Śeorinārāyaṇa) which was later named as Svaripur.[6] This place is within a distance of about 3 miles from the confluence of the river Jonk and the Mahānadi. This is the religious seat of the Pāṇḍus which is popularly known as Śabarinārāyaṇa. According to a traditional account, it is the place where Rāmachandra on his way to south met Śabari who worshipped him with ripe berries. So, the image of Nārayana being associated with the name, Śabari, has been worshipped there. It is situated on the left bank of the Mahānadi above its junction with the Jonk river, and is a very important place of pilgrimage.[7]

Inscribed Viṣṇu images dated to 2nd century B.C. are found at Malhar and Burhikhas sites in Bilaspur district. They show the Vaiṣhṇav impact in Upper Mahānadi valley. In early part of the Christian centuries, the Sātavāhanas rose as a political power. Gautamiputrā Satakarni who started his reign about 106 B.C. consolidated his strength in the Deccan by conquering the neighbouring territories. Gautamiputra apparently claimed a sort of suzerainty over the whole of trans-Vindhya India, as he is described as the lord of the Vindhya (the central and eastern Vindhyas as well as the Satpura), Rikshavat (portion of the Vindhyan range to the South of Malwa), Pariyatra (Western Vindhyas and the Aravalli), Sahya (Western ghats to the north of the Niligiri hills), Malaya (Travancore hills), Mahendra (eastern ghats) and mountain ranges encircling the peninsular of South India.[8]

A Sātsvāhana King of the Second century A.D. claimed to be equal to Rāma (Baladeva or Saṅkarshana) and Keśava (Vāsudeva-Kṛshna),[9] which is noteworthy, as it shows the growing importance of Vasudevism. The worship of Śiva and Kṛṣna was popular and votaries of the different faiths lived in harmony. Sometimes they even gave grants to one another.[10] This shows that assimilation of different faiths was taking place in society and Vaiṣhṇavism seems to have been popular in the whole Mahānadi river valleys then.

Samudragupta's expedition to the Deccan in 4th century A.D. brought the whole Mahānadi valleys under Gupta influence. Gupta emperors were devout follower of the Bhagavata religion, one of the many names by which Vaiṣhṇavism was known.[11] So, it seems that this invasion gave momentum to the popularisation of Vaiṣhṇavism in Mahandi river valleys.

In post Gupta period, the Nalas of Puṣkari were Vaiṣhṇav. It is known from the Podagarh stone inscription[12] that Skandavarman installed the foot-prints of Viṣṇu in a temple, which he built, the Kings of the Śarabhapuriya dynasty, ruling during 5th and 6th centuries were Vaiṣhṇav.[13] The early Sōmavaṁśi, known as Pāṇduvaṁśi, who ousted the Sarabhapuriyas were Vaisṇav Kings.[14]

In the coastal area epigraphic evidences reveal that Vaisnavism had its rise in Orissa during the Mathara rule in the fifth century of the Christian era.[15] In this manner there was spread of Vaisnav faith in whole of Mahānadi valley.

It will be interesting to know the view of K.C. Panigrahi,[16] when he states that the numerous copper plate grants and stone inscriptions of the ruling dynasties of Orissa do not refer to Lord Jagannāth. The absence of reference however, does not prove "that he did not exist in Orissa. It only shows that the Deity had not become so famous as he came to be later. This statement shows that K.C. Panigrahi did not go deep into the study of the use of 'Jagannāth' term in Sanskrit literature.

About the Origin of Jagannāth Deity, there are legends which are of highly conflicting character. Therefore the traditional narration of Jagannāth is given in Chapter I, the Introduction.

Religious revolution of Mahānadi valley is given in Chapter II. In early Christian centuries there was Religious Eclecticism.

Buddha was gradually observed into Vaiṣhṇav pantheon and was regarded as the 9th Avatara of Viṣṇu. This has been discussed in Chapter III.

Chapter IV has the study on the evolution of Puruṣottama-Jagannāth Deity, it has been proved that one ofthe icon of Buddha, signifying non-violence, was established or recognised as Puruṣottama-Jagannāth Deity by Ādi Śaṅkarāchārya. The author admires the Master Mind, who embellished this icon of non-violence for Buddha and has Salutations for that Individual.

Reverence and dishonour of Ādi Śaṅkarāchārya at Jagannāth temple of Puri, is a historical fact. This is a forgotten aspect, therefore, it is described in Chapter V.

The development of Jagannāth Trinity is dealt in Chapter IV. Single Jagannāth Deity is worshipped in different names, as Dadhibaban, Patitapabana and Trutyia. It has been discussed in Chapter VII.

A critical review of K.C. Mishra's view is done in Chapter VIII. Chapter IX has the Conclusion.

How much the author has succeeded in the study of the "Origin of Jagannāth Deity" is for the Readers and intelligentsia to judge. The author has done a humble service for the progress from darkness to the light of Jagannāth consciousness. Therefore the Universal Prayer :

असतो मा सद्गमय, तमसो मा जयोतिर्गमय, मृत्योर्मामृतं गमय।

Take me from evil to Good,

Take me from darkness to Light,

Take me from death to immortality.[17]

REFERENCES

1. (author ?), Glimpses of World Religions, Jaico Publishing House, Bombay, 1972, p. 9.
2. Lousis Renow (ed.), Hinduism, George Braziller, Inc. New York, 1961. p. 22.
3. Ibid., p. 37.
4. Sircar, D.C. 'Vaishṇavism.' THACOTIP, Vol. II, The Age of Imperial Unity, 1958, p. 431, 437.
5. CPOSK, pp. 303-304.
6. Cunningham, A. Archaeological Survey of India, Vol. VII, pp. 196-198.
7. Ibid., p. 196.
8. Sircar, D.C. "She Sātavāhānas," THACOTIP, Vol. II, The Age of Imperial Unity, 1968, pp. 201-202.
9. Ibid., p. 439.
10. Tripathi, Rāma Shankar, History of Ancient India, Motilal Banarsidass, Delhi, 1977, p. 198.

11. Sircar, D.C. "Vaiṣhṇavism," *THACOTIP,* Vol. III, the Classical Age, 1970, p. 419.
12. *Epigraphia Indica,* Vol. XXI, p. 153.
13. *CPOSK,* p., 305.
14. *Ibid.,* p. 305.
15. Behera, S.C. "Rise and Growth of Vaisnavism in Orissa", *Sidelights on History and Culture of Orissa,* ed. Das, M.N. Vidyapuri, Cuttack, 1977, p. 371.
16. Panigrahi, K.C. *History of Orissa, (Hindu Period),* Kitab Mahal, Cuttack, 1981, p. 337.
17. *The Bṛhadāraṇyana Upanisad,* Sri Rāmakrishna Math, Mylapore, Madras, 1968, pp. 43-44, 46.

Appendix-I

JAGANNĀTH STOTRAM OR ASHTAKAM WAS NOT COMPOSED BY ŚAṄKARĀCHĀRYA

Usually it is accepted that Jagannāth stotram or ashtakam was composed by Ādi Śaṅkārachārya. The author's critical study shows that like *Bhagavadgitā* is a remarkable interpolation (MAR. p. 15), and Purusottama Māhātmyam is an addition into *Skanda Purāṇa* in 12th century A.D. as dealt in this book, Jagannāth stotram or ashtakam was not composed by Śaṅkārachārya.

Jagannāth stotram (Prayer or Hymn) or ashtakam is a short work of eight stanzans. Each stanza ends with the verse जगन्नाथ: स्वामी नयनपथगामी भवतुमे. It has been studied in this book that Śaṅkarāchārya established or installed Jagannāth Deity as the Divinity, to be worshipped at Govardhan Matha of Puri, in 10th century A.D. Jagannāth became the Presiding Deity of Puri and the images of Śaṅkarāchārya and Padmapada were worshipped together with Jagannāth Deity. Later the other two images were removed. In Chapter VI, it has been dealt that Jagannāth Trinity or quarternary (including Sudarsana) worship developed in 12th or 13th century, A.D.

Jagannāth stotram praises Balabhadra and Subhadra also. So, it is definite that it was composed by some unknown Sanskrit poet during the development of the Trinity worship or after the Trinity were established in 12th, 13th century A.D. As name of the author is not mentioned, it came to be assigned as Śaṅkarāchārya's work. So, in Reality the author of Jagannāth stotram or ashtakam is unknown. For ready reference, it is given below.

श्री जगन्नाथाकष्टकम्

कदाचित् कालिन्दीतटविपिनसंगीत करवो,
मुदाभीरीनारी वदन कमलास्वाद मधुपः।
रमाशम्भुर्ब्रह्मा सुरपति गणेशार्चित पदो
जगन्नाथः स्वामी नयनपथगामी भवतु मे।।1।।

भृजे सव्ये वेणुं शिरसि शिखिपुच्छं कटितटे
दुकूलं नेत्रन्ते सहचर कटाक्षं विदधाते
सदा श्रीमद् वृन्दावन वसतिलीला परिचयो
जगन्नाथः स्वामी नयनपथगामी भवतु मे।।2।।

महाम्भोधोस्तीरे कनकरुचिरे नीलशिखरे
वरन् प्रासादान्तः सहजवलभद्रेण बलिना
सुभद्रामध्यस्थः सकल सुर सेवा वसरदो
जगन्नाथः स्वामी नयनपथगामी भवतु मे।।3।।

कृपापारावारः सजल जलद श्रेणि रुचिरः
रमावाणीरामः स्फुरदमल पद्मेक्षणमुखः
सुरैदिन्द्रैराध्यः श्रुतिगणशिखागीत चरितो
जगन्नाथः स्वामी नयनपथगामी भवतु मे।।4।।

रथारुढो गच्छन् पथिमिलित भूदेवपटलैः
स्तुतिप्रादुर्भावं प्रतिपदमुपाकर्ण्य सदयम्।
दयामिन्धुर्बन्धुः सकल जगतां सिन्धुसुतया
जगन्नाथः स्वामी नयनपथगामी भवतु मे।।5।।

परंब्रह्मापीड़यः कुबलयदलोत्फुल्लनयना
निवासी नीलाद्रौ निहिलचरणोहनन्तशिरसि।
रसानन्दो राधाा सरस वपुरालिंगन मुखो।
जगन्नाथः स्वामी नयनपथगामी भवतु मे।।6।।

न वै याचे राज्यं न च कनकमाणिक्यविभवम्
न याचे] हं रम्यां सकलजनकाम्यां वरवधूम्।

सदा काले काले प्रथमपतिन। गीतचरितो
जगन्नाथः स्वामी नयनपथगामी भवतु मे।।7।।

हर त्वं संसारं द्रततरमसारं सुरपते
हर त्वं पापानां वितातिमपरां यादवपते।
अहो दीनानाथ निहितमचलं निश्चिय पदं
जगन्नाथः स्वामी नयनपथगामी भवतु मे।।8।।

जगन्नाथाष्टकं पुण्यं यः पठेत् प्रयतः शुचिः।
सर्वपापविशु)त्मा विष्णुलोक सं गच्छति ।।9।।
इति श्री जगन्नाथ–स्तोत्रं संपूर्णम्।।

Appendix-II

ESTABLISHED FACT OF THE BOOK IS CONFIRMED BY NEW ARCHAEOLOGICAL FINDING

—Jitamitra Prasad Singh Deo

Tantra is a system that carries on the tradition that has been practiced throughout the world, since time immemorial. The word "TANTEA", is derived in the Kāsika-vṛitti from the root "Tan", to spread, i.e., to rise from little awareness to greater awareness or knowledge. Knowledge is of repetative, derigative, educative and intuitive types. Intuitive Knowledge is to be observed in different types of Consciousness alias Samadhis, acquired through Yogic process with the rise of Kundalini. Kundalini is the gift of Tantra to Human being.[1]

A Tantric text called the "Varahi Tantra", gives an elaborate description of the main subject of Tantra. They are summarized as follows :

1. Consciousness.
2. The Creation and destruction of the physical universe (Shristi and Pralaya).
3. Worship of Deities (Devi or Deva puja).
4. Classification of beings.
5. The heavenly bodies, astronomy and astrology.
6. The different levels of awareness (Lokas).

7. The psychic pathways and Centres in the human framework (Nadis and Chakras).
8. Laws and Duties in Society.
9. Sacramental - rites (Samskaras).
10. Consecration of forms of Deities (Murtis).
11. Incantation (Mantras).
12. Magic Circles (Mandalas and Yantras).
13. Symbolic and Invocative gestures (Mudras).
14. Spiritual practices (Sadhana).
15. Worship (Puja), both internal and external.
16. Consecration of houses, wells, etc.
17. Description of Holy Shrines.
18. Magic (Yogamaya Sadhana).
19. Ceremonial rites and incitations (Diksha).
20. Yoga including asanas, pranayama, meditative methods, etc.
21. Medicine of many types, including ayurveda which is a herbal Science combined with Yogic practices.
22. Science.

"To this list we would add all that Tantra also included alchemy, the art of living a fruitful and blissful life and the use of Sexual energy as a means to unfold higher awarenesss."[3]

Tantra gives importance to the Feminine aspect of Godhood, because Mother's love and care is more than the Father. "Though no Social sanction was received, the people continued to practise Tantra in the rituals and continued to attach to it a philosophical content. Tantra was a parallel cultural current along with the philosophical one is the Indian Culture.

"Other expression of the fertility rites is the philosophy of Tantra in India. Based on the dual perception of the Creation phenomenon with the participation of (Śiva) and (Śakti), the germinator and the nurturer, respectively, it is a highly complex system of philosophical thought. The Tantra practices, however, involved Sexual intercourse and other abhorrent methods."

Georg Feuerstein[4] is of opinion that one of the principal reasons for the decline of Hindu Tantrism was the inclusion of Sexual practices in its rich repertoire, which offended the sersipilities of Hindu puritans. It is a wrong notion, because Tantra wise, the Cosmic Sex is always continuing. A diagrammatic embodiment of the Creative Sexual activity of the Universe, is the "ŚRĪ YANTRA".[5]

The earliest conception of Śākti and Śiva in union has been discovered in Mahānadi Valley. Stone Sockets are found. It is of circular shape, with a Socket on the lower part and has component on the upper part, which fits into the lower Socket. The shape of this Socket owes its shape origin to the rock shelter painting of Yogimath Donger (hill) (vide: plate). Such a stone Socket was collected by the author from Mohangiri site of Kalahandi district in Orissa province and is preserved at the Museum of Bhawanipatna in 1992. It can be interpreted as union of Śiva and Śākti, which represents the Yoga of Sexual transformation. Later it developed as Vajroli and Sahajoli in Tāntric Hatta Yoga practice. Vajroli[6] is the thunder bolt attitude, in which the muscles of the male Sexual organ and lower urinary tract are contracted, redirecting Sexual energy upwards. A practice of Hatta Yoga and Tāntra. Sahajoli practice is the practice of Vajoli by a Woman, involving contraction of the lower urinary muscles. Such a Socket is collected by Pradeep Mohanty and Baba Mishra jointly from Kharligarh site of Balangir, Orissa. Such an object has been found from layer-III, (Early Historic phase), from Veerapuram of Andhra Pradesh, where it is interpreted as a votive Liṅga.'

T.N. Misra[8] inform that no representation of the Sexual art has been reported in the art and ritual objects yielded by the Indus Civilization. The earliest depiction of the Sexual art among the objects excavated so far in India, is found on a pot of the Chalcolithic period at Daimabad Another early representation of Sex has been noted in the Kupgallu Cave in Mysore.

These prove that before the crossing of Vindhya mountains by Vedic Rishi Agastya and coming to peninsular India. Yogic conceptions had already developed in peninsular India and Mahānadi valley in particular; the Yoga of Sexual transformation was popular.

While showing the Vedic origion of the Tāntric tradition in India, Sarbeswar Satpathy[9] informs, "The Vedās mostly deal with sacrifices which are divided into three Classes, viz. pāka yajña, homa yajña and Soma sacrifices. These sacrifices are based on the idea that Maithunikarana leads to Spiritual happiness. Sexual intercourse is agnihotra.[10] Maithunikarana is consecration.[11] This Maithunikarana is to be done secretly. The Śatapatha Brāhmana (VI. 5. 3. 5.) also indicates that bricks are made for the yajña because the making of the bricks causes generation. Even in the Aitareya Brahmana (II. 5. 3.) two pādas or caranas of an anuṣṭubh are raised in a manner to imitate Sexual union. A female devata is not worshipped unless she is coupled with a male Deva.[12] They use a couple of Chandās, or distinct as male from the other as female and the two taken together are believed to be the symbol of Maithuna or Sexual union and by such Maithuna the desired result of ritual is achieved.[13] They believe that the reading of the Ahanasya Mantra,[14] while confers bliss, it is said that the highest and the best Maithuna is Śraddhā and Satya, i.e., piety and truth[15] and this kind of Maithuna in the abstract is directed for Agnihotris who have purified themselves by observances of these acts in a religious spirit and everytime Maithuna performance is observed, Mantras are to be chanted.[16] Thus it is clear that one of the articles of faith of the Vedic people was that Sexual union led the ways to bliss hereafter and must be performed in a true religious spirit to ensure Spiritual welfare, wanton indulgence being severely deprecated.

After Vedic Rishies contact with peninsular people, the Yoga of Sexual transformation was elaborately later incorporated by the Vedic Rishis in Brihadaranyaka Upanishad of Sukla Yajurveda, as Upanishads listed or classified under the different Vedās in Muktikopanishad.[17]

Vedic culture has strength to observe everything into its field, because it is based on Cosmic Truth and its Principals. Whenever and where ever any Truth is found, it can be assimilated into Vedic Culture. As the earliest written record on Yoga of Sexual transformation, variously known as "From Sex to Salvation," "From Sex to Super Consciousness," etc. is found in Vedic culture, it can be said that this Yoga of Sexual transformation has Vedic origin. Later this Yoga was elaborated "HATTA YOGA PRADIPIKA" a Hatha Yoga text of early medieval period. Therefore, it is mentioned in Rigveda (I, 89, 1.), "Let noble thoughts come to us from every side."

Rigveda (5. 60. 5.) declares, "Here, there is none greater, none smaller. All have gathered together here for advancing common welfare of all." The studies of Vedās show that the Vedās constitute the root of all religious, social, cultural, political and economic thoughts of Mankind. The existential Blissful consciousness is the source of all Creation. The Energy of the Lord or by whatever name one recognises it, it is TRUTH, BEAUTY AND GOODNESS. The Vedās are his breath and Man is His expression. The tenets of Vedic Sanatana Dharma with its Scientific Yogic rationalism can help human beings in the flowering of their genius to its fullest potential. The fundamental Truths of Life as revealed to us by the Vedās, can make our lives healthy, wealthy and wise. The Vedās are the heritage of Mankind.

The shape of Stone Sockets, as discovered and dealt has been utilised for shape of Lord Buddha in Amaravati Crossbar railing, which shows the presentation of Rahula.[19] (Vide : photograph).

In two Seckets like shape of Buddha, two hands were added and such a shape is found in the monolithic figure near the south-east slope of Mahendragiri mountain, which area comes under Andhra Pradesh province. The Zone of Mahendragiri - Parlakhemandi has vast Buddhist remains.[19] One can also detect Buddhist remains in the vast archaeological wealth of the Gaṅga Capital Kalinganaara.[20] The monolithic Buddha image of Mahendragiri-Parlakhemandi zone is misunderstood as Lord Jagannāth, by S.N. Rajaguru.[21] There are many images of Lord Buddha at the Buddhist monastry of Ladhak (Jammu-Kashmir province) of north India, which resemble Lord Puruṣottama Jagannāth of Puri.

The new discoveries dealt, confirm that one of the images of Lord Buddha alias Puruṣottama Buddha Jagannāth evolved as Puruṣottama Jagannāth at Puri.

REFERENCES

1. Saraswati, Swami Satyananda - *Kundalini Tantra*, Bihar School of Yoga, Munger, 1992, passim.
2. Saraswati, Swami Satyananda - *A Systematic Course in the Ancient Tantric Techniques of Yoga and Kriya,* Bihar School of Yoga, Munger, second edition, 1989, p. 322.
3. Kulkarni, S.D. (General editor), *Bhishma's Study of Indian History and Culture*, Vol. I, Beginnings of Life, Culture and History, Shri Bhagavan Vedavyasa Itihasa Samshodhana Mandira (Bhishma), Bombay, (Thane), reprint 1997, p. 462.
4. Feuerstein, Georg—"FOREWORD", *Tantric Yoga and Wisdom Goddesses,* (Spiritual secrets of Ayurveda), by David Frawley. Motilal Banarsidass, Delhi, 1996, p. 11.
5. Bandhyopadhyay, Pranab - *The Goddess of Tantra*, Punthi Pustak, Calcutta, 1987, p. 48.
6. Saraswati, Swami Muktibodhananda - *HATHA YOGA PRADIPIKA BY YOGI SWATMARAMA*, Bihar School of Yoga, Munger, second edition, 1993, pp. 558, 564.
7. Sastri, T. V. G.—Bai, K. M. & Rao, J. V. P. *VERAPURAM*, Bhavani Printers, Hyderabad, 1994, passim.
8. Mishra, T. N. *Impact of Tantra on Religion and Art*, D. K. Print World Pvt., Ltd., New Delhi, 1997. p. 101.
9. Satpathy, S. *Sakti Iconography in Tāntric Mahāvidyās*, Punthi Pustak, Calcutta, 1991, pp. 4-5.
10. *Satapatha Brahamana*, XI. 6. 2. 10.
11. *Ibid.*, III. 2. 1. 2.
12. *Aitareya Brāhmana*, III. 5. 4.
13. *Ibid.*, V. 3. 1.
14. Sāmkhyāyana Śrauta Śutra, XII, 24. 1-10.
15. Aitareya Brahmana, VII. 2. 9.
16. *Ibid.*, VII. 2. 9.
17. Nathan, R. S. *OUR HERITAGE Book-I*, Central Chinmaya Mission Trust, Bombay, 1986, Appendix, p. 120.
18. Stone, E.R. *The Buddhist Art of Nagarjunakonda*, Motilal Banarsidass, Delhi, 1994, Illustration No. 32.

19. Dash, K.C. " Dantapura and Puspagiri," *The Journal of Orissan History*, Vol. IX, June 1989, p. 9.
20. Rāmaswami, N. S. *Monograph on Temples of Mukhalingam*, Govt. of Andhra Pradesh, Hyderabad, 1976, pp. 8-9.
21. Rajguru, S. N. Śrī Purushottam -O- Sri Mandira, (Oriya), Orissa Sahitya Academy, Bhubaneswar, 1996. pp. 35-52.

Glossary

Ādivasi.	Tribal.
Avatara.	Incarnation.
Anirudha.	Unrestrained, unhindered, ungovernable, self-willed, spy, a secret emissary, a rope for fastening cattle, name of the son of Pradyumna, grandson of Lord Kṛishṇa, God Śiva apte for Viṣṇu, name of a Buddhist Saint.
Anubhava.	Experience.
Abhaya.	Absence of fear or courage.
Brahma.	God of Creation.
Bhagavati.	Goddess Durga.
Bhairava.	Terrible forms of God Śiva.
Champakamāla.	A garland of Champaka flowers (Indian flower).
Divya drishti.	Supernatural insight.
Darurupi	The wooden idol of Lord Jagannāth.
Daitapati.	Individuals of Sabara origin, engaged in service of the Jagannāth Deity and they are the Ādivasi or tribals engaged in worship and services of the main Deities, in Jagannāth temple of Puri, specially at the time of the "Navakalevara" and the Car festival.

Dhaya.	Kindness, Compassion or Pity.
Devi.	Goddess.
Deva.	God.
Hari.	Viṣṇu.
Hrisikesa.	One of the name of Kṛshna.
Karma.	Action, Deed, Function or Work.
Kamandalu.	An eartheorn or wooden ware used by ascetics, having a semi-circular handle on the top (like a bucket)
Kaivata.	Fisherman.
Karana-sarira.	The causal frame enclosing the Soul (Vedanta philosophy). The original embryo or source of the body existing with the Universal impersonal Spirit and equivalent to Abidyā (equivalent to Māyā) and when investing the impersonal Spirit causing it to become the Personal God or Iswara.
Lokanātha.	Lord of Mankind or Universe.
Maheśa.	Śiva, Lord of Destruction.
Mauna.	Silence.
Madhyana.	Noon.
Narayana.	A name of Viṣṇu.
Narasimha.	An incarnation of Viṣṇu.
Naivēdya.	Offering to a Deity or oblation.
Paramananda.	Supreme delight or bliss, highest felicity or eternal happiness.
Pratyaksha.	Truth.
Pratyeka.	Each one and all.
Prakriti.	Nature.
Padmasana.	A posture in sitting, prescribed in the Sastras or holy scriptures.
Pradyumna.	Name of the eldest son of Śrī Kṛshna, i.e., Cupid.
Rishi.	Sage, anchorite, saint, a truthful person, a subduer of passions, the author of Sāstras. the author or the first recitor of a Vedic formuḷa.

Rāmbhakta.	Devotee of Lord Rāma.
Rathayatra.	Cart festival.
Raja.One of the three	attributes of Human nature, the passion in Human nature.
Śiva.	'Lord Mahādeva, one of the trinity of the Hindu pantheon.
Sūrya.	Sun.
Sattwa.	The best of the three qualities in the material nature, the aggregate of moral good qualities.
Sankarsan.	Elder brother of Śrī Kṛshna, Balarama.
Samādhi.	The unification of the human mind with the Divinity; the mental operation by which 'the God in man is one with the man iṇ God.'
Tama.	Darkness, gloom, or planet Rāhu (the ascending node in Hindu astronomy).
Vṛitti.	Profession or means of living.
Vhaikari.	Deterioration, Relating to the Sattwa quality.
Vedi.	A platform of worship or sacrificial altar or earth where all desires are obtained.
Varada-mudra.	A posture of the hand, granting a boon.
Vasudev.	Lord Kṛshna.
Yogi.	Saint.
Yoga.	Spiritual communion of man with God; the union of a man's Soul with the Divine Spirit.
Yajñapavita.	Sacred thread (Twice born).

Bibliography

Antiquaries, Catalogues, Journals, Magazines, Proceedings, Reports and Souvenirs

Annals of the Bhandarkar Oriental Research Institute, Vol. LXIV, parts I-IV.

Bajpai, K.D. & Pandey, S.K. *Malhar* 1975-77, Department of Ancient History, Culture and Archaeology, University of Sagar, 1977.

Beglar, J.D. Archaeological Survey of India, Vol. XIII, Varanasi, 1970.

Behera, S.C. (ed.), *Interim Excavation Reports,* P.G. Dept. of History, Sambalpur University, 1982.

Bhanja Pradipa, Oriya Quarterly, Vol. XI, 3, Sal 1349.

Catalogue of the Brahmanical Sculptures in the State Museum, Lucknow, Part-I, 1972.

Dhala, B.K. (ed.), *Sahitya Uchhaba (Lekhaka Samukhya),* (Oriya), Bhubaneswar, 1981.

Essays on History, Education and Culture, *COMPARATIVAS,* Nos. 3 & 4, Institute of Comparative Studies, Bhubaneswar, December 1987.

Gaekwad's Oriental Series, No. XLIV.

Govind, P. (ed.), *Mirror,* Vol. XXI, No. I, Bombay, November, 1985.

Indian Historical Quarterly, Calcutta, Vols. XV, XIX & XXII

Indian Antiquary, Vol. XV.

Journal of Mahakōśala Historical Society, Vol. II.

Journal of Ancient Indian History, Vol. XI.

Journal of the Gaṅganath Jhā Research Institute, Vol. I.

Journal of the Bihar and Orissa Research Society, Patna Vol. XVIII.

Journal of the Asiatic Society of Bengal (Old Series), Vol. LXVIII, 1898.

Kulke Hermann-"Some Remarks about the Jagannāth Trinity," SUDASIEN-INSTITUT, DER UNIVERSITAT HEIDELBERG (South Asia Institute of Heidelberg University, Germany), Reprints of Publications of Staff Members, No. 147.

Mahakōśala Historical Society's Papers, Vol. I, 1932.

Mathura Museum, Centenary Number, June-December, 1973.

Memoirs of the Archaeological Survey of India, No. 70.

Mohanty, U.N. (ed.) SOUVENIR, UGC. National Seminar on National Integration in India and the Cult of Lord Jagannāth, 25th-27th December, 1987, D.A.V. College. Titilagarh.

Orissa History Congress Proceedings of the Annual Session, B.J.B. College, Bhubaneswar, 1979.

Orissa Review, Vols. XI & XXVI, No. 12.

Pani, S. (ed.), UNMANA, Souvenir of Akhil Bharat Jagannātha Consciousness Conference, Cuttack, December 28-31, 1984, Charan Gosthi, Cuttack.

Patnaik, J.N. (ed.), Orissa Review, Vol. XLIII, No. 3, October 1986.

Proceedings and Transactions of the Seventh All India Oriental Conference, 1933.

Proceedings of the Indian History Congress, Vol. IV.

Prachya Pratibha, Vol. V, No. 1, January 1977, Agam Kala Prakashan, Delhi.

प्यारेलाल गुप्त, प्राचीन छत्तीसगढ़, रायपुर, 1973.

PURATAN, Vol. I, Nos. 3 & 4, 1984, Department of Archaeology and Museums, Madhya Pradesh.

Rai, C. (ed.), UTKAL PRASANGA, (Oriya monthly), Rathayatra Special Issue, Cuttack, July, 1984.

SOUVENIR, 422nd Geeta Gyana Yagna of His Holiness Swami Chinmayananda, 13th to 20th January, 1987, at Raipur.

Subas Pani (ed.), *Our Cultural Heritage,* (Souvenir), Golden Jubilee Celebration of the Orissa State Museum, Bhubaneswar, 1984.

SAPTARSI, (Oriya monthly magazine), Sambalpur University, January 1987.

SHREE JAGANNĀTH SMARIKA, Vol. I, Neelachala Seva Sangha, New Delhi, 19th December 1969.

Sahu, N.K. (ed.) *New Aspects of History of Orissa,* Vol. II, Sambalpur University, 1971.

The Journal of the Kalinga Historical Research Society, Vol. I, No. 2, September 1946 and Vol. II, No. 1, June 1947.

The Weekly Eastern Times, ed. Mahatab, H.K. Prajatantra Press, Cuttack, 29th November 1980.

The Orissa Historical Research Journal, Vols. III, No. 1 ; VI, No. 4 ; VII, No. I ; VIII, No. 1 ; XVI, No. 4 to XXII, No. 1 ; XI, No. 4 ; XXIV, XXV & XXVI; XXIX, No. 1 ; XXX, Nos. 2, 3 & 4 ; XXXI, No. 1 : and XXXII, Nos. 3 & 4.

Utkala Sahitya, Vol. 21, No. 10, Sal 1325.

Gazetteers

Kuanr, D.C. (State editor), *Gazetteer of India, Orissa, Puri,* (Chief editor) Senapati, N. Cuttack, 1977.

Kuanr, D.C. (State editor), *Gazetteer of India, Orissa, Kalahandi,* (Chief editor) Senapati, N. Cuttack, 1980.

Sahu, N.K. (State editor), *Gazetteer of India, Orissa, Balangir,* (Chief editor) Senapati, N. Cuttack, 1968.

Verma, R. (State editor), *Gazetteer of India, Madhya Pradesh, Raipur,* Bhopal, 1973.

Sinha, A.M. (State editor), *Gazetteer of India, Madhya Pradesh, Bilaspur,* (Chief editor) Shrivastav, P.N. Bhopal, 1278.

Mahanti, B.K. (State editor), *Gazetteer of India, Orissa, Sambalpur,* (Chief editor) Senapati, N. Cuttack, 1971.

Inscriptions

Corpus Inscriptionum Indicarum, Archaeological Survey of India, Vols. III & IV parts I & II.

Epigraphia Indica, Vols. I, IV, VI, VII, VIII, IX, XI, XII, XIII, XVIII, XXI, XXIII, XXVI, XXVII, XXVIII, XXXII, XXXIII & XXXV.

Rajaguru, S.N. *Inscriptions of Orissa,* Vols. I & IV, Orissa State Museum, Bhubaneswar.

Literatures

Bhagavadgitā — Being Reprint of the relevant parts of the Bhishmaparvan from the critical edition of the Māhabhāratā ed. by S.K. Belvalkar, Poona, 1945.

Brahmāṇḍa Purāṇa — Published by Venkatesvara Press, Bombay 1913.

Brahma Purāṇa — Anandāśrama Sanskrit Series Poona, 1895.

Bhāgavat Purāṇa — Ed. by V.L. Pansikar, Bombay, 1920.

English translation, M.N. Dutt, Calcutta, 1895.

Chetiya Jātaka — Jātaka ed. V. Fausboll, 7 vols, London, 1877-1897. English translation under the editorship of E.B. Cowell, 7 vols. Cambridge, 1895-1913.

Devi Bhāgavata

Harivamśa Purāṇa — ed. R. Kinjawadekar, Poona, 1936.

Kalika Purāṇa — Dealt in ŚĀKTA PIṬHA by D.C. Sircar, published by Motilal Banarsidāss from *Journal of the Royal Asiatic Society of Bengal* Letters, Vol. 14, 1948, pp. 1-108.

Mahābhārata — (Bombay ed.) with the commentary of Nilakantha, ed. by R. Kinjawadekar, Poona, 1929-33.

(Calcutta ed.) ed. by N. Siromani and others, Calcutta, 1834-39.

(Kumbhakonam ed.) ed. by T.R. Kṛishṇacharya and T.R. Vyasacharya, Bombay, 1905-10.

Matsya Purāṇa — Anandāṣrama Sanskrit Series, Poona, 1907.

English translation by a Taluqdar of Oudh.

Sacred Books of the Hindus 2 Vols., Allahabad, 1916-17.

Padma Purāṇa — ed. V.N. Mandlik, Anandīśrama Sanskrit Series, 4 vols, Poona, 1893-94. Pub. Venkatesvara Press, Bombay, 1895.

Raghuvaṁśa — ed. by S.P. Pandit, Bombay Sanskrit Series, Bombay, 1869-74. ed. with English translation by G.R. Nandargikar, 3rd edition, Bombay, 1897.

Vāyu Purāṇa — ed. R. Mitra, 2 Vols., Bibliotheca Indica, Calcutta, 1880-88.

Ānandāśrama Sanskrit Series, Poona, 1905.

Viṣṇu Purāṇa — English translation by H.H. Wilson, 5 Vols., London, 1864-70. Bombay, 1889,

English translation by M.N. Dutt, Calcutta, 1894.

Valmiki Rāmāyāna — Translation into English prose, by M.N. Dutt, Calcutta, 1892-94.

(North-Western India) ed. by Pandit Rāma Labhaya and others, Lahore, 1923 ff.

(North and South) Bombay, 1902. (South) Madras, 1933.

Vessantara Jataka — Jataka, ed. V. Fausboll, 7 Vols, London, 1877-97.

English translation under the editorship of E.B. Cowell, 7 Vols., Cambridge, 1895-1913.

Vrihad Samhita — ed. by H. Kern Bibliotheca Indica, Calcutta, 1865.

English translation by H. Kern, *Journal of the Asiatic Society of Great*

Britain and Ireland, London, 1870-1875; parts 1-5, London, 1870-1873.

ed. with English translation and notes by V. Subrahmanya Sastri and M. Rāmakrishna Bhat, 2 Vols, Bangalore, 1947.

Secondary Sources

Acharyay, P.M. *Odisār Itihāsa,* (Oriya), Cuttack, 1975.

Banerjea, J.N. *The Development of Hindu Iconography,* University of Calcutta, 1956.

Basham, A.L. *The Wonder that was India,* Delhi, 1982.

Bandyopadhyay, P. *The Goddess of Tantra,* Punthi Pustak, Calcutta, 1987.

Beal, S. *Buddhist Records of the Western World-Translated from the Chinese of Hiuen-Tisang* (A.D. 629), Oriental Books Reprint Corporation, Delhi, 1969.

Bhargava, M.L. *The Geography of Rgveda India (A Physical Geography of Sapta Saindhava),* The Upper India Publishing House Ltd. Lucknow, 1964.

Bhandarkar, R.G. *Vaisnavism, Śaivism and Minor Religious Systems,* Indological Book House, Varanasi, 1965.

Bhattacharyya, N.N. *The Indian Mother Goddess,* Manohar, New Delhi, 1977.

Cunningham, A. *The Stupa of Bharhut,* with introduction by Agarwala, V.S. Indological Book House, Varanasi, 1962.

Cunningham, A. *Archaeological Survey of India,* Vol. VII.

Cunningham, A. *The Ancient Geography of India, the Buddhist Period including the Campaigns of Alexander and the Travels of Hiuen-Tsang,* Varanasi, 1963.

Connelly, J.H. & Landsberg, L. (translators), *The Unknown Life of Jesus Christ,* Nababharat Publishers, Calcutta, 1981.

Datta, B.N. (Trans. into English), *Mystic Tales of Lāma Taranātha,* Calcutta, 1944.

Dās, Anirudha-*SABARA (Oriya),* Sathi Mahal, Cuttack, 1969.

Devadhar & Suru (ed.), *Ratnāvali of Śrī Harsa,* Poona Oriental Book House, Poona, 1954.

Dās, Suryanarayan, *Oriya Sahitya ra Itihas (Oriya).* part-I, (?), Cuttack.

Dās, M.B. (ed.), *Sidelights on History and Culture of Orissa,* Vidyapuri, Cuttack, 1977.

Dās, B. *The Bhauma-Karas-Buddhist Kings of Orissa and their Times,* Oriental Publishers, New Delhi, 1978.

Dās, H.C. *Cultural Development in Orissa,* Punthi Pustak, Calcutta, 1985.

Dās, A. & Sharma, S.R. *Śri Jagannāth and Nepal,* (Oriya), Vidyapuri, Cuttack, 1986.

Eschman, A.; Kulke, H. and Tripathy, G.C. (ed.), *The Cult of Jagannāth and the Regional Tradition of Orissa,* Manohar, New Delhi, 1978.

George Michell, *The Hindu Temple,* B.I. Publications, New Delhi, 1977.

Glimpses of World Religions, Jaico Publishing House, Bombay, 1972.

Ganguly, M.M. *Orissa and Her Remains-Ancient and Medieval, (District Puri),* Thacker Spink & Co. Calcutta, 1912.

Hunter, W.W. *Orissa,* Vol. I, London, 1972.

Jain, K.C. *Ancient Cities of Rajasthan,* Motilal Banarsidass, Delhi, 1972.

Jagadeb, Raja G.C.H. *Utkal Empire under Gaṅga Kings,* Berhampur, 1977.

Joshi, A. *New Light on the Cultural Heritage of Orissa,* Baneeshree, Cuttack, 1980.

Kṛishṇamacharlu, C.R. *The Cradle of Indian History,* The Adyar Library, Madras, 1947.

Kosambi, D.D. *An Introduction to the Study of Indian History,* Popular Prakashan, Bombay, 1975.

Lousis Renow (ed.), *Hinduism,* George Braziller, Inc. New York (?).

Kosambi, D.D. *Myth and Reality,* Popular Prakashan, Bombay, 1983.

Mitra, R.L. *The Antiquities of Orissa,* Vol. II, Calcutta, 1882.

Mullick, Sreeram Chandra, *Samkshipta Kōśala Itihasa,* (Oriya), Balangir, 1931.

Mohanty, A.B. (ed.), *Madala Pānji* (Oriya), Published by the Prachi-Samiti, Cuttack, (?).

Mukherjee, P. *The History of thc Gajapati Kings of Orissa and their Successors,* General Trading Company, Calcutta, 1953.

Mahatab, H.K. *The History of Orissa,* Vol. II, Prajatantra Prachar Samiti, Cuttack, 1960.

Mohanty, A.B. (ed.), *Saraḷa Mahābharata,* (Oriya), Cultural Affairs Department, Bhubaneswar, (Serially published in 15 vols.), 1965-68.

Majumdar, R.C. (ed.), *The History and Culture of the Indian People,* Vol. II, 1968 ; Vol. Ill, 1970 ; Vol. IV, 1964 and Vol. V, 1966, Bharatiya Vidya Bhavan, Bombay.

Mitra, R.L. *The Sanskrit Buddhist Literature of Nepal,* Sanskrit Pustak Bhandar, Calcutta, 1971.

Mishra, K.C. *The Cult of Jagannāth,* Firma K.C. Mukhopadhyay, Calcutta, 1971.

Mohapatra, G. *The Land of Viṣṇu,* B.R. Publishing Corporation, Delhi, 1979.

Mansinha, M. *The Saga of the Land of Jagannātha,* J. Mohapatra & Co. Cuttack, (?).

Mukherjee, P. *The History of Medieval Vaiṣhṇavism in Orissa,* Asian Educational Services, New Delhi, 1981.

Mohanty, S. *Lord Jagannāth - the Microcosm of Indian Spiritual Culture,* Orissa Sahitya Akademi, Bhubaneswar, 1982.

Miller, B.S. *Gitagovinda of Jayadeva,* Motilal Banarsidass, Delhi, 1983.

Mohanty, P. *Concept of Purusha and Puruṣhottama,* Gyan Publishing House, Delhi, 1986.

Madhava-Vidyaranya, *Sankara-Dig-Vijaya,* (The Traditional Life of Śrī Śaṅkarāchārya), Translated by Swami Tapasyananda, Sri Rāmakrishna Math, Madras, 1980.

Nema, S.R. *Political History of the* Sōmavaṁśi *Kings of South Kōśala and Orissa,* Oriental Publishers, New Delhi, 1978.

Pargiter, F.E. *Purāṇa Texts of the Dynasties of the Kali Age,* Oxford, 1913.

Panigrahi, K.C. *Chronology of the Bhauma-Kara and the Sōmavaṁśi of Orissa,* Bhopal, 1961.

Panigrahi, K.C. *Archaeological Remains at Bhubaneswar,* Orient Longmans, New Delhi, 1961.

Panigrahi, K.C. *History of Orissa (Hindu Period),* Kitab Mahal, Cuttack, 1981.

Paramahansa Yogananda, *Autobiography of a Yogi,* Jaico Publication, Bombay, 1971.

Pathak, V. *History of Kōśala upto the Rise of the Mauryas,* Motilal Banarsidass, Varanasi, 1963.

Puri, B.N. *India in the time of Patanjali,* Bharatiya Vidya Bhavan, Bombay, 1968.

Padhi, B. *Daru Devata,* (Oriya), Cuttack Students' Store, Cuttack., 1964.

Pearelal Gupta, *Prachin Chhattisgarh,* (Hindi), Ravisankar University, Raipur, 1973.

Pandey, R.K. *The Concept of Avatars,* B.R. Publishing Corporation, Delhi, 1978.

Pattanaik, P.K. *A Forgotten Chapter of Orissan History,* Punthi Pustak, Calcutta, 1979.

Patnaik, N.C. (ed.), *History of the Formation of the Orissa State,* (Oriya), Baruda Karyalayu, Berhampur, 1986.

Ragozin, Z.A. *Vedic India : As Embodied Principally in the Rigveda.* Munshiram Manoharlal, New Delhi, 1962.

Rajaguru, S.N. *History of the Gaṅgas,* Part II, Orissa State Museum, Bhubaneswar, 1972.

Russell, R.V. & Hiralal, *The Tribes and Castes of the Central Provinces of Orissa,* Vol. IV, Cosmo Publication, Delhi, 1975.

Rath, B.K., *Cultural History of Orissa,* Sundeep Prakashan, Delhi, 1983.

Singh Deo, J.P. *Cultural Profile of South Kōśala,* Gyan Publishing House, New Delhi, 1987.

Sahu, N.K. (ed.), *A History of Orissa,* (two Volumes), Susil Gupta (India), Ltd. Calcutta, 1956.

Sankalia, H.D. *The Rāmayana in Historical Perspective,* Macmillan India Limited, Delhi, 1982.

Sircar, D.C. *Studies in the Geography of Ancient and Medieval India,* Motilal Banarsidass, Delhi, 1971.

Sahu, N.K. *Khaveda,* Orissa State Museum, Bhubaneswar, 1984.

Schwartzberg, J.E. (ed.), *A Historical Atlas of South Asia,* Chicago University, U.S.A. 1978.

Sahu, N.K. *History of Orissa,* Utkal University, Vol. I, Vani Vihar, Bhubaneswar, 1964.

Sahu, N.K. *Buddhism in Orissa,* Utkal University, 1958.

Sahu, K. (ed.), *Sabara Śrī Kshetra,* Vol. II, (Oriya), Sabora Sanskrutic Gabesana Kendra, Koraput, 25th February, 1988.

Siddhantrashastree, R.K. *Śaivism through the Ages,* Munshiram Manoharlal, New Delhi, 1975.

Singhal, J.P. *The Sphinx Speaks : The Story of Pre-historic Nations,* Sadgyan Sadan, New Delhi, 1963.

Subuddhi, U. *The Bhauma-Karas of Orissa,* Punthi Pustak, Calcutta, 1978.

Sircar, D.C. *Studies in the Religious Life of Ancient and Medieval India,* Motilal Banarsidass, Delhi, 1971.

Sri Jagannātha Sanskrutic, (Oriya), ed. Orissa Cultural Forum, Bhubaneswar, 1978.

Swami Chinmayananda, *A Manual of Self-Unfoldment,* Central Chinmaya Mission Trust, Bombay, 1985.

Swami Rāmakrishnananda, *Life of Śrī Rāmānuja,* Śrī Rāmakrishna Math, Madras, 1965.

Swami Chinmayananda, *Vedanta the Science of Life,* Part-I, Central Chinmaya Mission Trust, Bombay, 1983.

Sah, A.P. *Life in Mediaeval Orissa (circa.* A.D., *600-1200),* Chaukhamba, Varanasi, 1976.

Sankara The Missionary, Central Chinmaya Mission Trust, Bombay, 1978.

Singh, F. *The Vedic Etymology,* National Publishing House, Delhi, (?).

Swami Shivananda, *Mind Its Mysteries And Control,* The Divine Life Society, Shivananda Nagar, 1974.

Sengupta, S.R. *Mother Cult,* Firma KLM Private Limited, Calcutta, 1977.

The Brhadaranyana Upanisad, Śrī Rāmakrishna Math, Mylapore, Madras, 1968.

Tripathi, R.S. *History of Ancient India,* Motilal Banarsidass, Delhi, 1972.

The Cultural Heritage of India, Vol. II, Rāmakrishna Mission, Institute of Culture, Calcutta, 1969.

Tod, J. *Annals and Antiquities of Rajasthan,* Vol. II, (?), 1914.

Thakur, V.S. *RAJIM,* (Hindi), Madhya Pradesh Hindi Grantha Academy, Bhopal, 1972.

Vatsyayana's Kamasutra, Translated by Burton, R. & Arputhrcot, F.F. Orient Paperbacks, Delhi, 1977.

Walters, *Yuan Chwang's Travels in India,* part I & II, Munshiram Manoharlal, New Delhi, 1973.

Index

Illustrations and Maps

Fig. 1. Lord Puruṣottama Jagannāth.

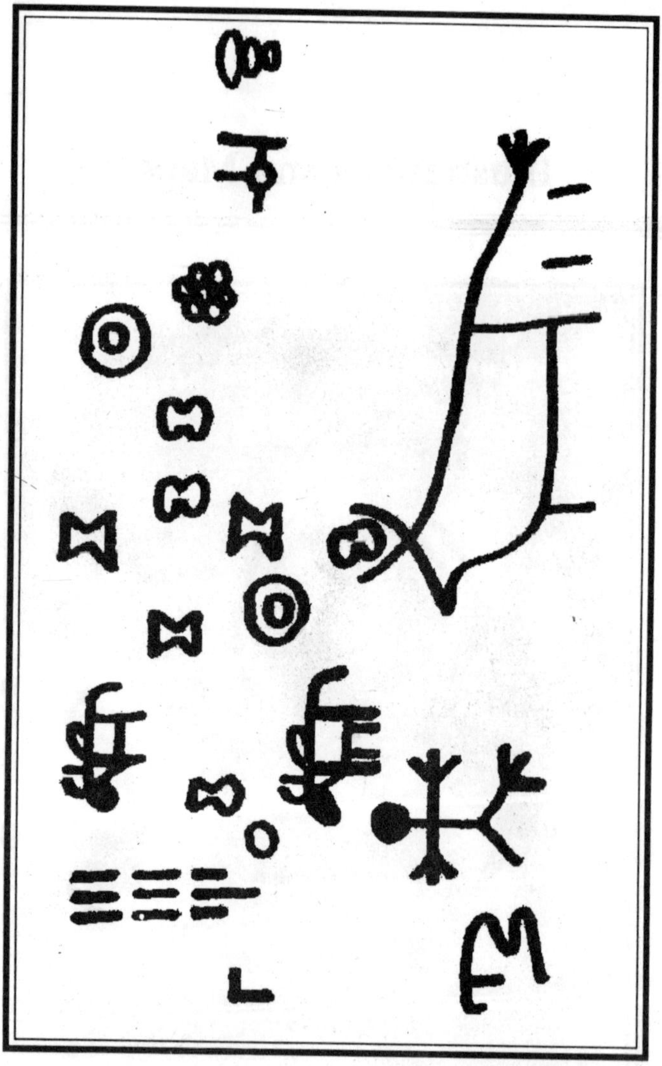

Fig. 2. Pre-historic cave painting of Yogimath Donger (Neolithic period). Discovered by Jitamitra Prasad Singh Deo on 21st December, 1970 (The Painting is in Red)

Fig. 3. Lord Sri Jagannāth with elder brother Balabhadra, sister Subhadra and Sudarsana.

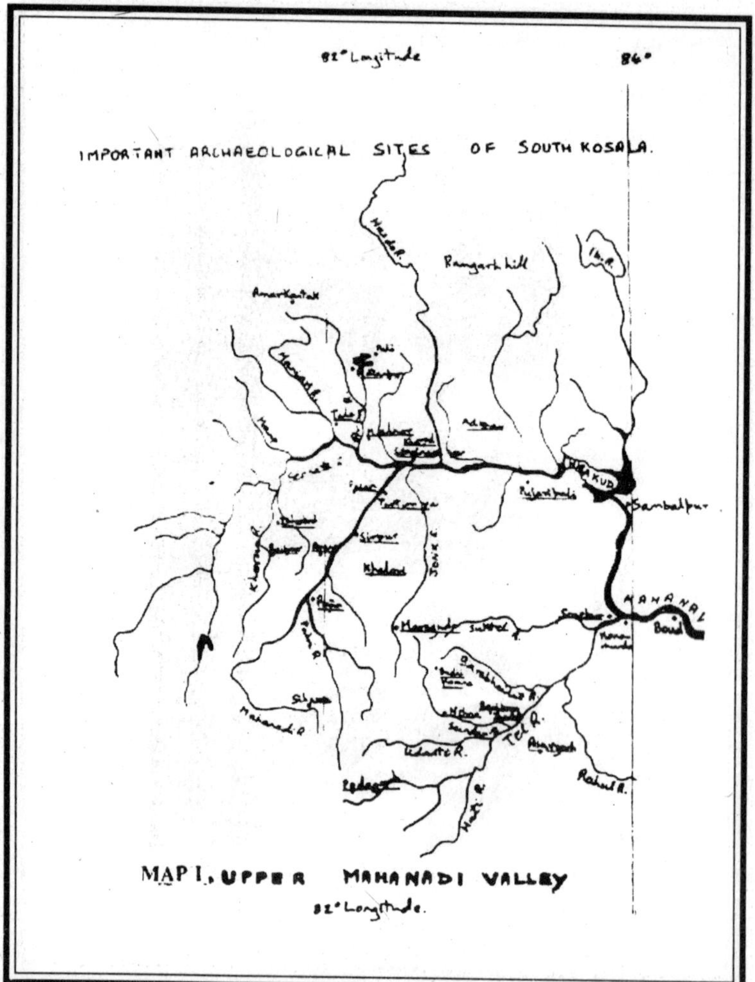

Fig. 4. Upper Mahanandi Vally

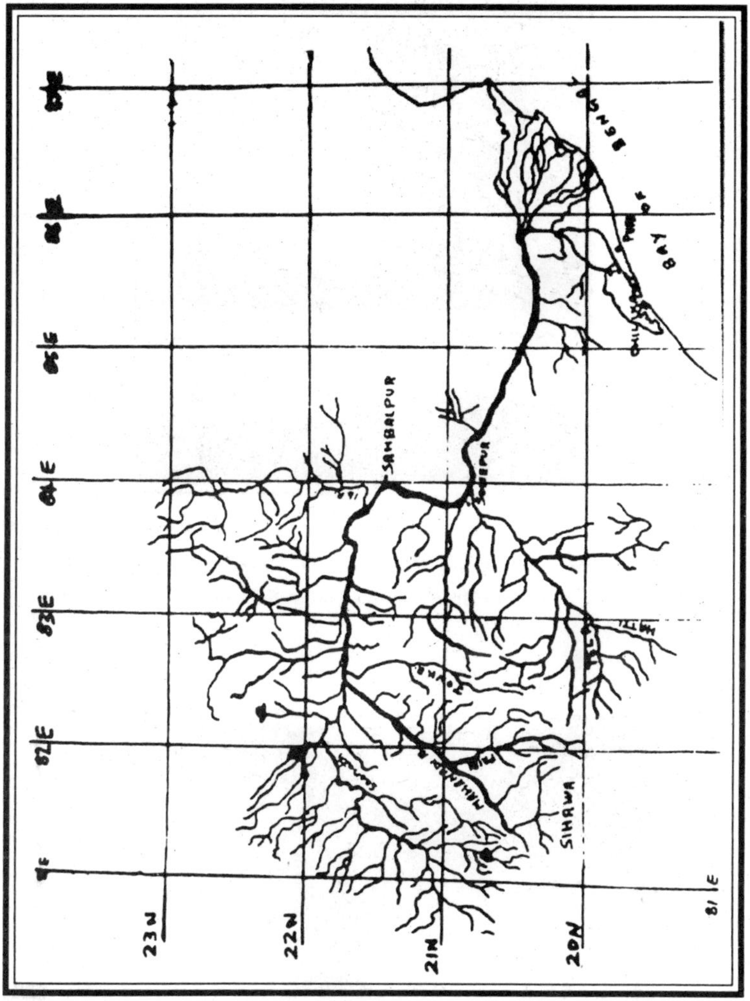

Fig. 5.

Fig. 6. Stone Socket set, showing the union of Male and Female principals (i.e. Śiva and Śākti), Find Spot : Mohongiri (Kalahandi district Orissa), preserved at Manikyapur Museum, Bhawanipatna, Post neolithic period.

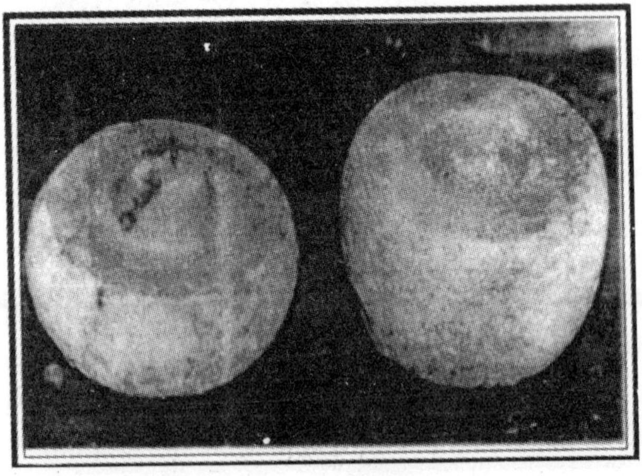

Fig. 7. Exposed stone sockets, Find Spot : Mohongiri.

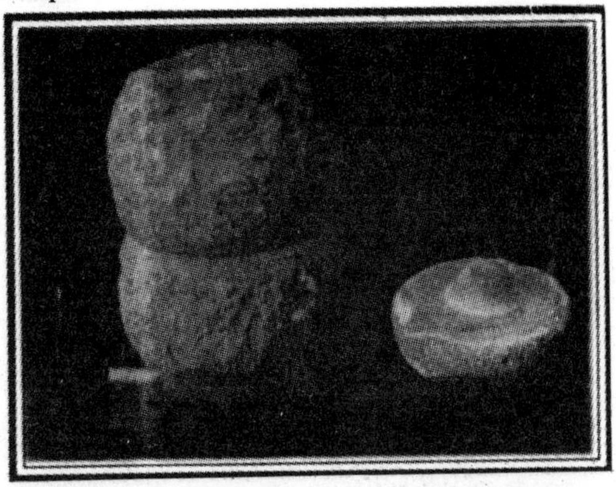

Fig. 8. Stone Socket set, Find Spot : Kharligarh (Balangir district, Orissa). Post neolithic period.

Fig. 9. Exposed Stone Sockets, Find Spot : Kharligarh.

Fig. 10. Presentation of Rahula, Crossbar from Amaravati railing, Archaeological museum, Amaravati. (The Central Figure represents Lord Buddha)